# Food, Development, and Politics in the Middle East

## Also of Interest

*The New Arab Social Order: A Study of the Social Impact of Oil Wealth,* Saad Ibrahim

*OPEC: Twenty Years and Beyond,* edited by Ragaei W. El Mallakh

*Economic Growth and Development in Jordan,* Michael P. Mazur

*The United Arab Emirates: Unity in Fragmentation,* Ali Mohammed Khalifa

*Libya: The Experience of Oil,* J. A. Allan

*King Faisal and the Modernisation of Saudi Arabia,* edited by Willard A. Beling

*South Yemen: Profile of a People's Democratic Republic in Arabia,* Robert W. Stookey

# About the Book and Author

## Food, Development, and Politics
## in the Middle East
### Marvin G. Weinbaum

As the reality of a food deficit emerges in the Middle East, rural society and the agricultural sector—once widely viewed as peripheral to national development—now are high on the policy agendas of nearly every Middle East country. This book looks at the complex interrelationship of food production, development schemes, and politics in these countries.

Dr. Weinbaum considers the origins, nature, scope, and political dimensions of the potential food shortfall and explores how food deficits could lead to changed international relations among states in the Middle East. He specifically examines the physical and technological limitations to increased food production, then assesses the major social, economic, and political hurdles in the way of agricultural development, the effects of—and pressures for—agrarian reform, the bureaucratic policymaking process, and the domestic impact of foreign assistance policies. He concludes with an examination of the linkage between food supply availability and political stability.

Dr. Marvin G. Weinbaum is associate professor of political science at the University of Illinois, Urbana-Champaign, and has conducted extensive field research in Iran, Afghanistan, Pakistan, and Egypt.

# Food, Development, and Politics in the Middle East

Marvin G. Weinbaum

Westview Press • Boulder, Colorado
Croom Helm • London, England

Published in 1982 in the United States of America by
    Westview Press, Inc.
    5500 Central Avenue
    Boulder, Colorado 80301
    Frederick A. Praeger, President and Publisher

Published in 1982 in Great Britain by
    Croom Helm Ltd.
    2-10 St John's Road
    London SW11

Library of Congress Catalog Card Number: 81-16098
ISBN (U.S.): 0-89158-947-3
ISBN (U.K.): 0-7099-2726-6

Printed and bound in the United States of America

To my wife, Francine

# Contents

# Tables and Figures

# 1
# The Region: Its Food Potential and Constraints

Strains on the international monetary system and the unbalancing of budgets in the industrialized West and the Third World are largely credited to the exercise of economic power by the Middle East's oil-exporting countries. States of that region, including the less prosperous, also share heavy responsibility for a challenge of another kind — to global food security. With the new affluence of principal oil-producing countries after 1973 and the steep increase in food consumption from Morocco to Pakistan, the Middle East has emerged as a leading competitor for the world's food stocks and foreign assistance. Countries that only a decade or two ago were self-sufficient or showed a favorable net food trade now turn to international markets as their domestic food production lags behind an accelerating demand. Government projects and programs designed during the 1970s to close the wide gap between domestic supplies and consumption have succeeded instead in increasing reliance on imported technologies and in more closely integrating countries into a world economy. Although capital reserves drained off for food imports have not neutralized the influence acquired from oil wealth, even the region's richest states have become uneasy about their food dependence and potential economic vulnerability. Among the Middle East's poorer states, heavy financial burdens and lowered self-reliance have slowed development and threaten economic independence.

The Middle East mirrors most of the problems of food production and conditions of rural poverty faced throughout the less developed world. Despite distinctive institutions and copious oil revenues that permit high-cost solutions, the region resembles most of the Third World in its limited ability to sustain effective and profitable agricultural systems. Behind the rising food imports is a legacy of decades of low agricultural productivity and public policies that slighted the rural sector. As elsewhere, large segments of the region's labor force remain engaged in agricultural pursuits, and the vast majority of farmers cultivate the land by traditional means. Scarce farm inputs, inappropriate technologies, and weak producer incentives contribute to low productivity, and the remedies sought through improving rural incomes and ensuring adequate public investments and services are familiar ones. Much as in other regions, agrarian reform and balanced sectoral policies in the Middle East may be impossible without structural changes and redistribution of income and power. Yet progress, or the lack of it, by Middle East governments in managing food problems and rural development is likely to have, aside from the expected bearing on the quality of rural and urban life, a unique impact on a dwindling world food reserve and conditions for global economic and political stability.

The following study of food and agricultural policies in the Middle East is framed by the view that constraints on production and major obstacles to development—familiarly described as physical and technological or conceived in economic and social terms—are also inescapably political. Although political factors are very likely no more relevant in the Middle East than elsewhere, the imprint of politics on the region is unmistakable and sometimes profound. Factional fighting in Lebanon or Turkey, a war between Iran and Iraq, Soviet armed intervention in Afghanistan, and the enduring Arab-Israeli struggle are only the more dramatic events that have had a bearing on food production and distribution and on hopes for agricultural development. Regional conflict and domestic instability disrupt programs, divert resources, and distract policymakers. On a more continuous basis, political cultures and institutions, political ideologies and interests contribute to shaping policies and determining how they are executed. Frequently, seemingly technological choices in development in fact incorporate political values and priorities. Government food strategies supposedly dictated by economic imperatives may actually be the price exacted by ascendant domestic interests. And what is so often described as societal resistance to programs can be found to be the result of bureaucratic conflict, confusion, and lethargy.

Government actors plainly dominate the formulation of food strategies and planning for agricultural modernization. Price guarantees, input subsidies, import and export regulations, and public investments are, with other policies, the instruments of public officials and their legions. Their decisions, frequently political, have a direct bearing on farmers' planting choices, use of inputs, and incentives to produce. The private sector often shares responsibility for investment and is, in some cases, nurtured by government policies. But in the Middle East the public sector is expected to finance the lion's share of agricultural expansion and improvement and to satisfy demands from the countryside for increased economic and social equity. Government alone possesses the legitimacy and resources necessary to overcome entrenched interests that stand in the way of fundamental change. Because the stakes in agricultural and food policy decisions at times are nothing less than a regime's survival, few policies are likely to escape the test of how they alter configurations of national and local political power and privilege.

## The Food Deficit

The Middle East is not normally identified with hunger and mass starvation. Periodically poor rains and runoff, fragile food distribution systems, and limited foreign exchange bring some countries in the region precariously close to famine conditions. Yet by contrast to the famine-prone areas of South and East Asia or Africa's Sahel, the contemporary Middle East appears to have averted the worst consequences of droughts and man-made calamities. Dietary energy supplies in the Middle East have, in fact, been rising in recent decades, especially in relation to other regions. Table 1.1 indicates gains between 1961–1965 and 1975–1977 for all but two of sixteen countries examined. In some cases, the improvements were dramatic, in particular among countries with previously low caloric levels. Whereas Table 1.1 indicates that only three Middle East states were above the world average in 1961–1965, seven were higher in 1975–1977 and twelve of the sixteen were above the average for all developing countries. Moreover, by 1977, Middle East countries had close to or better than the per-capita daily dietary energy requirement estimated by the Food and Agriculture Organization (FAO). With a protein intake of 70.9 grams per day per person, the Middle East was slightly above the world average and compared favorably with other developing areas.[1]

The statistics in Table 1.1 reveal much variation among Middle East states, with general dietary conditions during the 1970s apparently least sufficient in Afghanistan and Jordan, and most satisfactory in Israel, Iran, and Turkey. In a 1976 listing of forty-four "food priority countries," the World Food Council identified Afghanistan, Egypt, Pakistan, and the two Yemens. National comparison, however, throws little light on the differential caloric or protein intake within a single country. As a rule, nutritional levels in the region have been rising far more rapidly in urban areas than in rural areas, and the gap between the middle classes and the poor in the cities is believed to be widening. In any case, to the extent that chronic malnutrition exists among groups in the Middle East, it is presently no more severe than elsewhere in the Third World.

Countries of the Middle East have the distinction, nevertheless, of forming the world's most rapidly growing food deficit area. Between 1973 and 1980, the value of agricultural imports rose from about $4 billion to more than $20 billion.[2] Wheat, the major component in the Middle East diet, was

TABLE 1.1
Daily Per Capita Calorie and Protein Supply for Middle East Countries and Other Regions

| Country or Region | Daily Calorie Supply Per Capita | | | Percentage of Energy Needs, 1977 | Protein Per Capita Per Day in Grams, 1975-77 |
|---|---|---|---|---|---|
| | 1961-65 Average | 1975-77 Average | Percentage Change 1961-65 to 1975-77 | | |
| Iran | 1890 | 3139 | +69 | 130 | 84.3 |
| Libya | 1854 | 2946 | +59 | 126 | 74.8 |
| Tunisia | 1985 | 2657 | +39 | 112 | 72.5 |
| Algeria | 1897 | 2357 | +24 | 99 | 63.0 |
| Pakistan | 1838 | 2255 | +23 | 99 | 62.0 |
| Sudan | 1873 | 2247 | +20 | 93 | 66.7 |
| Iraq | 2028 | 2306 | +14 | 89 | 60.9 |
| Morocco | 2251 | 2568 | +14 | 105 | 67.7 |
| Saudi Arabia | 2185 | 2474 | +13 | 88 | 65.0 |
| Israel | 2869 | 3145 | +10 | 122 | 104.6 |
| Syria | 2416 | 2616 | +08 | 108 | 73.0 |
| Turkey | 2771 | 2916 | +05 | 115 | 82.3 |
| Egypt | 2605 | 2716 | +04 | 109 | 74.4 |
| Lebanon | 2434 | 2495 | +02 | 101 | 67.4 |
| Afghanistan | 2108 | 1974 | -06 | 110 | 60.8 |
| Jordan | 2214 | 2067 | -07 | 62 | 55.9 |
| Middle East* | 2201 | 2413 | +09 | | 70.9 |
| Africa | 2086 | 2208 | +06 | | 54.9 |
| Latin America | 2413 | 2552 | +06 | | 65.2 |
| Far East | 2025 | 2053 | +02 | | 49.6 |
| All Developing | 2126 | 2282 | +07 | | 57.8 |
| World | 2436 | 2590 | +06 | | 69.3 |

SOURCES: FAO Production Yearbooks, 1977, 1978 (Rome: Food and Agricultural Organization, 1977, 1978). World Bank, World Development Report, 1980 (New York: Oxford University Press, 1980).

*The 16 countries shown in this table.

the principal food commodity imported. Nearly 60 percent of the region's wheat requirements now come from nondomestic sources, as do between 15 and 20 percent of its meat supplies. In 1972, countries in the region purchased some 8.3 million metric tons of wheat and wheat flour abroad. But, although the region's needs and available supplies varied over the decade, the trend was clear: In 1978 wheat imports reached 17 million tons.[3] Egypt's imports went up 53 percent between 1970 and 1980. Morocco, whose wheat purchases abroad averaged only 500,000 tons annually in the early 1970s, more than tripled this volume in 1979–1980. With Turkey the single notable exception, food imports in the Middle East absorbed an ever larger share of national requirements. Iran, with 7 percent of its food consumption from imports in 1972, turned to foreign suppliers for between 30 and 40 percent at the decade's end. Egypt in 1980 was importing 40 to 45 percent of its needs, Jordan more than 50 percent, Libya 60 percent, and Saudi Arabia as much as 75 percent.

The cost to national treasuries has been enormous and is growing. Economically hard-pressed Egypt spent $2 billion for food imports in 1978, and such other foreign currency–short countries as Morocco and Israel set aside between $700 and $800 million in the same year for imports. However, the oil-exporting countries, forced to divert an ever larger proportion of their revenues to agricultural imports, made the best new customers. Iran's bill for food from all sources ran over $2 billion in 1978, up from just $330 million in 1973–1974. In 1979 Algeria devoted more than $1 billion to food imports; in 1980 Iraq budgeted $1.4 billion—four times the 1973 level. Predictably, the costs for Saudi Arabia topped those of the others; its projected bill of $4.5 billion in 1980 represented a 50 percent increase in just a single year.[4]

Overall advances in domestic food production during the 1970s barely kept ahead of population growth in most Middle East countries. Average population growth rates for the 1970–1978 period ranged from a surging 4.1 percent in Libya and 3.5 percent in Saudi Arabia to a relatively modest expansion rate of 2.0 percent in Tunisia; the regional average was 2.9 percent (see Table 1.2). Meanwhile, food production regionwide grew only between 3 and 4 percent during the late 1970s. Table 1.2 indicates that food output rose in 1976–1978 (on a per-capita basis from a 1969–1971 base period) only moderately in six countries of the region and actually fell behind in another six. Among countries with substantial agricultural systems, Syria and Tunisia alone registered impressive gains. Higher per-capita production fails, in any case, to measure the strong food demand in the region stimulated by larger disposable incomes and public policies to raise nutritional levels. Thus, an official and satisfactory 5.5 percent average annual increase in Iran's agricultural production in 1970–1978 pales alongside the

TABLE 1.2
Population, Average Annual Growth Rates and Index of Per Capita Food Production
for Middle East Countries

| Country | Population in Millions 1980 | Average Annual Pop. Growth Rate 1970-78 | Index of Per Capita Food Prod. (1969-71=100) Average 1976-78 |
|---------|------------|------------|------------|
| Afghanistan | 15 | 2.2 | 100 |
| Algeria | 19 | 3.2 | 82 |
| Egypt | 42 | 2.2 | 93 |
| Iran | 38 | 2.9 | 113 |
| Iraq | 13 | 3.3 | 84 |
| Israel | 4 | 2.7 | 113 |
| Jordan | 3 | 3.3 | 77 |
| Lebanon | 3 | 2.5 | 85 |
| Libya | 3 | 4.1 | 123 |
| Morocco | 20 | 2.9 | 80 |
| Pakistan | 82 | 3.1 | 101 |
| Saudi Arabia | 9 | 3.5 | 135 |
| Sudan | 18 | 2.6 | 108 |
| Syria | 9 | 3.2 | 150 |
| Tunisia | 6 | 2.0 | 128 |
| Turkey | 45 | 2.5 | 110 |
| Average for 16 Countries | | 2.9 | 105 |

SOURCE:   World Bank, World Development Report, 1980, pp. 110-111, 142-143.

country's yearly estimated 8 to 12 percent growth in food consumption after 1974.[5]

Optimism has largely waned that the region's increasing food consumption can be met by a Green Revolution. The relatively easy gains from improved seed-cum-fertilizer and water application were realized in many countries in the late 1960s and early 1970s. Cereal yields rose between 1961–1965 and 1969–1971 by a regional average of 6 percent, and this improvement climbed to 10 percent between 1969–1971 and 1976–1978 (Table 1.3). There was, however, little consistency or uniformity in the performance of most countries. Of the seven countries that registered substantial increases in cereal yields by 1969–1971, only four were able to maintain these impressive rates during the 1970s. Among the states that either failed to improve yields or saw a falloff in the 1960s, more than half made substantial gains in the 1970s. Still, many countries like Tunisia and Libya remained far behind in relative productivity. Others—namely, Algeria, Sudan, and Jordan—appear to have been bypassed entirely by the Green Revolution in cereals. The performance of the region as a whole has been unimpressive in terms of both yields attained and comparative rates of growth. In every period, the Middle East yield averages rank ahead only of Africa, and by the late 1970s they were far behind Latin America, the Far East, all developing countries, and the world average. The Middle East's relative position,

TABLE 1.3
Cereal Yields in the Middle East and Other Regions

Yields in kg/ha

| Country | 1961-65 Average | 1969-71 Average | Percentage Gain, 1961-65 to 1969-71 | 1976-78 Average | Percentage Gain, 1969-71 to 1976-78 |
|---|---|---|---|---|---|
| Afghanistan | 1076 | 1132 | +5 | 1303 | +15 |
| Algeria | 623 | 614 | +2 | 636 | +4 |
| Egypt | 3310 | 3847 | +16 | 2975 | +3 |
| Iran | 930 | 823 | -12 | 1151 | +38 |
| Iraq | 831 | 1079 | +30 | 984 | -9 |
| Israel | 1471 | 1145 | -22 | 1803 | +57 |
| Jordan | 726 | 738 | +2 | 426 | -42 |
| Lebanon | 1027 | 870 | -15 | 1082 | +13 |
| Libya | 251 | 293 | +17 | 467 | +59 |
| Morocco | 820 | 989 | +21 | 928 | -6 |
| Pakistan | 874 | 1206 | +44 | 1453 | +28 |
| Saudi Arabia | 1356 | 1435 | +6 | 1088 | -24 |
| Sudan | 815 | 773 | -5 | 680 | -12 |
| Syria | 816 | 611 | -25 | 868 | +42 |
| Tunisia | 428 | 516 | +21 | 607 | +18 |
| Turkey | 1146 | 1351 | +18 | 1789 | +32 |
| Middle East* | 1031 | 1089 | +6 | 1202 | +10 |
| Africa | 735 | 803 | +9 | 818 | +2 |
| Latin America | 1331 | 1477 | +11 | 1662 | +12 |
| Far East | 1128 | 1334 | +18 | 1530 | +15 |
| All Developing | 1087 | 1423 | +31 | 1608 | +13 |
| World | 1460 | 1773 | +22 | 2011 | +13 |

SOURCES: FAO Production Yearbook 1978 and Yearbook 1976.

*The 16 countries shown in this table.

moreover, seems to be deteriorating. Whereas in 1961–1965 cereal yields in the sixteen countries were 71 percent of the world figures, in 1969–1971 they were just 61 percent, and in 1976–1978 they had declined to 60 percent. And if Egypt is excluded, in 1976–1978 the Middle East had little better than half the world average yields.

With population growth rates expected to keep pace with domestic agricultural production and food demand rising more rapidly than either, national food deficits are likely to continue to increase. Although more than two-thirds of cultivation is in cereals, the region is expected by the mid-1980s to have a shortfall of 22 million tons.[6] Egypt, which in 1980 imported nearly 4 million tons of cereal a year, will probably need to buy twice that amount by the year 2000. For the region as a whole, the United Nations has estimated that by 1985 food demand, assuming a 4 percent growth rate per annum, will have jumped 80 percent over 1970, while production will increase, if 1961–1973 rates are maintained, by 57 percent. And at the century's end, production is projected to stand at 148 percent above the 1970 figure, but demand will have risen 227 percent.[7] These production trends would maintain mid-1970s per-capita levels but make self-sufficiency a far more distant goal, and they would do nothing to improve the nutrition of low-income groups. To make progress toward these goals would probably entail an additional 70 to 100 percent rise in food production above what is projected.[8]

### The National Picture

The physically limiting factors in agricultural expansion in the Middle East are formidable. Above all, there is a dearth of land suitable for farming and climatic conditions yield insufficient rainfall. To be sure, the Levantine Coast, Egypt's Nile Valley and Delta, the Caspian Sea and Black Sea regions of Iran and Turkey, and Pakistan's Indus River Basin have usually adequate water resources. Other areas, especially the Tigris-Euphrates systems and Sudan's Nile savanna below Khartoum and its semitropical south, can support major soil restoration programs and transformation into regions of extensive cultivation. But overall, the climate and soils of the Middle East are not hospitable to agriculture intended to support large populations. The same ecological constraints in the region also largely preclude the kind of production take-off through modern technology experienced in areas like India's Punjab.

Arable land presently cultivated amounts to only a small fraction of the total land mass of the region, and much of this is set aside for nonfood crops. Table 1.4 indicates the extent of arable land under cultivation in the sixteen countries, its proportion of total land, and the amount of cultivated

TABLE 1.4
Arable Land Under Cultivation, Percentage of Total Land Mass, and Man-Land Ratios in Middle East Countries

| Country | Cultivated Land* in 1977 (1,000ha) | Percentage of Total Land Area | Cultivated hectares per capita in 1977 |
|---|---|---|---|
| Afghanistan | 8050 | 12 | .40 |
| Algeria | 7524 | 3 | .48 |
| Egypt | 2831 | 3 | .08 |
| Iran | 15950 | 10 | .48 |
| Iraq | 5290 | 12 | .46 |
| Israel | 430 | 21 | .12 |
| Jordan | 1365 | 14 | .65 |
| Lebanon | 348 | 34 | .12 |
| Libya | 2544 | 1 | 1.00 |
| Morocco | 7840 | 17 | .42 |
| Pakistan | 20300 | 26 | .27 |
| Saudi Arabia | 1110 | a | .15 |
| Sudan | 7495 | 3 | .46 |
| Syria | 5509 | 29 | .71 |
| Tunisia | 4410 | 28 | .73 |
| Turkey | 27929 | 36 | .66 |

SOURCE:   FAO Production Yearbook 1978 , pp. 45–52.

*Includes land in fruit tree and field crops and land that may be temporarily fallow.

[a]less than 1 percent.

land per capita. The extent of land in crops varies considerably in the region, from 27.9 million and 20.3 million hectares in Turkey and Pakistan, respectively, to a mere 348,000 in Lebanon. The cultivated area in Turkey, Lebanon, Pakistan, Syria, and Tunisia occupies more than a quarter of the total land, but in Algeria, Egypt, Sudan, Libya, and Saudi Arabia it amounts to 3 percent or less. Although the average productivity of the land must be taken into account, the per-capita figures in Table 1.4 offer a rough measure of the pressure of population on domestic food production. Egypt, with approximately 0.08 cultivated hectares for each person, is severely pressed, although multiple cropping in effect nearly doubles the area harvested. Ratios for Lebanon, Israel, and Saudi Arabia are also extremely poor. By themselves, the figures here suggest that Libya, Tunisia, Turkey, and Syria are in the best position to absorb proportionally large population increases.

By some calculations, the amount of agriculturally productive rainfed and irrigated land could increase by more than 50 percent regionwide. Surface and underground water resources might eventually be doubled, extending areas of cultivation and also irrigating cropland that is presently at the mercy of uncertain rainfall. The average efficiency of use of available water, currently about 50 percent, could be improved.[9] More progressive farming methods are expected to increase cropping intensity and yields. Out of the approximately one billion hectares of land in the Arab Middle East, 400 million have some economic potential, and 140 million would be suitable for crops, with the rest available for pasturage.[10] However, during the 1970s, no more than 50 million hectares in these Arab countries were being cultivated, and less than a fifth of this was irrigated. Much of the land already in production is threatened by desertification resulting from both drought and poor usage. Even in the region's developed agricultural areas, problems of drainage and poor water management have reduced crop yields and taken once good acreage out of production.

Prospects for increased food production and rapid progress in agricultural development in the Middle East are, on balance, not bright. A more complete picture warrants a brief survey of country prospects, especially against natural constraints, and a general classification of agricultural systems. Figure 1.1 roughly aligns the sixteen countries by their effective use of factors of production, estimated from overall yields, cropping intensities, and labor utilization; and their potential for further agricultural development, based primarily on known water and soil resources. Four systems have relatively greater natural endowments and exploitable potential: Sudan, Pakistan, Iraq, and Syria, in Class A, all possess considerable arable land not yet intensively cultivated, and Sudan has the most ample scope for reclamation.

As much as half of the region's projected horizontal expansion in cultivation is expected to come from Sudan. Ideally, cropping would be increased from the current 7.5 million hectares, less than one-fourth of which is irrigated, to as much as 32 million, with a large proportion of farmers assured of access to water on a regular basis. The greatly accelerated reclamation from new dams and irrigation schemes, exploiting the ample resources of the White Nile and the Blue Nile, is expected to open up vast new lands. Much stock is placed in the 270-kilometer Jonglei canal, now scheduled for completion in the mid-1980s. The canal is designed to recover at least 4 million cubic meters of White Nile water lost annually to evaporation, seepage, and stagnation in the country's enormous, Florida-sized Sudd marshes. But to realize its potential of becoming the region's major provider of grains, sugar, and edible oils, Sudan must also transform a system in which 80 percent of the agrarian population is engaged in traditional farming. Aside from building a physical infrastructure of roads, storage, and power supplies, all of which require massive transfusions of unreliable exter-

Figure 1.1
Classifications of Middle East Countries by Agricultural
Productivity and Development Potential

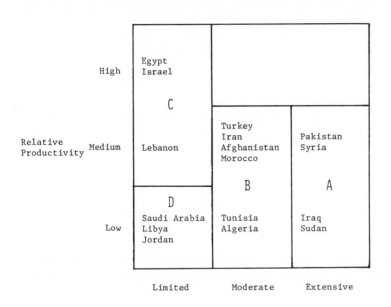

nal capital, the proper institutional framework and supporting services to farmers are critical to production growth. In the meantime, Sudan remains a net importer of food, forced to secure a quarter of its needs elsewhere. Production of the country's major export earner, cotton, has sagged in recent years.

If only on account of its 20.3 million hectares under cultivation and its population of 80 million, Pakistan must figure prominently in any food plans for the region. The country has some notable advantages and much underutilized potential. It possesses, as a legacy of its colonial experience, the world's most extensive network of irrigation canals, allowing two-thirds of the land in production to be irrigated. This distributive capacity, combined with rich soil and a long growing season, has led some to call the Indus River Basin "the great food machine."[11] By the early 1990s, Pakistan could more than triple its cereal grain production, far more than would be necessary to meet a domestic increase in demand of between 3 and 5 percent per annum. Already a major supplier of rice to the Middle East, the country could conceivably take first place as exporter in the world's rice trade.[12] Most of the increased output would come from vertical expansion, in higher yields and cropping intensities. But this growth turns on the affordability of imported fertilizer and other costly inputs by a country with meager foreign exchange reserves. It is doubtful that even by 1990 more than a quarter of the harvestable area will be covered by mechanization. There are also impediments to growth in a poorly rationalized farm price structure, and serious water management and administrative problems. The country has made little progress in recovering land lost to salinity and waterlogging created, ironically, by the extensive but unimproved canal system. Despite favorable weather conditions into the early 1980s, Pakistan had still not reached its long-sought goal of self-sufficiency in wheat production and was forced to reach out to international markets for commercial and concessional purchases.

Two other states, Iraq and Syria, are believed to have high potential for agricultural expansion, horizontally as well as vertically. Both countries have the advantage of a major river system and relatively favorable arable land-to-man ratios. Iraq, at least, is able to draw on usually reliable oil export revenues for agriculture-related investments. Planners have projected self-sufficiency in the 1980s, but this is based on the restoration of much of the once fertile, now highly saline alluvial plain between the Tigris and Euphrates rivers. In all, about half of the country's land is potentially arable, with just a quarter currently under cultivation. The hope is that an increase in irrigated land and more extensive double and triple cropping achieved by control of the seasonal flow of the rivers will enable Iraq again to become the region's granary.[13] But even with the enormous investment in irrigation and land supposed to be reclaimed in the early 1980s, low productivity in the country's long-neglected agricultural sector will not be easily reversed.[14] Much cropland, especially in cereal production, will remain in dryland farming in which primitive practices are still the rule. Moreover, little progress took place in the 1970s in creating the rural institutions and tenure patterns needed to retain motivated and skilled farmers. Although by 1980 Iraq had begun to question its heavy capital-intensive and sometimes doctrinaire approaches to agricultural development, it had not yet discovered how to overcome a fragmented system of agricultural administration nor settled on workable alternative structures for land ownership and production.

Syria's agriculture, by contrast to Iraq's, has benefited in recent years from a somewhat more sophisticated and open system of policymaking.[15] More pragmatic approaches to development and land tenure allowed skepticism to surface in government circles about the probable returns from a newly completed Euphrates dam and expensive irrigation projects. As a result, increased interest has been shown in upgrading dryland farming through improved extension services, research, and marketing arrangements. Still, with 80 to 90 percent of the cropland in the country rain-fed and subject to the vagaries of climate, any long-term plans must also include schemes to extend further the amount of irrigated land in use. Water resources in both Iraq and Syria are contingent on cooperation between them and with Turkey over the sharing and rational use of the Euphrates flow. Yet, as the 1980s began, there were once again tensions between the Baathist governments of Syria and Iraq. More significant, perhaps, with Syria's increased political isolation in the region and internal political challenges, the earlier flexibility might fall victim to the suspicions of a beleaguered regime.

The largest number of Middle East states is grouped in Figure 1.1 into Class B, those with moderate potential for further agricultural growth and low to moderate current productivity. Turkey, Morocco, Tunisia, Algeria, Iran, and Afghanistan have all been, in the not too distant past, essentially self-sufficient in major food crops but have failed over the last two decades to keep pace with rising national demand. Most allowed their agricultural sectors to stagnate or worse. Each faces difficulty in involving a large unemployed or underemployed rural population in productive activities. None of the countries in this group are likely to become major, reliable exporters of foodstuffs, although agriculture remains in all except Iran and Algeria an important source of foreign exchange. Citrus products are the second most important source of export earnings for Morocco, and olive oil is an export staple for Tunisia. Turkey, in some ways the region's brightest spot after six consecutive years of good harvests, has an exportable wheat surplus.[16]

All six countries rely for the most part on dry farming and traditional methods of cultivation. Except in small regions of adequate rainfall, agricultural output, especially grain production, is vulnerable to limited and unreliable rainfall. But each country has substantial undeveloped water resources. Turkey could increase its present 12 percent of irrigated land by three to four times; Morocco hopes to have 15 percent of its cropped land, or 1.1 million hectares, irrigated by the end of the decade. Afghanistan can theoretically add another 40 percent to its presently irrigated regions. Tunisia expects to increase its irrigated 132,000 hectares by up to 25,000 more hectares with several dam projects in the 1980s. Algeria has plans to raise its irrigated cropland from 300,000 to 500,000 hectares. A critical choice for these countries is whether efforts to restore self-sufficiency, particularly in food grains, should be made at the expense of cash crops and at the price of increased erosion as a result of intensive farming of converted pasture land.

The countries in Class B also have in common with most other countries in the region a familiar list of problems, headed by their need for increased capital investment in numerous small development projects, more input credits, and technical assistance for farmers. It is usually conceded that infrastructural weaknesses underlie much of the difficulty in reaching agricultural targets. The dearth of modern roads and transport, as well as inadequate storage, restricts the purchase of crops, helps to create spoilage, and interferes with the delivery of commodities to processors and urban markets. Limited port facilities slow agricultural exports while delaying and hiking the costs of food imports. Policymakers are further hampered by a lack of accurate data on which to base planning decisions. These countries have yet to find either a satisfactory way to consolidate fragmented production activities or to raise productivity levels under newly introduced industrial and cooperative models of farmer organization.

Another set of countries, Egypt, Israel and, marginally, Lebanon, are grouped in Class C. They are characterized by high to moderate productivity but a limited capacity for further agricultural growth. These countries have realized a high intensity of cultivation in many crops while they have also largely exhausted economically attainable water and land resources. New lands are likely to be of only marginal quality, opened for cropping only after costly public investment. Meanwhile, in each country, industry and housing are in increased competition with agriculture for use of land and water.

By most measures, Egypt's agricultural system is the region's most successful. Its perennial irrigation, allowing in large areas two and three crops yearly, and the outstanding yields obtained make it one of the most agriculturally prolific systems in the world. Yet this country is also unable to feed itself. Farmed land-to-man ratios have dropped throughout the century under pressures of population growth. Egypt loses roughly 20,000 hectares a year to urban sprawl, and waterlogging resulting from poor drainage and misuse of water resources has ruined once highly productive land. Food grain hectarage has declined over the last twenty years while agricultural imports have risen dramatically.[17] Expanded mechanization and further application of fertilizers, improved seeds, and plant protection can boost output in the Nile Valley and Delta, Egypt's "old lands." Aspirations of planners for further growth are also horizontal; plans call for extension into the West Desert and Sinai to reclaim between 2 and 3 million hectares over a twenty-year period.[18] Yet experiences to date with new land development must be sobering; the low productivity obtained reveals difficulties as much technological, administrative, and social as economic. Moreover, ambitious horizontal expansion is contingent on an increased volume of water from projects in Sudan to minimize the loss of Nile water and from other sources,

including better conservation. The government's inability to control cropping decisions or provide suitable incentives for farmers also leaves little
reason for optimism. In any event, shortage of investment capital makes any
grandiose schemes for old or new lands in Egypt highly problematic without
massive foreign investment.

While Egypt is probably approaching maximum use of available water
from the current Nile flow, the scarcity of water in Israel has been a continual and acute problem. At independence in 1948, only 30,000 hectares
were under irrigation. But with completion of the country's integrated water
system during the 1960s, irrigated areas were broadly extended and totaled
186,000 hectares by the mid-1970s. Full exploitation of the Jordan River, its
tributaries, and two major aquifers—the country's most expensive development undertaking—left no other promising sources of water.[19] At least in
the Jewish sector, production can increase only with incremental productivity gains, mainly on irrigated modern farms. New techniques, including
cloud seeding, desalinization, and sewerage reclamation, are of doubtful
short-run value. Notable progress in conservation, including efficient irrigation methods—Israel already gets between 70 and 80 percent efficiency—is
needed to overcome rapidly growing nonagricultural consumption. Israel
has long settled for a policy of foregoing self-sufficiency in its concentration
on export crops. Even with diversification, grains, meats, and vegetable oils
must be imported. Although agriculture has for most of the country's
history claimed a small and declining fraction of the labor force and gross
domestic product (see Chapter 2), agricultural exports have remained an important component of the economy. In the late 1970s, their value and
volume rose handsomely against the tide of a rapidly worsening trade
deficit. At the same time, the increasing costs of water to agriculture have
had an impact on traditional water-intensive export crops, such as oranges
and some vegetables, leading to a gradual switch to other crops.[20]

Lebanon has a ratio of cropped land to population similar to those of
Egypt and Israel, and its prospects for increased output and greater efficiency in production are, if for somewhat different reasons, also limited.
Certainly, Lebanon has been no match for Egypt and Israel in productivity.
The country does have some assets, however. Much of the coastal plain and
terraced hills are well-watered fertile soil, normally providing Lebanon with
a sizable export crop of fruits and vegetables. The broad, more arid Bekaa
Valley contains much of the country's grain production and many of its
larger, more modern farms. A relatively high proportion of arable land is in
production, and a high intensity of irrigation exists in many zones. At best,
though, the country can produce only one-half to two-thirds of its domestic
food needs. The cost of improving marginal areas through irrigation is very
high. Aside from the Litani River in the south, there are no obvious new

sources to be tapped. Nor are the chances of boosting productivity much better. A diminishing rural labor force, the result in large part of dismal farm income among smaller producers, obliges Lebanon to import a seasonal agricultural workforce of 100,000.[21] The mechanization, technology, and training necessary to help overcome this labor shortage and raise productivity have had to compete for funds in the postwar recovery. Only the larger, prosperous growers are in a position to invest in machinery in the farm economy, which is still dominated by the private sector. Struggling governments have been slow to adopt policies that would make it possible for small farmers to qualify for credit for equipment purchases.

The balance of available water and consumption in agricultural and nonagricultural uses is especially precarious in Jordan, Libya, and Saudi Arabia, all identified in Class D in Figure 1.1. Low potential and productivity in these countries reflect their sparse arable and irrigable land and still largely traditional agricultural systems. The aridity and poor soils that are typical of much of the Middle East are unrelieved in Saudi Arabia and Libya by any perennial rivers or streams. Although the scope of planned development in Jordan is limited by most regional standards, the country has ambitious schemes for irrigation systems, dams, reservoirs, and canals to maximize water resources. The first phase of an extended scheme to increase Jordan's water supplies was reached with completion of the East Ghor Canal in 1966. Full achievement awaits the building of the Marqarin Dam on the Yarmouk River near Syria which, before the souring of relations between the two countries, was scheduled for completion in the early 1980s. The major objective of the numerous projects, financed with World Bank, Arab, West German, and U.S. loans, is the continued development of the Jordan Valley, described as "a natural hothouse" for vegetables.[22] The Yarmouk project is designed to attract thousands of farmers to the valley and to expand sprinkler irrigation up to 36,000 hectares. The water is also expected to ease demands on the depleted underground reserves that have supplied industry and two-thirds of the country's population in the Greater Amman region.[23] A development authority created for the valley is meant to serve as a model of agricultural administration as well as of irrigation for the rest of the country. It directly involves an agency of the central government in overseeing land distribution, production, rural services, crop research, and cooperative marketing.[24] Even with the plan's success, some 80 to 90 percent of cultivable land in the Hashemite kingdom will remain in the dry farming sector where 40 percent of food production takes place and where yields in most seasons are among the lowest in the Middle East.

Oil-rich Saudi Arabia and Libya share many of Jordan's physical constraints but few of its financial ones. High-cost agricultural projects and related public works and services can prepare these largely desert countries to meet a larger, if still minor, share of their domestic food requirements. Although Saudi development budgets for agriculture are small relative to other outlays, the government provides generous credits to the sector. More of a hindrance to development and higher productivity are problems of effective absorption of funds in a sector short on technicians and skilled administrators, lacking a skilled agricultural labor force, and burdened by a traditional land tenure system. Radical Libya gives greater priority to agriculture in its budget, with expenditures heavily targeted for infrastructural and social projects and large subsidies to growers. Yet in both states rapid modernization has been slow to penetrate the agricultural sphere, and there are even doubts about its suitability; for example, mechanization and intense cropping are questionable practices in shallow soils that are probably better left to animal grazing. Libyan planners have become more sober about the chances of any dramatic new increases in domestic food production; their ambitious land reclamation plans were laid on the basis of coastal aquifers, which are now being rapidly depleted, and inland fossil water reserves, now quickly dropping. Conservation and new technologies in the reclamation of oases are feasible, and improved irrigation methods can release high-quality water for expanded use. Hydroponics may have a role to play in cultivation of high-value crops, and the partial substitution of desalinized water for underground sources is well under way. These prosperous countries, along with the oil-exporting states of the Gulf, also have the option of ensuring future availability of food by underwriting agricultural projects in other Middle East countries, notably those in Class A. In the meantime, Saudi Arabia and Libya seem resigned to a high level of imports from outside the region. That they are also determined to use their considerable oil income to strengthen domestic and regional sources is due as much to political as to economic reasons.

## Food and Assistance Systems

In an important sense, the production, distribution, and consumption of food in countries of the Middle East are governed by decisions reached within the context of largely distinct but interacting systems. Each contains mechanisms, both formal and informal, that regulate the behavior of those engaged in food trade and aid and agricultural development assistance. At the broadest level there exists a global system of which the Middle East is an increasingly critical component. Transactions at this level frame much of what Hopkins and Puchala have referred to as an international "food regime,"[25] a prevailing set of rules and institutionalized expectations that govern food affairs among nations. These normative international parameters have the effect of both limiting choices and prescribing actions, public and private. The world food regime, which Hopkins and Puchala recognized as having undergone change during the 1970s, had long been characterized by norms supporting free-market aspirations, a low priority on national self-reliance in food, an absence of concern for chronic hunger, and respect for national sovereignty.[26] A corresponding set of food aid and development assistance norms have included those that ensure ample dividends for donor countries' economies, avoid creating future commercial competitors among the recipient countries, and give priority to high-technology transfers. To the extent that these constraints have been undermined in recent years by changes in the economic and political order, and especially by attitudes in the Third World, the Middle East has made a sizable contribution.

A set of governing rules and expectations also suitably fits the concept of a regional food and assistance system. Although the normative elements in the Middle East are not nearly so well developed or enforced as those at the global level, the region is increasingly characterized by exchanges of food commodities, development capital, research findings, and skilled and unskilled personnel, together with the rules for regulating these activities. In the area from Morocco to Pakistan, there was evidence throughout the 1970s of a growing self-consciousness and assertiveness. Although drawing strength from symbolic ties of culture and religion, the region felt as well the pulls of economic interdependence and convergent political aspirations. Notwithstanding the continuing ideological differences and increasingly disparate national incomes, countries of the region shared an intensifying rejection of foreign modes and values. In the agricultural sphere, conditions of soil, climate, and population growth that are often similar gave the region a coherence that was reflected in many common problems of development and food requirements. There emerged from all of this, if still more at the level of rhetoric than action, the desire for regional agricultural cooperation and joint development that would replace many global food policy dictates.

A national system contains rules and expectations governing food and development policies that are more numerous and potentially more competitive than those imposed by regional or international systems. These national, usually elite-held values carry significant implications for the behavior of domestic food producers, distributors, and consumers. Support for the view that agriculture now warrants higher priority in national planning and increased public investment is among the more salient national norms found in Middle East countries. There is a growing conviction among policymakers that industrial and agricultural sectors are complementary and that national development will be stunted or illusory unless both are considered and somehow balanced. A related norm calls for a new look at self-reliance in food. The need for imported commodities and technologies, if possible on the best terms, is presumed to continue but there is a consensus that the deepening reliance on foreign sources of aid and trade must somehow be reversed. Normative support is also apparent for a larger government responsibility for increasing social and economic justice for agriculturally productive populations. Although slow in emerging in many countries, this norm has become a major ingredient in prevailing government formulas for national legitimacy and integration, regardless of prevailing economic or political ideologies. Equity that results in higher rural employment, larger farm incomes, and generally better standards of living is also recognized as a part of the solution to weak domestic demand for industrial products, excessive rural migration, and the raising of agricultural-sector productivity. Often the foremost consideration is that the boundaries for food and agricultural development policy are established by the norm that policies are expected to contribute to, or at least not compromise, the political security and control of those holding power nationally and often locally.

National system norms are likely to be manifested in government-regulated commodity pricing, food and farm-input subsidies, import-export controls, and the choices of development projects and programs. The rules and expectations also find expression in elite attitudes toward land tenure reform, institutional strategies of rural development, and farm modernization. The national system is, to be sure, not all-inclusive; large segments of the agricultural sector—namely, the majority of farmers outside the market economy—may remain, for the most part, insulated from the governing rules. But even these subsistence producers, by their inability or reluctance to participate in a national system, help to shape its norms.

At the global level the major system norms affecting policies have, over time, been largely parallel and reinforcing, and usually powerful economic sanctions have been available to discourage deviation. The more inchoate norms at the regional level may have a high level of consensus but lack mechanisms of enforcement. Nationally, the controlling norms that serve as guides and handy rationalizations for policy may not always be clear or easily applied. Either a strong elite consensus on normative priorities is lacking, or the expectations, and more especially their policy applications, are to some degree incompatible. Moreover, the costs for the maintenance of the system of trying to impose one set of values to the exclusion of others can run high. The task of policymakers is often to find the means to acknowledge and balance competing sets of expectations and policy goals.

Despite these contrasts, the three systems are essentially interdependent. A global system cannot be sustained without normally supportive policies by regional and national actors. Should a more meaningful regional system emerge in the Middle East, it will be at the initiative of those national decision makers able to impose some conformity on the trade and aid policies of other countries. In the formation of global norms, the food- and capital-exporting countries have played the dominant role in the postwar period, and Middle East states, along with others in the Third World, have learned to live within the constraints imposed by the developed states' values and interests. To the extent that global system priorities have changed during the 1970s, bringing different expectations about Third World food autonomy and new criteria for food and development aid recipients, as well as questions about capital-intensive approaches to rural development, countries of the Middle East have played no small part in these changes.

This book takes into account the constraints imposed by the three system levels on food and agricultural development policies in the Middle East. The chapters are focused mainly, however, on comparative national policies and their normative, sometimes changing parameters. The discussion identifies areas of public policy and decision processes in which these norms and the different perspectives and interests they reflect come into contact and possible conflict. Chapter 2 describes the competing claims of sectoral interests and underscores how the political bases for investment and development strategies are intertwined with social and economic factors. Chapter 3 examines from the perspective of class structures and relations agricultural-sector tensions arising from simultaneously pursued policy goals and the consequences of reform, subsidization, and reorganization programs. In Chapter 4, the implementation of policy is examined in the context of bureaucratic decision styles and biases whose origins are traced to institutional and broader system norms and interests. Global and regional rules and expectations are described in Chapter 5, which considers, among other topics, the possible distortions of national economies and production disincentives in bilateral and multilateral assistance and foreign trade. The chapter also discusses the likelihood that food exports can serve as an instrument of foreign policy directed at Middle East states. A final chapter draws attention to the coincidence of political strategies with development strategies and to the close interaction of food shortages and prices with political instability in the region.

## Notes

1. Also see Hossein Askari and John Cummings, "Food Shortages in the Middle East," *Middle Eastern Studies* 14, no. 3 (October 1978):347. The authors note the need for higher-quality protein in the region's diet and point out that it cannot be satisfied through increased quantities of the cereals cultivated in the region. Wheat is the basic protein source.

2. These figures are based on actual and projected statistics in John B. Parker, Jr.,

"North Africa-Mideast Fastest Growing Market for Agricultural Imports," *Foreign Agriculture* (U.S. Department of Agriculture), January 1, 1979, p. 2; *Outlook for U.S. Agricultural Exports* (U.S. Department of Agriculture), August 20, 1980, p. 1.

3. "FAO's Saouma: Co-operate or Starve," *Middle East* (London), March 1981, p. 68; *Middle East Economic Digest,* July 7, 1978, p. 19; and *Foreign Agriculture,* December 1979, p. 25. (Hereafter all tons are metric tons.)

4. "Saudi Farm Imports Head Toward 4.5 billion," *Foreign Agriculture,* September 1980, p. 14. Also see, "Secrets of Iraq's Oil Sale Surge," *Middle East,* August 1980, p. 53; and "Which Land is My Land," *Middle East,* September 1980, p. 75.

5. Ann Schulz, "Food in Iran: The Politics of Insufficiency," in Raymond F. Hopkins, Donald J. Puchala, and Ross B. Talbot, eds., *Food, Politics, and Agricultural Development: Case Studies in the Public Policy of Rural Modernization* (Boulder, Colo.: Westview Press, 1979), p. 173; also, M. G. Weinbaum, "Agricultural Policy and Development Politics in Iran," *Middle East Journal* 31, no. 4 (Autumn 1977):436. Using figures from *MERIP Reports* 43 (1976), p. 6, Schulz found that per-capita agricultural production in Iran was considerably lower than in 1935 ("Food in Iran," p. 173). Lester R. Brown, *Redefining National Security,* Worldwatch Paper 14 (Washington, D.C.: Worldwatch Institute, October 1977), p. 40, claimed that Iran had suffered a 42 percent per-capita decline in grain production in the previous quarter century.

6. International Food Policy Research Institute, *Meeting Food Needs in the Developing World: The Location and Magnitude of the Task in the Next Decade,* Report no. 1, February 1976.

7. United Nations, *Assessment of the World Food Situation: Present and Future* (New York: United Nations, 1974), p. 79. Also, "Arab Food Experts Say: Co-operate or Starve," *Middle East,* November 1978, p. 137. The Food and Agriculture Organization estimates that by 1985 the wheat deficit for the Middle East will reach 10 million tons, sugar 3.3 million, meat 1.1 million, and rice 2.1 million. "Regional Land Reform Bears Little Fruit," Ibid., September 1979, p. 79.

8. Askari and Cummings, "Food Shortages," pp. 333, 338. The authors' estimates are apparently exclusive of the Maghreb countries, Afghanistan, and Pakistan.

9. Food and Agriculture Organization, *State of Food and Agricultural Production, 1977* (Rome: Food and Agriculture Organization, 1977), p. 2; idem, *State of Food and Agricultural Production, 1978,* p. 43. Also, *Middle East Economic Digest,* May 25, 1978, p. 9.

10. From a study by agronomist Mustapha al-Gabali in the *Christian Science Monitor,* December 27, 1976, which quoted an article in *al-Ahram,* January 17, 1974. Also see discussion in John Waterbury, "Aish: Egypt's Growing Food Crisis," *American Universities Field Staff Reports* Northeast Africa Series 19, no. 3 (December 1974), p. 11.

11. John Cool, "The Great Indus Food Machine," *Pakistan Economist,* March 18, 1978, pp. 13–17. The author at the time headed the Ford Foundation mission in Pakistan and based his conclusions on a Ford-sponsored study by Roger Revelle and Walter P. Falcon.

12. Ibid.

13. Richard F. Nyrop, ed., *Iraq: A Country Study,* Foreign Area Handbook Series (Washington, D.C.: American University, 1979), p. 157. Also see *Middle East Economic Digest,* February 10, 1980.

14. Six major irrigation projects, expected at least on paper to add 650,000 hectares of improved land, were slated for completion in the early 1980s. "Iraq's Cloud with the Silver Lining," *Middle East,* January 1981, p. 48.

15. Particularly instructive are the observations, even if they are to some extent dated, by Robert Springborg in "Baathism in Practice: Agriculture, Politics and Political Culture in Syria and Iraq," unpublished paper delivered at the meetings of the Middle East Studies Association, November 1980, Washington, D.C.

16. About 1.2 million tons were likely to be exported in 1980-1981. "Turkey: Recent Wheat Crop Brightens Export Prospects," *Foreign Agriculture,* November 1980, p. 30.

17. James B. Fitch, Hassan A. Khedr, and Dale Whittington, "The Economic Efficiency of Water Use in Egyptian Agriculture: Opening Round of a Debate," a paper presented at the 17th International Conference of Agricultural Economists, September 3–13, 1979, Banff, Canada, pp. 2 and 8.

18. See discussion in "Farming in the Arab East," *ARAMCO World Magazine,* May-June 1978, pp. 33–38.

19. Richard Nyrop, ed., *Israel; a Country Study,* Foreign Area Handbook Series (Washington, D.C.: American University, 1979), p. 191. See this volume for a good summary of the state of Israel's agriculture.

20. *Foreign Agriculture,* May 1980, p. 28.

21. *Arab Economist,* no. 100 (January 1978), p. 12. International aid is projected to inject $1.5 billion into comprehensive development of the Bekaa Valley. *Middle East,* August 1980, p. 26.

22. "Farming in the Arab East," p. 7.

23. "Maqarin Dam: A Project in Need of People," *Middle East,* September 1978, p. 117; "Jordan Faces Drought Disaster," *Middle East,* September 1979, p. 39.

24. A full description of the Jordan Valley development can be found in Oddvar Aresvik, *The Agricultural Development of Jordan* (New York: Praeger Publishers, 1976), p. 339.

25. Raymond F. Hopkins and Donald J. Puchala, "Prospects on the International Relations of Food," *International Organization* 32, no. 3 (Summer 1978):598.

26. Ibid., pp. 600–603.

# 2
# The Agricultural Sector
# in Development Policy

Indifference and calculated neglect of agricultural development and rural interests are evident in more than two decades of public policy in the Middle East. In blueprints for economic growth, the agrarian sector throughout most of the region rated secondary attention and was often allowed to languish. Using advanced industrial countries of the West as models, governments sought a remedy for the region's economic backwardness in capital accumulation to provide for rapid urban-industrial expansion and competitive exports. Public investment in heavy industry, as well as in communications and defense, promised the desired national self-determination, while an agriculture-dominated economy supposedly sentenced a country to an impotent future. In countries in which agriculture had been the prime source of national income, new sources were indispensable in view of the limitations on agricultural productivity inherent in the region's soil and climate. Transition to an urban-industrial society was most easily justified where agricultural systems were already small and tenuous and countries survived off handsome oil revenues. Many of the Middle East's most traditional countries led the way in accepting the vision of a consumption-oriented, urban society as the key to national prosperity, power, and respect, which would sustain them in a future of declining oil revenues. But in their willingness to leave agriculture largely unimproved and to tolerate chronic underproduction, states of the Middle East necessarily failed to optimize their food production potential, assuring themselves of a deepening dependence on foreign imports. The region's policymakers, aware that agriculture had historically contracted as a source of employment and income in the world's more developed states, largely ignored the fact that, along with urban and industrial expansion, these modern countries had usually evolved a highly efficient, technologically advanced agriculture.

Agriculture was understandably not invited to make strong, competing claims on national resources. At most, the sector would assume a supportive role in supplying needed raw materials, manpower, and food. The rural areas were also expected to make a critical contribution to the mobilization of savings for industrial growth. Massive dams, ambitious water projects, and other capital-intensive, prestige undertakings, ostensibly designed to benefit agriculture, were also substantially used to meet the water requirements of industry and a growing urban population. By the early 1970s, no more than 15 percent of public investment in the region was going to the agricultural sector, broadly defined. Officials periodically voiced concern about stagnant production of certain crops and the need to solve the problem of rural unemployment. The region's more progressive regimes championed the cause of the disadvantaged peasants and the fuller use of their resources. Yet many rural economic problems and social injustices were expected to be alleviated in an accelerated migration from the countryside.

The traditional city and village in the Islamic Middle East have always stood in some contrast. Preindustrial cities and larger towns grew up as commercial, religious, and administrative centers, serving and acting upon often diverse populations. The villages, the focus of settlement for the vast majority who tilled the soil, were largely homogeneous and undifferentiated in their institutions and social roles. The village was frequently isolated and fundamentally conservative; the city was a crossroads of people and ideas. Societal change, however slow, originated in the cities and was absorbed there almost entirely. City dwellers had adopted much from village and nomadic cultures, and many continued to idealize rural life; but the urbanized also held village peasants in contempt as ignorant and backward folk.[1]

With expanded industrialization in the region, rural and urban areas often seem even more contrasting in their value systems and material conditions. Western products and practices, so inescapably tied to modernization, are embraced by most urban middle-class elements and envied in the working-class stratum, but they are slow to penetrate the countryside. In other respects, however, the distance between city and village has been narrowed. Mass migrations to the cities and larger towns have ended the classic isolation of village life. The economic attractions of the urban areas, along with the availability of health, education, and other facilities, initially absorbed large, cheap labor surpluses from the provinces for construction and other industries. The region's largely inefficient industries ensured a high labor intensity. A steady stream of unemployed from the hinterlands acted, meanwhile, to restrain demands by urban labor for better working conditions.

Yet during the 1970s a diminishing share of the potential work force was employable in the cities. Excessive transfers of population from rural to urban areas, especially evident in Iran, Algeria, Turkey, and Egypt, created serious problems for both urban and rural sectors. Much public investment was allocated to maintaining and expanding urban services and social programs for the recent arrivals. Social problems emerged from the concentration of transplanted labor in the cities, and income disparities between urban and rural areas increased tensions. On the fringes of the largest Middle East cities appeared shantytowns that were fertile grounds for economic discontent and political unrest. The continuing migration from the countryside transformed people who had once been agriculturally productive, if only marginally self-sufficient, into full-time consumers. Rising incomes in the urban middle class, coupled with newer, mass-based dietary preferences, also created wider demand, including markets for high-value food imports. Although the lure of good salaries in the expanded labor markets of the Gulf states and Libya relieved some of the pressures on urban employment and offered a welcomed safety valve and source of foreign exchange for a number of hard-pressed countries, the solutions it offered were only temporary. A revived rural sector would be needed to help ensure both reliable food supplies in the rapidly growing urban areas and the raw materials on which industry was dependent.

Policymakers in most Middle East states took a second, hard look at their agricultural sectors during the 1970s. Rural society and agricultural development, so long viewed as peripheral to national progress and a drag on modernization, were accorded higher standing on policy agendas across the region. Extractive economic policies that relieved the rural areas of capital and labor for an expanding urban-industrial sector began to give way, in official pronouncements at least, to development strategies that recognized sectoral balance and interdependence. The hinterlands that had previously satisfied central governments through a trickle of taxes and periodic expressions of loyalty were increasingly incorporated into national economic planning. The aspirations and basic needs of the rural poor now figure prominently in the rhetoric of conservative as well as radical regimes. Using modern modes of communication and social and economic organization, authorities have turned to their own agents to supervise and direct local affairs, replacing local status elites as intermediaries with the peasantry.

Without abandoning ambitions for a larger industrial base, governments appreciate better the limits of technology and the social costs of growth. Earlier goals have also been questioned in the light of experience. Plans for industry were often found to be unrealistic and projects mismanaged. Capitalization was inadequate in the poorer states, and long-term foreign indebtedness became identified as a serious burden. Efforts to induce rapid change were discovered to carry strong inflationary pressures and other

strains, even for the more affluent economies. Worker productivity has remained low across the region, a result of both poor skills and poor motivation. Most industrial goods have turned out to be uncompetitive in international markets, and domestic demand is normally too weak to absorb these
finished products.

But for all the increased traffic of people and ideas between city and
village, and the heightened awareness of their mutual dependence, the rural
areas of the Middle East have remained largely backwaters in the process of
national development. The lot of the small farmer and landless worker,
never very good, has improved very slowly in most countries of the region
and has actually deteriorated in others.[2] The inequalities between villages
and the cities and larger towns have generally widened. The countryside receives levels of public services that pale by comparison with those in cities,
even next to the inadequate delivery to urban slums. Rural dwellers are
distinctively worse-off in education and health. There is little debate that
the problems of the rural masses are traceable to low incomes. Less agreement exists on the means to relieve poverty. Land fragmented through
inheritance and redistribution often leaves uneconomic-sized farms. Unpro-
gressive methods of cultivation contribute to low productivity and ensure
that traditional farming is almost everywhere a marginal economic activity.
Many planners stress the need for laws and policies to create greater incentives for cultivators and improved access to farm inputs. Others insist that
these changes would be superficial and that only a radical restructuring of
the social and political system will produce the desired economic changes. In
any case, public policies in the region have done little to relieve the hardships of rural majorities and, whether deliberately or inadvertently, have
perpetuated the poor conditions of the countryside.

## A Sectoral Profile

Despite demographic and social changes, the rural sector continues to
bulk large in the Middle East as a source of employment and in its economic
contribution. As Table 2.1 shows, a high proportion of the labor force in the
region remains tied to agricultural pursuits. Although the share has dropped
between 1960 and 1977, in some cases sharply, only in Israel and Lebanon is
agricultural employment less than 20 percent. The heaviest exodus of people
from agricultural occupations has occurred in Algeria, Libya, and Lebanon,
with notable movement also in Iran, Jordan, and Turkey. Regionwide, there
is reason to believe that increasing numbers will try to earn their livelihood
away from the rural areas and that, by the century's end, the Middle East

TABLE 2.1
Share of Labor Force in Agriculture in 1960, 1978

| Country | Percentage in Agriculture | |
| --- | --- | --- |
| | 1960 | 1978 |
| Afghanistan | 85 | 79 |
| Algeria | 67 | 30 |
| Egypt | 58 | 51 |
| Iran | 54 | 40 |
| Iraq | 53 | 42 |
| Israel | 14 | 7 |
| Jordan | 44 | 27 |
| Lebanon | 38 | 12 |
| Libya | 53 | 21 |
| Morocco | 62 | 53 |
| Pakistan | 61 | 58 |
| Saudi Arabia | 71 | 62 |
| Sudan | 86 | 79 |
| Syria | 54 | 49 |
| Tunisia | 56 | 45 |
| Turkey | 78 | 60 |

Source: The World Bank, World Development Report, 1980 (New York: Oxford University Press, 1980), pp. 146-147.

may become a heavily urbanized region. At least presently, agriculture continues to support a large segment of the population, roughly 50 percent or more of those gainfully employed in half of the countries examined.

Agriculture also makes a substantial contribution to national wealth in much of the region. Table 2.2 indicates that the sector is dominant in Afghanistan and Sudan; and in Pakistan, Egypt, and Turkey, it accounted for between one-fourth and one-third of the gross domestic product (GDP) in 1978. In three other countries its share was roughly one-fifth. That these statistics in fact underestimate the importance of agriculture to the region's economies is made clearer in Table 2.3, in which food and related commodities are shown as a share of merchandise exports. Aside from the major oil-exporting states, in all but two countries the percentage of exports is appreciably higher than the contribution to GDP; the particular dependence of Sudan, Afghanistan, Turkey, Egypt, Pakistan, Jordan, and Morocco on

TABLE 2.2
Distribution of Gross Domestic Product by Major Sectors

| Country | Percentage in Agriculture 1960* | 1978** | Percentage in Industry 1960* | 1978** | Percentage in Services 1960* | 1978** |
|---|---|---|---|---|---|---|
| Afghanistan | - | 55 | - | 14 | - | 31 |
| Algeria | 21 | 8 | 33 | 56 | 46 | 36 |
| Egypt | 30 | 29 | 24 | 30 | 46 | 41 |
| Iran | 29 | 9 | 33 | 54 | 38 | 37 |
| Iraq | 17 | 8 | 52 | - | 31 | - |
| Israel | 11 | 7 | 32 | 37 | 57 | 56 |
| Jordan | - | 11 | - | 29 | - | 60 |
| Lebanon | 12 | - | 20 | - | 68 | - |
| Libya | - | 2 | - | 72 | - | 27 |
| Morocco | 23 | 18 | 27 | 32 | 50 | 50 |
| Pakistan | 46 | 32 | 16 | 24 | 38 | 44 |
| Saudi Arabia | - | 1 | - | 76 | - | 23 |
| Sudan | 58 | 41 | - | - | 27 | - |
| Syria | - | 20 | - | 28 | - | 52 |
| Tunisia | 24 | 18 | 18 | 30 | 58 | 52 |
| Turkey | 41 | 27 | 21 | 28 | 38 | 45 |

Sources: The World Bank, World Development Report, 1979, pp. 130-131; and Report, 1980, pp. 114-115.

*Some figures are for 1961.
**Some figures are for 1976 and 1977.

TABLE 2.3
Percentage Share of Merchandise Exports

| Country | Percentage of Food and Related Commodities* 1960*** | 1977 | Percentage of Fuels, Minerals, and Metals 1960*** | 1977 | Percentage of all Manufactures** 1960*** | 1977 |
|---|---|---|---|---|---|---|
| Afghanistan | 82 | 74 | (.) | 13 | 18 | 13 |
| Algeria | 81 | 2 | 12 | 97 | 7 | 1 |
| Egypt | 84 | 49 | 4 | 25 | 12 | 27 |
| Iran | 9 | 1 | 88 | 99 | 3 | (.) |
| Iraq | 3 | 1 | 97 | 99 | 0 | (.) |
| Israel | 35 | 19 | 4 | 11 | 61 | 80 |
| Jordan | 96 | 38 | 0 | 31 | 4 | 31 |
| Lebanon | - | - | - | - | - | - |
| Libya | 84 | 0 | 6 | 100 | 10 | 0 |
| Morocco | 54 | 33 | 38 | 46 | 8 | 21 |
| Pakistan | 73 | 36 | 0 | 5 | 27 | 59 |
| Saudi Arabia | 0 | 0 | 100 | 100 | 0 | (.) |
| Sudan | 100 | 95 | 0 | (.) | 0 | (.) |
| Syria | 81 | 28 | 0 | 62 | 19 | 10 |
| Tunisia | 66 | 17 | 24 | 49 | 10 | 34 |
| Turkey | 89 | 67 | 8 | 8 | 3 | 25 |

SOURCES: The World Bank, World Development Report, 1979, pp. 142-143, and Report 1980, pp. 126-127.

*Includes food and live animals, beverages and tobacco, inedible crude materials, oils, fats, and waxes.
**Includes textiles and clothing, machinery and transport equipment, and other manufactures.
***Some figures are for 1961 rather than 1960.

food and related commodity exports is indicated. Israel, whose agricultural sector contributed merely 7 percent of GDP, relied on this sector for 19 percent of its merchandise exports in 1977.

The larger picture for the Middle East is of course one in which agriculture's economic role has contracted relative to the roles of other sectors. For every country for which comparative figures are available, the contribution made by agriculture has diminished over the nearly two decades examined. Oil-rich Libya and Algeria show the expected contraction in agricultural exports, but precipitous falloffs have also occurred in the share of exports in more agriculturally active Syria, Egypt, Pakistan, and Turkey, as well as in Tunisia, Jordan, and Morocco (Table 2.3). Between 1960 and 1978, industry's expanded contribution to national income in nonoil-exporting Tunisia, Egypt, Pakistan, and Turkey (Table 2.2) showed at least a 25 percent increase, usually at the expense of agriculture.

A plausible interpretation of the data in Tables 2.1 and 2.2 leads to the conclusion that the region has also experienced a declining efficiency of agriculture, measured by the ratio of the sector's contribution to GDP to its share of the agricultural work force. Table 2.4 shows that between 1960 and 1978 the much-heralded shift of labor away from rural areas did not keep pace with the more rapid contraction of agriculture's contribution to national income. The most efficient use of the agricultural work force occurred in Israel, Pakistan, and Sudan in 1960, but only Israel bettered this ratio by 1978. More modestly, Egypt and Jordan had also improved between 1960 and 1978; in all other countries studied, however, there was declining efficiency. Some of the sharpest losses are noted for Iran and Iraq. But the list of countries with steeply declining ratios also includes more agriculturally dependent Sudan, Pakistan, and Turkey. Overall, these data support the view that across most of the Middle East, despite rural migrations and local labor shortages, there exists an expanding, underproductive rural work force.

Several growth rates are more revealing of the changing status of agriculture in countries of the Middle East and suggest, to some extent, the relative public priorities. Table 2.5, which presents World Bank figures for average annual growth in agriculture, industry, and services for the periods 1960–1970 and 1970–1978, indicates considerable variation in rates of expansion.[3] The figures confirm that production was sluggish in the agricultural sector in many countries of the region. They also reveal, however, that the average rate of growth for all sixteen countries, 4.3 percent in the 1970s, had improved over the 3.8 percent registered during the previous decade. For many states in the Middle East, the 1970s was also a period when the gap between agricultural and industrial growth, although wide, had narrowed somewhat.

TABLE 2.4
Agricultural Efficiency as Measured by the Ratio of
the Sector's Contribution to GDP to its Share of the
Labor Force

| Country | Efficiency Ratio | |
| | 1960 | 1978 |
| --- | --- | --- |
| Afghanistan | – | – |
| Algeria | .31 | .26 |
| Egypt | .52 | .57 |
| Iran | .54 | .22 |
| Iraq | .32 | .19 |
| Israel | .79 | 1.00 |
| Jordan | .36 | .41 |
| Lebanon | .32 | – |
| Libya | .26 | .09 |
| Morocco | .37 | .34 |
| Pakistan | .75 | .55 |
| Saudi Arabia | – | .02 |
| Sudan | .67 | .52 |
| Syria | .46 | .41 |
| Tunisia | .43 | .40 |
| Turkey | .53 | .45 |

SOURCES: Calculated from data in The World Bank,
World Development Report, 1979 and Report, 1980.

Table 2.5 divides into four categories the countries for which there is comparative agricultural growth data. In the first are Algeria and Egypt where, although the countries differed sharply in their rate of expansion, the magnitude of change between periods was similarly minimal. Stagnant agricultural growth in the two countries contrasts with higher rates for other economic activities, particularly in Egypt's industrial and service sectors during the 1970s. A second category of states includes Iran, Israel, and Turkey, in which average annual growth rates for agriculture improved moderately between the 1960s and 1970s.[4] Gains in Turkey came after a relatively low rate of expansion during the earlier decade. The table also indicates that once wide differences between agriculture and industry disappeared in Iran and Israel in the 1970s, although Iran had experienced a spectacular rate of development in its service sector.

Libya, Sudan, Tunisia, and Syria form a third group of countries, those with high agricultural sector growth rates during the 1970s and substantial improvement over the previous decade. The 1970–1978 growth for Libya, in particular, is exaggerated by a small agricultural base, but the expansion through the 1970s recorded by Libya and Sudan is among the highest in the

TABLE 2.5
Average Annual Growth Rates by Sector, 1960–70, 1970–78

| Country | Agriculture Percentage 1960–70* | Agriculture Percentage 1970–78** | Industry Percentage 1960–70* | Industry Percentage 1970–78** | Services Percentage 1960–70* | Services Percentage 1970–78*** |
|---|---|---|---|---|---|---|
| Category I | | | | | | |
| Algeria | 0.4 | 0.2 | 12.9 | 5.9 | -3.0 | 5.5 |
| Egypt | 2.9 | 3.1 | 5.4 | 7.2 | 5.1 | 12.0 |
| Category II | | | | | | |
| Israel | 5.0 | 6.6 | 15.6 | 5.3 | 1.5 | 5.4 |
| Iran | 4.4 | 5.2 | 13.4 | 4.0 | 10.0 | 16.1 |
| Turkey | 2.5 | 3.9 | 9.6 | 8.8 | 6.9 | 7.9 |
| Category III | | | | | | |
| Libya | 2.2 | 12.7 | - | -2.7 | - | 16.7 |
| Sudan | 3.3 | 8.8 | 1.7 | 2.8 | - | - |
| Syria | 4.4 | 7.2 | 6.3 | 11.6 | 6.2 | 9.5 |
| Tunisia | 2.0 | 5.6 | 8.7 | 8.1 | 4.2 | 8.7 |
| Category IV | | | | | | |
| Iraq | 5.7 | -1.5 | 4.7 | 12.2 | 8.3 | 13.5 |
| Jordan | 5.0 | 2.6 | 9.9 | - | 6.4 | - |
| Morocco | 4.7 | 0.1 | 4.0 | 7.9 | 4.0 | 7.6 |
| Pakistan | 4.9 | 1.9 | 10.0 | 4.8 | 7.0 | 6.2 |
| Others | | | | | | |
| Afghanistan | - | 3.5 | - | 5.3 | - | 6.1 |
| Lebanon | 6.3 | - | 4.5 | 12.0 | 4.8 | - |
| Saudi Arabia | - | 4.0 | - | - | - | 11.6 |
| Country Average | 3.8 | 4.3 | 8.2 | 6.8 | 5.1 | 9.7 |

Sources: World Bank, World Development Report, 1978, Report, 1979 and Report, 1980.

*Some figures are for 1961–70.
**Some figures are for 1970–77.

world.[5] Table 2.5 indicates, by contrast, that both countries made little or no progress in their fledgling industrial sectors, although services grew at a rapid rate in Libya. Over the same period, Syria and Tunisia were able to manage relatively high rates of change in all sectors.

Four countries in the region, Iraq, Jordan, Morocco, and Pakistan, went from high rates of expansion in agriculture during the 1960s to dismal showings in the 1970s. Lebanon, for which there are no statistics for 1970–1978, undoubtedly also falls into this category. The negative growth in Iraq's agricultural production is particularly remarkable during a time when industry and services were expanding by more than 12 percent and 13 percent respectively. Agriculture's nearly stagnant condition in Pakistan in 1970–1978 follows a period between 1965 and 1970 when the rate had actually reached 6.3 percent.[6] In Pakistan and Morocco, moreover, industry and services performed considerably better in 1970–1978. For all countries in this fourth category, as well as Algeria in the first, agricultural production lagged well behind population growth rates (see Table 1.2).

A number of factors contribute to the rising and declining agricultural growth rates. From season to season, production in most systems fluctuates widely with favorable or adverse weather. At least a few countries find difficulty in some years in purchasing costly fertilizers and pesticides and experience reduced crop yields. As new irrigation and water systems have come on line, agricultural output has often been boosted but, as in the case of improved seed varieties, usage peaks and high growth rates are impossible to sustain. In the 1970s, many countries in the region ran into serious problems as a consequence of poor water management and drainage, inappropriate cultivation, and inadequate credit. Rates of change have been affected over time by policies that alter farm tenure arrangements and other structured reforms. In no small way, however, public sector investments influence long-term expansion, particularly for agriculture in a languishing condition. These sectoral priorities accorded by planners and governing elites, to be fully understood, must be viewed as part of a political process.

## The Political Context

Dualism in underdeveloped market economies almost everywhere in the Middle East is a manifestation of uneven economic and political power. Public funds have gone disproportionately toward underwriting industry and subsidizing food for city dwellers—in preference to higher prices for farmers' crops and easier farm credits—in no small part because influential elites, both in and out of government, are preponderantly urban. As such, they have had a strong stake in an overall growth strategy based on the preeminence of urban-based industry and commerce. Established economic interests welcome the stimulus of public expenditures in the larger cities and value the role of low agricultural prices in holding down the costs of raw materials. They have usually opposed policies that might attract larger private investment to agriculture through restricting opportunities for capital speculation in the urban sector.

Urban middle and working classes are no more anxious to divert resources in order to increase the profitability of agriculture. Importantly, government policymakers can ill afford to be unresponsive to public employees and other middle-class groups that constitute highly mobilized and attentive political constituencies. The expanded urban labor force includes many recent peasants whose increased expectations of a better life leave them impatient to share in the fruits of urban progress. Programs carrying immediate and tangible benefits to the cities and well-publicized projects that promise increased employment and improved services are one price paid for urban peace. By contrast, rural programs have long been viewed as offering fewer political dividends to regimes. The more passive, geographically dispersed populations have traditionally had little or no effective bargaining power with which to attract public expenditures and are of doubtful value as political allies. Even older rural elites normally have supported policies that slight rural development in a tacit exchange for effective government consent to tenure laws and a social order that permits their continued exploitation of the peasants.

Extractive sectoral policies have not been applied evenly among rural dwellers. Nor are the long-term biases against agricultural interests always consistent or self-evident in government decisions. If measured by direct taxation, agriculture appears, in fact, to have been spared its fair contribution to the mobilization of development capital. It has been frequently documented that publicly subsidized farm inputs and outlays for rural improvements outweigh the levies on agricultural producers. Nearly everywhere in the Middle East, taxes on land and agricultural income are low, inefficiently collected, or nonexistent. In Egypt, small farmers are entirely exempt from levies on land. As there was no meaningful tax on agricultural property or income, wealthy industrialists, merchants, and urban professionals in Pakistan had transferred savings into agricultural land. During the 1970s, Iranian authorities gave up trying to collect a 2 percent tax on farm produce from cooperatives, and during the Daoud-led republic (1973–1978) in Afghanistan, a steady decline occurred in revenue collected directly from the agricultural sector. In general, the major beneficiaries of rural tax policies in many countries have been the larger landed families. Low taxes made it possible to maintain their clientist and tenurial systems and high consumption patterns, even if these policies did not normally make it profitable to modernize agricultural production.

Economic policies are rigged against most farmers through indirect forms of taxation. By a system of depressed crop prices, agriculture over much of the region has been made to bear a great deal of the burden of capital formation for industry and the urban sector. State bureaucracies are variously engaged in establishing production allocations for crops and determining the costs of key farm inputs. They also peg retail food prices and strictly regulate food imports and exports. But the setting of artificial crop prices and efforts to monopolize the purchase of designated crops exercise the most control over the behavior of producers and serve as the basis for a sectorally biased, de facto taxation. Although official procurement prices are proclaimed a guaranteed or floor price, in many states in the Middle East they work instead as a ceiling and are typically below real market value or international commodity prices. On basic food grains and other crops, for example, the Egyptian government's official prices were until recently substantially less than world market prices. Even where governments offer more competitive prices, set at or above international rates, farmers are forced to agree to private sales far below the supported price because purchasing centers may be scattered and storage and handling facilities inadequate.

Higher guaranteed prices, it is argued, would result in rising food costs and fuel rapid inflation. Crop price increases allowed to reach consumers could be expected to lead to higher urban wage demands and greater labor unrest. The consequent increase in the costs of industrial products would make investment less attractive to the private sector and leave domestic industry, whether under state or private ownership, uncompetitive in external markets. A reduction in urban dwellers' disposable income through higher food costs is also bound to slacken demand for the country's domestically produced goods.

Governments further justify their refusal to increase official prices by arguments that farmers are well enough compensated through publicly subsidized inputs. Fertilizers, seeds, and pesticides are usually distributed to farmers at considerably less than their market value, or even at production cost. In Iran, producers of basic crops were offered seeds at 50 percent of production cost and fertilizer at 20 percent. Water charges are typically nonexistent or minimal, and reduced power rates for agricultural use are not uncommon. Subsidies are also applied in many countries for irrigation equipment and other farm machinery. In all, input assistance in Pakistan during the mid-1970s came to nearly half of all budgetary expenditures for agriculture, about a third of this sector's allocations going for fertilizer subsidies. Where farmers have received land under reform legislation, public officials also imply that a debt is owed that should be repaid by accepting lower crop prices.

In general, an input-support rather than incomes strategy should help the least well-off farmers who have little if any crops to market, but for whom subsidized inputs can be used to increase yields on the land. Fixed procurement prices, especially for small farmers with no storage facilities, can protect against fluctuating prices as well as ensure delivery of fertilizer and seeds at affordable costs. At the same time, this strategy should enable governments to control farmers' planting decisions in a manner designed to meet national goals, including agricultural export quotas.

In fact, aside from those few countries that, like Egypt, have a functioning cooperative system, the subsidized inputs rarely reach farms of more modest size. Few small cultivators qualify for the credits needed to purchase the offered inputs, and for many the scale of farming is too small to warrant their effective use. Assistance is absorbed almost entirely by the larger, commercially oriented farmers and, even then, often reaches them too late or in insufficient quantities. On the whole, farmers with regular surpluses prefer the stimulus of a free market for sale of their crops, despite the uncertainties. They would be satisfied with higher incomes to purchase inputs through private investment choices, although most continue to insist that government has a responsibility to intervene should fertilizer, seed, and other input costs become excessive or prices for crops drop too low.

In the urban areas, administered food prices are frequently portrayed as redistributive, aimed at benefiting lower-income groups. In fact, there is considerable leakage to other urban groups, those not in need of public relief or nutritionally needy. Critics charge that the subsidized foodstuffs regularly enjoyed by the urban middle classes are an economic waste and a misallocation of resources. Yet if government workers and others in this class were not allowed to benefit together with the poor, most programs that hold food prices artificially low would not be politically feasible. Based on a similar political calculus, policymakers have shied away from trying to discourage through higher prices the rising demand for high-value foodstuffs, notably red meat, rice, and edible oils. Using the elasticities of demand to drive down consumption is viewed as politically risky. In addition to the certain popular reaction to removing food subsidies or narrowing their coverage, allowing prices to rise invites an inflationary spiral that is especially injurious to the middle classes and wealthy investors. Through policies that absorb the costs of domestically produced food and expensive imports in a single price, governments accept gross distortions in their economies and overburdened exchequers.

Food subsidies take a large bite out of state budgets. Consumer supports, mainly of wheat, cooking oil, sugar, rice, and tea, drained off $2.2 billion, or nearly 20 percent, of Egypt's projected outlays in 1980. In Iran almost $1 billion was slated for direct food subsidies, intended to hold down prices during 1978–1979. A wide range of foodstuffs, including sugar, poultry, and dairy products, was covered. The shah's government bought foreign wheat in the late 1970s for about $400 a ton and sold it domestically at less than $100. But it was the depressed prices paid to crop and livestock producers that, in Iran as elsewhere in the region, provided the principal means of containing the heavy costs of consumer food subsidies. By keeping procurement prices to farmers low, many governments not only absorb less of the consumer price differential but also ensure a wider profit margin in the sale of export crops. Elsewhere, restrictions and bans on exports are used to control consumer prices and domestic supplies. Whatever the kind of intervention, public policy has normally, if also unintentionally, created production disincentives domestically and, over the long haul, increased requirements for agricultural imports.

The combined effects of low agricultural prices and cheap food in the cities are behind much of the push and pull of peasants to urban areas and foreign labor markets. Uneconomical farming and more attractive employment opportunities in industry have created in many countries acute shortages of skilled and even unskilled farm workers. Attempts to hold labor in the countryside can drive up the costs of agricultural production, often to a point at which domestic crops become uncompetitive with food imports. Across much of the region, government price and subsidy programs have often tended to discourage private investment in agriculture and to perpetuate the economic marginality of small farmers. Public policies are thus a major contributor to the spreading differences between urban and rural incomes. Perhaps most significant, the loss by the rural areas of their most ambitious and enterprising sons deprives them of some of the very people who are best qualified to lead agricultural sector development.

## National Investment Strategies

The symbiotic aspects of rural and urban development have gained increasing, if not yet uniform, attention among the region's policymakers. The mutual dependencies were inevitably overshadowed during the earlier phases of economic development, when the normally dominant agricultural sector was forced to husband much of the capital required for industrial expansion. But the dichotomy between urban and rural sectors, so long overdrawn in development planning, could not be defended as the inherent contradictions of uneven sectoral growth became more visible. There is now a better appreciation that the agricultural sector can serve an important and even dynamic role in sustaining economic growth. Regimes may be disturbed by the backward conditions in the countryside and the injustices felt by rural majorities. More commonly, changes in official attitudes reflect worries about lagging agricultural production and surging food imports.

Public policies that fix the terms of domestic trade against the agriculturists begin to be reexamined when they are seen as adversely affecting the operations of industry. The movements of rural populations also become a concern as they threaten rational urban planning and question traditional mechanisms of political control.

Policymakers are anxious to moderate the rural exodus, both because of its increasingly negative impact on urban life and because of the way it has affected rural economies. Few planners question that the way to stem the migration of people is to narrow urban-rural income differentials and to upgrade the conditions of rural life through improved health, education, and other social services. There is also agreement that the attractions of rural areas must eventually include local, nonagricultural supplementary or alternative employment, at first through public works that mobilize underemployed labor, but over the longer term in small, consumer-oriented industries.

Industrialization in much of the Middle East, as elsewhere in the Third World, cannot progress very far without an expansion of domestic demand for its products. With the population of the region still predominantly rural, a large, impoverished, unproductive agricultural sector denies industry an enormous potential market. In a region where as many as two-thirds of the rural population virtually limit their consumption to foodstuffs, increased disposable income among rural consumers could result in a stronger demand for nonagricultural goods and services that, through its multiplier effects, would also improve industrial workers' incomes.[7] Progress in modernizing agriculture can also be expected to stimulate demand for domestic production of farm machinery, fertilizer, and other inputs. And wider rural prosperity through rising income can generate savings that, if effectively taxed, will provide new capital for industry.

Other intersectoral links are difficult to ignore. Table 2.3 suggests that for about half the countries in the Middle East, agricultural exports are a prominent source of foreign exchange. A sizable portion of these revenues goes toward the purchase of industrial equipment and raw materials, as well as consumer items. The unstable international price structure for agricultural commodities creates uncertainty in the profitability of production, but on the whole, the region's cash crops are more competitive than its exported manufactured goods. Domestic agriculture serves, moreover, as a major source of raw materials for local factories. By one estimate, at least 50 percent of Egyptian industry depends on agriculturally based activities.[8] The textile industry in Pakistan stands or falls on the availability of relatively inexpensive domestic cotton. Industry must also pay for agricultural sector failures by having to yield to demands for higher wages by urban workers. To maintain cheap prices for food, governments are usually obliged to increase food imports, assume the costs of added subsidies, and as a last resort, offer higher prices to farmers in order to stimulate crop production. In any case, low agricultural output may force the diversion of public investments that might otherwise have gone for urban-industrial development or, for that matter, to finance agricultural modernization.

The pivotal sector role of agriculture was fully accepted in Egypt during the Nasser era. By 1967–1968, the share of agricultural investment in total public capital expenditures had risen to 16.8 percent, up from 11.6 percent in 1952–1953. If allocations for the Aswan Dam are added, closer to a quarter of expenditures in the mid-1960s were oriented toward agriculture.[9] Nasser's emphasis on bringing new lands into cultivation was replaced by Sadat's stress on industry and related economic activities in his Open Door economic policy. In 1975, agriculture's share of public investment had declined to just 7 percent of the total; by 1978 it had dropped to about 4 percent.[10] Agriculture's preeminent position was weakened as the government realized increased revenues from overseas workers' remittances, Suez Canal tolls, tourism, and foreign aid and set out to attract foreign capital and technology for industry. Yet Egypt's agriculture continued to provide the country with important foreign exchange. And when, by the end of the 1970s, the widening gap between farm wages and productivity had begun to show up in the declining output and profitability of agricultural exports, plans were accelerated for the rapid mechanization of Egyptian agriculture and interest in land reclamation was renewed. The 1980–1984 development plan gives food and agriculture top priority, with an investment of more than $6 billion, outspending all other sectors, including industry. There has been no retreat, however, from the expectation that private capital investment would also make a sizable contribution to further agricultural development.

Pakistan had a postindependence flirtation with the notion of building the country into an industrial society in which the large agricultural sector would hold its own without much priming. By contrast, every government since 1958 has publicly acknowledged agriculture as the linchpin of Pakistan's economy. A preferred position for agriculture was reflected in two successive development plans between 1960 and 1970. Over the decade, agriculture was allocated approximately 11 percent while industry averaged 8 percent of total public outlays. The rural areas loom still larger in development appropriations when expenditures for the separately budgeted water sector are included. In fact, water-related investments claimed by far the largest share of development expenses in the sector, and the publicly subsidized installation of private tubewells was probably the single most important factor in agriculture's upsurge in the 1960s. During the Bhutto years, the sector's share of expenditures climbed to more than 13 percent. Between

1970 and 1976, outlays for rural development, including agriculture, grew impressively in national and provincial budgets. Yet much of this growth was wiped out by increased costs of farm inputs and an annual inflation rate of 15.2 percent for this period. In general, it has been conceded that public investment in agriculture has been insufficient to sustain productivity in the sector. More important, investments have been misdirected. An approach that devoted as much as 90 percent of allocations to land and water schemes and mechanization undervalued farm support services, rural institutions, and economic incentives for producers.[11]

Buoyed by improved agricultural performance and eased budgetary pressures in the late 1970s, Pakistan's planners envisioned heavier investment in agriculture and a 5 percent expansion rate during 1980–1981. Seeking to revive the sector growth strategies that had worked so well during the 1960s, the government strengthened farmer incentives with higher crop procurement prices. The federal government also cushioned higher fertilizer prices with subsidies to cultivators that increased from $170 million in 1979–1980 to $350 million in the following year. Private investment in the agricultural sector was slated to rise by 22 percent during 1980–1981.

Investment policies in Syria are tied to plans seeking a better balance between industrial and agricultural development. Syrian officials continue to pin their hopes for a strengthened, more independent economy on light and heavy industry, more than 75 percent of which is in the public sector. But slowed agricultural growth in the late 1970s raised alarm in government circles in light of import figures for foodstuffs, which jumped in value from $295 million in 1977 to $411 million the following year and were continuing to rise.[12] Overall budget increases were pushed up largely by higher defense outlays, but they also reflected the increased costs of subsidizing basic consumer commodities, including bread, sugar, rice, and vegetable oils. The total real investment in industry, which stood at 47 percent in 1977 after rising from 33 percent in 1973, fell back to 35 percent in 1979. Public investment for agricultural development, for dams, irrigation canals, land reclamation, and village infrastructural schemes meanwhile went from roughly $300 million in 1977 to $400 million in 1978 and remained at about that level in 1979. For the full term of the Fourth Five-Year Plan that ended in 1980, agricultural projects captured just less than 10 percent of total national investment.[13] As elsewhere, however, the problems in Syria were as much in the effective use of development funds as in gaining increased expenditures for agriculture.

Libya no doubt provides the most striking example of a reassessing of sectoral priorities. Although less than 2 percent of the country's land area is arable, in the five-year plan beginning in 1981 the government authorized more than $10 billion for agricultural development, up from roughly $3.3

billion in the previous plan.[14] Of total investment slated for the period, agriculture, with about 16 percent, ranked ahead of housing, transport, communications, and electricity and was second only to industry. With an income from oil that grew to more than $16 billion in 1979, Libya's difficulties in realizing its ambitious objectives for agriculture have obviously had little to do with finding the financial resources. But allocated funds frequently cannot be spent in the absence of timely development planning. Despite the leadership's claim that Libya would soon become self-sufficient in food, the country had in the late 1970s experienced damaging mismanagement of its scarce water resources and severe rural labor shortages as a result of the rapid exodus of rural people to the population centers for employment in a booming industrial sector.

After years of lavishing funds on prestigious industrial projects, Algeria gave new emphasis in its Five Year Plan inaugurated in 1980 to agricultural development and light industry, enough to encourage officials to suggest the possibility of the country's feeding itself once again.[15] The Tunisian government's renewed interest in agriculture (which still accounts for the bulk of employment, provides coveted export earnings, and furnishes 40 percent of domestic industry's raw materials) is reflected in a strong financial commitment in the country's most recent Five Year Plan.[16] Iraq set aside $10.5 billion in its 1976–1980 National Development Plan for agriculture, a 72 percent increase over the previous Five Year Plan. A determination to speed irrigation and land reclamation prompted a 30 percent increase to $677 million in 1980 for the completion of projects.[17] The aborted Sixth Plan in Iran, slated to get under way in 1978, had been expected to stress rural development, particularly the overcoming of infrastructural bottlenecks. Public investment for agriculture in Iran warrants more extended examination, however, as a case of relative neglect in the 1960s, distorted expansion in the 1970s, and promised promotion by the revolution's leaders in the 1980s.

Prior to Iran's Fifth Plan (1973–1978), little effort was made to hide an official de-emphasis of agriculture. When dams and other primarily capital-intensive schemes are separated from agricultural development outlays in the Third Plan (1962–1967), the country's first comprehensive one, the sector received officially 11.7 percent of all allocations.[18] Of this amount, public expenditures for agriculture were in part diverted after 1963 to administer the shah's much-advertised land reform program.[19] At the same time, the private capital freed through compensation to landlords relinquishing land under the reform was allowed to escape the agricultural sector. Many former landlords transferred their wealth to the cities for often lucrative investments in real estate and industry. A smaller number found commercial agricultural enterprise sufficiently profitable to convert holdings into modern farming operations in order to take advantage of exemptions in the law.

The subsequent 1968–1973 plan was still more clearly designed to focus public investment on industry, although it also banked heavily on a role for private capital. Actual government expenditures for agriculture in the Fourth Plan came to 8.1 percent of the development budget.[20] Despite a relatively low target set for agricultural growth during the plan period, this sector was alone in failing to attain or exceed the established goals. By the end of the Fourth Plan, Iran had largely accomplished the transformation of the country's economy from one strongly reliant on agriculture to one in which once secondary and tertiary activities were dominant. A token of the shift to an urban-industrial society is the fact that by 1971, public investment for a person in Tehran was almost three times more than for someone living elsewhere in the country.[21]

Iran's Fifth Plan (1973–1978) proclaimed the regime's intention to spread the socioeconomic benefits of rapid economic growth and to deal with those sectors, such as agriculture, that had been left behind in the country's rapid economic expansion. Reflecting growth targets that were revised after the country's oil revenues rose steeply beginning in 1974, the Fifth Plan initially allocated $4.5 billion to agriculture, 5.8 percent more than in the previous plan, and projected a 7 percent average yearly expansion rate in crop production. In execution the Fifth Plan, like its predecessors, fell short of its goals for agriculture, and although government reported an increase higher than 5 percent, independent observers claim the actual rate was well below that figure. Actual disbursements often ran far behind the funds allocated. Agriculture had, to be sure, ceased to be merely an afterthought in development, but the heaviest sector concentration fell on electricity, industry, and transport. During the penultimate year of the Fifth Plan (1976–1977), some 21 percent of expenditures went to agricultural activities (not including allocations for water projects). But roughly half of this amount was set aside for consumer food subsidies.[22] The actual budget for agriculture, including farm services, cooperatives, and credit, was no more than 12 percent of the total. Agribusiness, the regime's pampered but sinking flagship of agricultural modernization, absorbed as much as a quarter of this budget.

The grand design for Iranian agriculture in the 1970s had called for a deliberate policy to reduce the rural share of the population to no more than 25 percent and to cut the actual farm population to less than 20 percent.[23] In the vision of Iran as a Great Society, on a par economically with the developed West, the country was to become fully industrialized, leaving only a limited labor force in a highly mechanized agricultural system. But rather than have peasants continue to flock to the overcrowded urban centers, authorities decided in the mid-1970s to relocate them in expanded villages and towns. The abandonment of many remote villages would bring peasants to those areas offering the most natural resources for agriculture, where they could expect to receive a disproportionate share of technical services and credits and of social assistance. These so-called agricultural poles were expected to become the focus for capital-intensive agricultural enterprises, particularly agribusinesses and new consumer industries.[24]

In the turmoil of 1978, the Sixth Development Plan never left the drawing boards. In it the shah's planners had shown a greater willingness to admit that all was not well in domestic agriculture and that early measures were required to improve the sector's performance. There was to be an effort to reverse the rapidly declining contribution of agriculture to national wealth, bringing it eventually back to 20 percent of GDP. In the first year of the Sixth Plan, 1978–1979, the development budget had authorized agricultural expenditures to increase 53 percent over the previous year.[25] Planners did not abandon their belief in large-scale, high-technology solutions to agriculture, either through agribusiness or some form of state farms. Yet they could not ignore the country's poor physical infrastructure and weakly motivated farmers in setting national goals. There also appeared by the late 1970s rude reminders that by slighting agriculture over two decades, public policies had destroyed the basic social and economic fabric of the countryside. Many traditional sources of food production, most notably tribal meat supplies, had been permanently destroyed, and the government had helped to create a rootless and politically alienated rural population.

The Islamic republican government, installed in power in February 1979, rejected the development strategies of the shah's regime but not all of its goals. Top billing in economic plans went to reducing the country's massive reliance on food imports through revitalization of the rural sector. The revolutionary government believed that agriculture's reverses could be quickly stemmed with a healthy dose of social and economic justice in the countryside that would not only restore faith in the government but also spur production and attract excess migrant rural labor from the cities. Despite these intentions officials had to admit in mid-1980 that there were probably an additional 1.5 million people who had settled in the outskirts of Tehran since the revolution.[26] It was also difficult to change the demand for food based on the high level of consumption reached in the 1970s. The government had been unable as well to halt the spiraling prices for most food items. Initially at least, the exhortations of the Ayatollah Khomeini to increase the area under cultivation paid off. Helped by ample rains, the 1979 wheat crop was probably 50 percent larger than in the previous growing season. No relief was found in 1980; domestic upheavals and difficulties in importing farm inputs caused the rate of growth in Iran's agricultural production to fall to near zero. It was possible that the country's 1981 agricultural imports could reach a new high of more than $3 billion in value.[27]

The new government's approach to agricultural development differed mainly in its call for small-scale projects and its willingness to increase loans to small farmers. Yet professional planners had no illusions that Iran's food problems would be solved by a simple return to traditional agriculture or that the country could expect in the near future to do without subsidies to middle and large farmers to obtain marketable food surpluses. While suggesting the need for new land reforms, authorities publicly acknowledged the responsibility of more prosperous farmers to lead the sector and to ensure a substructure of modern agricultural practices.[28] The budget expenditures for agriculture, projected for 1980–1981 at $2.1 billion, were, despite several earlier austerity cutbacks, among the few budget categories to be promised real dollar increases over the amounts proposed by the shah's planners.[29] The promise to provide financial aid, technical assistance, and other farm services was of course indivisible from broader efforts by government supporters to win sympathy for the regime among villagers and to establish an effective means of provincial political authority.

National investment strategies throughout the Middle East, despite their differences, reflect a comparable set of development norms. With only a few, usually eccentric exceptions the states of the region have since the 1960s fostered modernization rather than suppressed it. Some have moved vigorously and even precipitously to impose change; others have acted more cautiously. But on the desired material benefits of development, there is a high convergence of aspirations, whatever the caveats about the preservation of traditional values. No small part of the rules guiding modernization has been the belief in a need to transfer people and capital from rural to urban sectors of society. The indirect taxation of land, people, and products and the unequal allocation of resources between the sectors manifest the prescribed direction of change and its supporting doctrines and interests. This chapter, while underlining these patterns of policy, has also indicated the normative shift in expectations and rules governing sectoral policies that was evident in the 1970s. In most countries reexaminations have only begun to involve such issues as the undesirable effects of industrial centralization, urban land use, environmental pollution, and deterioration of national resources. Further along as subjects of concern are slowed agricultural output, increased disparity of income, and the social and political implications of rapid urbanization. In efforts to cope with these problems in rural-agricultural sector policies, government decision makers have to choose regularly among normative goals of growth, equity, and political control. The next chapter describes these goals, the policies they inspire, and the differential benefits they confer.

## Notes

1. For a good discussion of contrasting patterns of village and city life, see Morroe Berger, *The Arab World Today* (Garden City, N.Y.: Doubleday and Company, Anchor Edition, 1964), pp. 57–73.

2. Waterbury found several sources to show the declining conditions for Egypt's farmers. From data provided by Samir Radwan, *The Impact of Agrarian Reform on Rural Egypt (1952–75)* (Geneva: International Labour Office, January 1977), Waterbury reported that the percentage of rural poor increased between the mid-1960s and mid-1970s. The share of the rural population below the poverty line is given at 17.0 percent in 1964 after falling from 22.5 percent in 1958–1959. By 1974–1975, however, it had risen to 28 percent. John Waterbury, "Administered Pricing and State Intervention in Egyptian Agriculture," an unpublished version of "Egyptian Agriculture Adrift," *American Universities Field Staff Reports*, Africa Series, no. 47 (October 1978), p. 2.

3. The World Bank statistics used here define the agricultural sector as including forestry, hunting, and fishing. The industrial sector comprises mining, manufacturing, construction, electricity, water, and gas. All other forms of economic activity are classified as services. (World Bank, *World Development Report, 1979* [New York: Oxford University Press, 1979], p. 178.)

4. Official agricultural growth statistics for Iran are open to question. Looney indicated a growth rate of 2.5 percent for the 1960s. Robert E. Looney, *The Economic Development of Iran* (New York: Praeger Publishers, 1973), p. 13; but see also M. G. Weinbaum, "Agricultural Policy and Development Politics in Iran," *Middle East Journal* 31, no. 4 (Autumn 1977):434–435.

5. Growth in agricultural production in Libya is reported to have been a more modest 8.5 percent from 1978 to 1979. "New Libyan Faces to Tackle Same Problems," *Middle East*, March 1980, p. 62.

6. International Bank for Reconstruction and Development, *Pakistan: Special Agricultural Sector Review*, Vol. 1 (Washington, D.C.: World Bank, November 1975), p. 4. Also see Marvin G. Weinbaum, "Agricultural Development and Bureaucratic Politics in Pakistan," *Journal of South Asian and Middle Eastern Studies* 2, no. 2 (Winter 1978):42. Official Pakistan government statistics claim that for 1978–1980, agriculture had climbed back to 4.2 percent annual growth, industry to 7.4 percent. "Pakistan Economic Survey 1979–1980," *Pakistan Affairs* (Embassy of Pakistan) 32 (August 1980):7.

7. See discussion in World Bank, *World Development Report, 1979*, p. 61.

8. Alan Richards, "The Agricultural Crisis in Egypt," *Journal of Development Studies* 16, no. 3 (April 1980):303.

9. Ibid, p. 309.

10. Ibid. p. 311. Also see "Egypt: Torn Between Food and Energy," *Arab Economist*, April 1981, p. 45.

11. Much of this discussion is taken from Weinbaum, "Agricultural Development and Bureaucratic Politics in Pakistan," pp. 42–44. See also *Pakistan Affairs* 32 (August 1980), pp. 7–8.

12. *New York Times,* November 16, 1979.

13. Ibid. Also see "Syria: Ahead With Agricultural Development," *Arab Economist,* June 1981. p. 18.

14. *Middle East,* January 1980, pp. 58–59, and *Middle East,* May 1981, p. 52.

15. *New York Times,* April 20, 1980.

16. "Releasing Fair Weather Hold on Crops," *Middle East,* August 1979, p. 105.

17. "Water Resources Will Outlast Oil," *Middle East Economic Review,* February 15, 1980, p. 7.

18. Fahad Daftary, "Development Planning in Iran: An Historical Survey," *Iranian Studies* 6, no. 4 (Autumn 1973):197.

19. Weinbaum, "Agricultural Policy and Development Politics in Iran," 434.

20. Daftary, "Development Planning in Iran," p. 217.

21. *Report of the Tehran Development Council,* November 1976, Table 11, p. 24a.

22. *Keyhan International,* March 12, 1977. The $1.7 billion that went to agriculture, including urban food subsidies, compared to outlays in 1976–1977 of $7.8 billion for the defense budget.

23. Ibid., August 14, 1976.

24. Ann T. Schulz, "Food in Iran: The Politics of Insufficiency," in Raymond F. Hopkins, Donald J. Puchala, and Ross B. Talbot, eds., *Food, Politics, and Agricultural Development: Case Studies in the Public Policy of Rural Modernization* (Boulder, Colo.: Westview Press, 1979), pp. 171–191.

25. Schulz, "Food in Iran," p. 182, quoting An-Nahar, *Arab Report and Memo* 2, no. 7, (February 13, 1973):3.

26. *New York Times,* June 1, 1980.

27. Ibid., December 14, 1979, and April 6, 1981. Also see "Iran's Farm Imports Could Hit Record High in 1981," *Foreign Agriculture,* April 1981, p. 7.

28. *Iran Voice,* September 19, 1979.

29. U.S. Congress, Joint Economic Committee, *Economic Consequences of the Revolution in Iran,* (Washington, D.C.: Government Printing Office, 1980), p. 63.

*3*

# Agrarian Development Goals and
# Strategies, and Class Inequalities

Varying economic and natural endowments make it probable that no single set of development strategies can be optimal regionwide. Contrasting domestic power configurations further ensure that different choices will emerge from dissimilar decision processes. Still, in the face of very common experiences with inefficient food production systems, widening social and economic disparities, and political insecurities, public policies for the region's rural sectors respond to three principal development norms and goals. The most conspicuous of these dictates growth-related strategies intended to bring about a rapid increase in national food and fiber production. Even states that under the best of circumstances have only a limited ability to feed their citizens or to export crops accept the critical need for a more effective, rationalized agricultural system. Second, development strategies in the Middle East are expected to address objectives of social and economic equality. Proposals for a greater measure of social justice for small farmers and improved incomes for rural majorities are publicly endorsed by policy leaders, whatever their supposed class biases. Third, agrarian policies are shaped to further a regime's efforts to manage conflict and secure authority. Rural development may help to realize promised revolutionary reforms as well as stave off forces of radical change. Programs are often geared to augment the status and power of groups with which a government shares values and common political objectives. Very rarely are the three goals, growth, equity, and political control, pursued with equal vigor or dedication. Efforts fail as often from a weakness of administrative capacity as of regime will. A high priority assigned to any one of these ends may leave little energy for the others.

Increased productive capacity, reduction of social and economic inequities, and enhanced regime maintenance are frequently conceived as competitive if not incompatible objectives. Strategies employed to optimize one goal often seem inimical to progress toward another. Hard choices are often confronted in efforts to obtain a more equitable distribution of national income without sacrificing agricultural production increases. Policies aimed at ending the economic exploitation of small farmers and restructuring rural class relations may threaten gains in agricultural production and be held responsible for stimulating rural unemployment and urban migration. Large private estates can be transformed into small, uneconomic, often fragmented units, unable to afford or effectively employ modern farming methods. The material assistance and administrative attention given to subsistence farmers in order to overcome these problems are often said to divert scarce resources that could otherwise be used to secure agricultural surpluses.

Yet a good case is regularly made that greater economic and social equality in the region is a prerequisite for agricultural systems to realize their full potential. As long as those who work the land are denied by landlords or government a fair share of their labor, are insecure about tenure rights, and are in constant debt, they can hardly be expected to adopt more progressive farming methods. Tenants and smallholders are poorly motivated to improve their lands and adopt new practices until they are free of oppressive social and economic obligations to local elites. Increased productivity from the great mass of cultivators is unlikely while government-assisted farmers experience differential access to basic inputs and are denied opportunities to participate in decisions affecting their economic well-being. In practice, then, the major goals in agrarian policies are unavoidably interdependent. If the overall employment picture is healthy, rising farm income can stimulate economic growth and provide incentives for productivity gains. Conversely, a sound and expanding economy, combined with structural reforms, provides the resources and mechanisms for redistributive economic policies. Still more, unresolved inequities and a lagging agricultural sector are bound to release potentially dangerous political fallout for most regimes in the Middle East.

Whatever the normative priorities in agrarian development goals, several strategic choices are at the center of national policy discourse. The first of these can be characterized as a distributive strategy. It encompasses policies involved with the promotion and distribution of material and technical resources-cum-incentives to cultivators. Although primarily conceived to ensure sustained agricultural growth and modernization, those policies can be used to improve the incomes of farmers as well as to allow for politically motivated economic rewards and sanctions. The approach basically accepts the prevailing legal and administrative constraints of the system. A second orientation, the reformative strategy, is aimed at regulating or reassigning the rights and obligations of those engaged in agricultural activities. These policies typically deal with land tenure and titles, crop sharing, water rights, and tax obligations. Intended to modify ongoing rules and relationships, reform strategies are usually associated with a quest for social and economic justice and are ostensibly redistributive. But they can be justified also in terms of strengthening farmers' incentives and capacity to accept agricultural modernization. Reform policies are no less often a powerful symbolic and tactical means for regimes to build and hold loyal rural clienteles. A third orientation, an institutional strategy, seeks a more fundamental reorganization of agricultural production and, sometimes, of rural life. This restructuring may try to alter the relations of labor, land, and capital in the name of raising agricultural output or bettering the economic conditions of peasants, or both. It seeks to create new rural institutions and farm structures, both large and small in scale, either voluntary or compulsory. Because the institutional strategy often determines the degree of farmer's participation in decisions affecting them and may shift the locus of authority for policy, it also has direct import for political legitimacy and control.[1]

The several policy approaches are of course not mutually exclusive, and a mix of strategies is commonly pursued. It is very difficult to conceive of, for instance, either reform or institutional changes succeeding in raising production levels without active technical assistance programs, or new units of management emerging in the absence of changes in the rules that regulate land tenure rights. Most development plans assume a broad spectrum of programs. Every regime in the Middle East has, at one time or another, engaged in distributive policies; all but a few have introduced species of reform; and the majority have attempted basic reorganization schemes. The actual emphasis given to a particular set of strategies often reflects differing philosophies of national development, a country's resources, and its administrative capabilities.

This chapter examines how distributive, reformative, and institutional policies have been used in countries of the Middle East to realize objectives of expanded production and to meet demands for equity. It points out how these sets of strategies are reconciled with regime efforts to ameliorate perceived domestic threats and problems of legitimacy. Much of the discussion focuses on class structures and relations in countries of the region. A class-oriented analysis aids an understanding of how priorities are arrived at in setting development goals and of the motives behind particular strategies. More directly, class helps to identify the benefits of agricultural development for various segments of a society. It also offers insights into the differential costs imposed when the terms of trade are turned against agriculturalists. A class perspective is perhaps the best means to assess the potential for domestic conflict and system transformation in the region's states.

Class structures and inequalities do not offer, to be sure, a complete description of the dynamics of change in the rural Middle East. Rural interests at times make common cause against urban, industrially oriented forces and their attempts to impose colonial-style domination over the countryside. A study of the pace and direction of agrarian development in the region cannot ignore, moreover, the persistent loyalties rooted in rural clientele systems. The reciprocal benefits based on patronage and deference relations tie together people of contrasting local status and power. Primordial societal divisions provide the structure for endemic factionalism. Distinctive clan, tribal, ethnic, and religious groups continue in many countries to mark the major fault lines of rural conflict and, like other factional groups, they typically cross economic lines, inhibiting class consciousness and mediating class differences. Income derived from nonagricultural employment by those working in the cities or abroad has also helped to soften rural status and economic tensions. The rising real income in a number of countries of the region has no doubt taken the edge off the widening gap between rural rich and poor. At the same time, the political and class consciousness that characterizes many economically marginal city dwellers is increasingly shared by villagers, mainly younger men, who commute to the cities or spend extended periods in urban jobs, but who retain their ties to the land and rural life.

Traditional rural factionalism is giving away throughout the region to class-based activities and tensions. The newer cleavages in some cases transcend, but do not replace, older social divisions. In other instances, they have strained or ruptured interpersonal loyalties that integrated rich and poor and superseded clan and other group rivalries. No doubt the widening income gap that has accompanied technological innovation in the countryside has contributed to breaking down once meaningful vertical structures. Commercialization of agricultural production, in which social and economic obligations are replaced by monetary ones, figures directly in the changes. Mobilization of the rural areas by elites stressing economic themes, and the interventions of government on behalf of particular class interests, are increasingly evident. These processes, much further along in some countries than in others, have almost nowhere brought to the rural areas the kinds of class antagonisms already visible in larger urban areas of the region. But the direction of change is unmistakable, and the forces created are ones that national ruling elements have sought both to overcome and to use.

## The Structure of Classes

Agriculturally engaged populations are described by relationships rooted in their control and use of land. It is customary to identify, among many other categories, absentee owners and cultivators, large and small holders, cash rental and share-cropping farmers, casual laborers and regular salaried workers. The resulting complex economic and social stratifications contain, however, no simple hierarchy of roles, and they often obscure major class differences. To uncover these requires that such relationships to the factors of production as access to scarce resources and contributions to a larger economic system be taken into account. With this in mind, there are found in most Middle East countries five broad agrarian classes: traditional landlords, agricultural entrepreneurs, market-oriented middle farmers, subsistence cultivators, and an agricultural proletariat. These strata distinguish rural elites whose income is derived mainly from nonproductive uses of capital from other larger holders with an investment in managed agricultural enterprises. They also divide farmers who earn their livelihood from the proceeds of progressively farmed land from those who, using more traditional methods, can rarely subsist on the land they till and from still others, irregularly employed, who have only their labor to sell.

The several classes have different potential for developing consciousness and solidarity and different capacities for political organization. They have often responded differently to agrarian reform policies, have had different attitudes toward technological change, and have been variously touched by the economic policies of central governments. Even then, many distinctions among the classes, it will be argued here, have become less meaningful in the face of contemporary forces. As class-based interests sharpen in most states of the region, class structure is simplified, leaving just the surplus and nonsurplus producers.

There exists in the Middle East a chasm between those in the rural areas who are able to profit from the increased productivity of the land and others without the means to extract a decent living from their land or labor. Classic distinctions between cultivating and appropriating classes are by no means inappropriate to the Middle East. But the advantages of the privileged are not found solely or even primarily in their direct exploitation of tenants and wage laborers; the relative prosperity of a region's surplus farmers is frequently a result of their differential claims on the state's resources. Where modernization, mobilization, and commercialization have had their heaviest impact on rural life, there emerge two agricultural societies, one commercially oriented and favored, the other composed of either neglected or administratively oppressed subsistence farmers and agricultural workers.

Agricultural wage earners are normally located at the bottom of the rural class structure. Often only seasonally employed, this agrarian underclass offers its labor to wealthier peasant farmers and larger commercial farms, private or state-owned. The wage labor force constitutes a substantial proportion of rural families over most of the Middle East. Recent comparable statistics are lacking for most countries, but data (taking as farm wage workers both the landless and families with very small landholdings who are obliged to work for others) are available for several countries in the 1960s. This labor force is roughly 20 percent of the agriculturally active population in Morocco and Tunisia respectively and as much as 60 percent in Algeria. It stood at 25 percent in Iran and 38 percent in Egypt.[2] A 1967 survey in Afghanistan found about 40 percent of rural families in the landless category.[3] By most accounts, the ranks of the agricultural proletariat expanded during the 1970s. A 1976 survey in Iran found that one-third of the agriculturally active were in the wage labor category.[4] Between 1961 and 1972 the proportion of the landless in Egypt had risen from 40 to 45 percent of all agricultural families.[5]

A rural labor surplus in many countries of the region forces the poorly paid agricultural wage earners to supplement their incomes where possible with money earned in casual, nonfarm employment. Many laborers will migrate to more prosperous farming areas or find jobs in larger cities or abroad. Indeed, the great majority of the critical labor transfers involve unemployed or underemployed agricultural workers. In a few countries of the region, the lure of economic opportunities elsewhere has resulted in pushing up wages for farm laborers. Yet an accompanying inflation usually manages to ensure that real income will rise little, if at all, for the rural poor. Then too, high production costs for labor-intensive cultivation merely stimulate increased mechanization and lead to fewer jobs.

Significant by-products of geographic mobility, manifested in family resettlement, commuting village workers, and expatriate workers, are the gradual breakdown of the rural sector's classic insularity and a better sense among agricultural workers of their relative deprivation. Aside from sporadic and isolated cases, however, dissatisfied rural labor has very rarely sought expression or found allies in political movements. Nor has it, when given an opportunity to participate in popular elections, acted as a bloc, throwing off allegiances to economic patrons and local status figures. A notable exception occurred in 1970 with an election victory by Z. A. Bhutto in West Pakistan that was based on an appeal to a newly politicized majority of landless laborers and tenant farmers. Once in power, the Pakistani leader rewarded supporters with symbolic actions while allowing older economic elites to reassert their local influence and more prosperous farmers to continue to reap much of the benefit from development programs.[6] At most, the landless in the Middle East can expect their interests to be promoted by a few sympathetic officials in the central ministries or by national party ideologues. If this lowest rural class is mobilized at all by government, it is on specific issues rather than on a continuous basis, and then very cautiously.

Small owner-cum-tenant farmers make up the numerically dominant rural class in the Middle East. In contrast to wage laborers, those farmers normally have long-term attachments to the land they till, either through title or contract. Regionwide, at least 80 percent of small farmers are at the subsistence or near subsistence level. Most work an uneconomic plot of land. Holdings in Egypt of less than 5 feddans (one feddan is equal to 0.42 hectares) constitute about one-half of the arable land, a proportion that has changed very little over the last two decades.[7] After Iran's White Revolution, which began in 1962, 2.2 million farmers, or three-quarters of all those owning land, held 10 hectares or less, and almost half of these farmed less than 3 hectares.[8] A 1965 survey of Jordan's East and West banks found that 71 percent of the agricultural holdings contained 5 hectares or less.[9] Morocco in 1977 had about 960,000 farms smaller than 5 hectares.[10] Some 80 percent of the landholders in Afghanistan owned less than 4 hectares in the early 1970s, and in Pakistan those holding less than 2 hectares made up, by one account, 64 percent of the country's proprietor farmers.[11]

The ordinary failure of those small farmers to innovate or shift to cash crops stems not from a lack of motivation so much as from inadequate opportunity and experience. Despite the institutional and commercial obstacles that commonly frustrate change, poor farmers, as Griffin and others have observed, are often as sensitive as their better-off neighbors to price signals in the fluctuating markets. Given the technology, the necessary inputs, and the markets, they will not reject a more productive and profitable agricultural system. But in the absence of these requirements, the small farmer follows a risk-spreading strategy. By keeping to mixed cropping and intercropping practices, the farmer foregoes the increments to income that he might have gained by planting single, high-value crops in order to ensure income and a regular source of food for family consumption.[12]

With few in this farmer class producing agricultural surpluses on a recurring basis, little savings can be accumulated for land improvement and increased crop yields. Sharecropping tenants may be expected to give the landowners as much as two-thirds of the produce and to contribute a portion of the inputs along with the animals used in cultivation. Most small peasant proprietors and tenant farmers, liable to suffer rapid decline in their fortunes from crop failures, lack the assurance that they can afford, from season to season, essential agricultural inputs. The great majority are forced to borrow to meet basic needs and personal obligations and find themselves caught in a perpetual state of debt to larger farmers and local merchants.

Subsistence farmers in the region participate in two largely opposing trends. On the one hand, there is a continuing fragmentation of holdings that results both from Islamic inheritance laws that distribute land equally among male offspring and from the division of large private estates and state-owned land in periodic reform programs. On the other hand, a consolidation of land proceeds from smallholders' inability to keep from mortgaging or selling off their land to wealthier neighbors, from landlords' eviction of tenants and resumption of land for mechanized farming, and in several countries, from collectivization in state-managed farms. The poverty of marginal farmers may be less extreme than that of the traditionally landless, and important status distinctions often persist between those who have access to land and those who do not. Many smallholders and sharecroppers continue to identify more with better-off farmers than with the agricultural proletariat. But, by most objective measures, small subsistence farmers have become, like wage laborers, individuals whose labor is reduced to a commodity of exchange. Faced with similar insecurities and hardships, they form a single, growing underprivileged class.

Few subsistence farmers throughout the Middle East succeed in becoming firmly established in a third agrarian class, the middle farmers. These usually wealthier peasants and a fourth, less numerous class of agricultural entrepreneurs are together the commercial agricultural classes, the source of most food reaching consumer markets. In Iran, for example, farms of more than 10 hectares accounted for 42 percent of gross agricultural production for the country and more than three-quarters of the marketed output.[13] Although the boundaries between the two commercial classes are seldom sharp, their scales of activity, proximity to productive forces, and very frequently, social origins do bear comparison. In some countries, middle farmers own or lease 60 hectares or more, but more typically they cultivate less than 20 hectares. Many hire salaried help in periods of peak activity, although much of the labor comes from members of their families. Fields owned by middle farmers that cannot be directly worked or managed are likely to be rented to others. A great many belong to a village's socially more prominent, though not major, landholding families.

The principal source of status and income among many in the entrepreneurial class, as opposed to that of the middle farmers, lies outside agriculture and beyond the local area. The entrepreneurs are normally a disparate class of noncultivators, including scions of the landed aristocracy, provincial merchants, and active or retired bureaucrats and military officers. Normally absentee landowners, they are better described as investors than farmers. The holdings of the entrepreneurs may be no larger than those of the wealthier peasants, and legal ceilings in many countries of the region place restrictions on size. In some cases, however, holdings may be in the hundreds of hectares. Entrepreneurs frequently rent land, but the most productive part is usually placed in the hands of professional farm managers. Along with the middle farmers, they form a class of economic maximizers that has mobilized capital and is willing to assume (or has succeeded in shifting) risks for increased production. Both classes are committed to more advanced, innovative farming methods and, where possible, land expansion. Notwithstanding the often wide status and income differences between as well as within the two commercially minded classes, middle farmers and entrepreneurs have stakes in the agricultural policies of government that are often similar.

Income disparities drive a sharp wedge between the market-oriented innovating classes and the precapitalist subsistence farmers. Thus more than 60 percent of all rural income in Pakistan during the early 1970s was accumulated by those with more than 10 hectares of land, a group numbering no more than 10 percent of rural families.[14] A handful of entrepreneurial larger landowners control much of Morocco's valuable citrus and vegetable export crops. The small modern sector produces 25 percent of all crops but 85 percent of those sold abroad.[15] Throughout the Middle East higher consumption by well-off farmers is a major factor in inflating the prices that the rural poor must pay for basic farm and nonfarm products. Economic exploitation of small farmers in a market economy takes many forms, but few are so resented as the selling of crops at harvesttime to larger farmers in order to pay off debts and meet immediate needs, only to have to buy grain later at a higher price. The greater financial resources of the wealthier peasants and entrepreneurs enable them and their agents to determine access to credits and water rights and to exercise control over the critical employment of subsistence farmers and the landless. By and large, efforts by the commercial agricultural classes to make land more profitable come at the expense of security of tenure and the earnings of tenant farmers and wage labor.

There exist, of course, possibilities for the coexistence of feudal and capitalist modes of production. Tenant and mechanized farming occurring alongside one another, not just as a transitional phase but as a logical system of production, can be identified in several countries of the region. Hamza Alavi has described this development in Pakistan, insisting that each system is not entirely viable without the other. Commercial enterprise, for example, can offer seasonal employment to sharecroppers who, in turn, provide the needed labor for mechanized operations.[16] Seasonal workers, moreover, risk unemployment or underemployment in the event that middle farmers and entrepreneurs succumb in an adverse market. Yet this interdependence cannot replace the older, binding reciprocities between landlord and tenant. Nor can it remove entirely the tensions between those classes for whom agriculture is essentially a source of profit and those for whom it remains a condition of survival.

The economic polarity of the commercial and lower classes is more than matched by their dissimilar capacities for voicing political demands. The wealthier peasants have always maintained close ties with local and district government officials. More recently, with the increased recognition of their central role in national food systems, they have come to enjoy, along with the entrepreneurs, a hearing among national policymakers. Although the usually common objectives of the middle farmers and entrepreneurs are not necessarily inimical to the mass of smallholders, tenant farmers, and the landless, their interests and ambitions diverge on important issues. Small farmers place their hopes on land and tenurial reform and on better terms for credit; the landless profit from public works, minimum wages, improved working conditions, and cheaply priced food. Commercially oriented farmers petition, however, for higher prices through market support and for subsidies for machinery, pesticides, and other inputs. The privileged access of the surplus-oriented, innovating classes to the means of production is often a function of their success in getting government to assume or reduce their risks as farmers. John Waterbury has noted that the influence of Egypt's middle farmers also permitted a direct challenge to legislative protection for smaller farmers. He described how, through parliamentary amendments, middle landowners succeeded in raising artificially low rents that had come to have little relation to land scarcity. Government measures to bring more peasants into the political process were blunted, moreover, by the placing of the peasant clients of wealthier, higher-status farmers in parliamentary office.[17] At the local level, popular institutions designed to allow broad rural political participation have ordinarily not prevented the more prosperous farmers and their allies from easily dominating village councils and other institutions. Particularly in their aversion to many redistributive policies, the middle farmers may be every bit as conservative as the urban-based entrepreneurs and as resistant to change as their long-time adversaries—the landed elites.

For a fifth agrarian class, the region's traditional landlords, control over land is as much a social and political resource as an economic value. In societies where the possession of land is often the only solid basis of wealth, ownership of large estates (and access to water) carries with it high social status. The usually absentee traditional landlord assumes a nonproductive role; his income derives largely from rents, land speculation, and moneylending. The landlord's exploitative relationship with small farmers is highly paternalistic, offering peasants minimal economic protection and the services of an intermediary with higher authority.[18] In return the landlord expects social deference and peasant loyalties that can form, when needed, a political constituency. In many Middle East societies the landlords may seem "parasitic," but this term often underestimates the extent to which local status elites can offer security against rapacious government officials, as well as the mutually beneficial exchanges and close interpersonal ties that are embodied in many clientele relationships.

Among traditional landlords, the economic returns on rented land, even if modest, are a reliable source of income and, importantly, require little personal attention. The class usually lacks the managerial skills required for serious economic rationalization of the land. Improved cultivation methods are normally resisted, as they involve costly investment in farm inputs and gains that will, in any case, be shared with tenants. Yet land ownership also remains attractive in those countries in which it provides a continuing base of power and prestige, and its light or inefficient taxation offers in several countries a shelter for more heavily taxed wealth derived from urban ventures.

The traditional landlord class in the Middle East has been considerably diminished in recent decades. Regimes that have risen to power on the strength of egalitarian appeals and that have sought a political base among the peasant classes have moved quickly to destroy the most visible symbols of the past—the feudal aristocrats. In Iraq and Sudan, the institution of large landlords had weak roots, being the creations of British administrations that had implanted it on tribal lands. Algeria's landed elite was a nonindigenous class. It was eliminated in the postindependence period when the departing French colons deserted their large agricultural estates. By the early 1960s the Baath socialist leaders in Iraq and Syria had established their credentials by dispossessing large landlords, and Marxist governments in South Yemen and Afghanistan followed suit later. Very probably the single most popular undertaking of Egypt's revolutionary government was the breaking up of the largest holdings, including former royal lands.

An erosion of the traditional landlord class in conservative states has resulted from government policies that encourage transformation rather than forced destruction of the class. Landed elites in several countries, most notably Jordan, Morocco, Lebanon, and Pakistan, remain visible and influential. Local economic and political privileges have not been seriously curbed, and the partnership of the class with national elites is largely intact. Comprehensive programs to end the concentration of land in private hands have been largely sham exercises. Rural elites remain well ensconced in countries with no ideology to challenge their legitimacy and without the need to mollify popular demands. Their acceptance is also strongest in countries with deep ethnic and religious differences, where prominent landed families furnish contending groups with much of their material resources and leadership.

Despite this, the political and economic costs of retaining an unreconstructed landlord class are rising; a landed aristocracy is viewed as a liability in growth-oriented development strategies and is of declining value in organizing support in the countryside. With few conservative states able to tax effectively the wealth of rural elites, policymakers have been anxious to have these elites channel their usually substantial capital more productively, replacing classic patterns of high personal consumption. In fact, most rural elites have required little prodding where investment opportunities in the urban-industrial sector provide high-yielding returns. This process can be accelerated, as occurred in Iran when the shah determined that the comfortable landlord class was a major obstacle to rapid economic transformation of the country. The extensive land reform program instituted in the early 1960s, although limited in its impact on the lower rural classes, did enable the regime to more quickly mobilize the assets of the rural rich for urban expansion. By substituting central authority for the peasants' allegiance to a feudal aristocracy, the Tehran government additionally hoped to involve the rural population directly in its modernization plans.

Other regimes have been more active in fostering among traditional landlords the attitudes and behavior of a landed entrepreneurial class. Development subsidies, more favorable price structures, and legislated means to circumvent agrarian reforms are all tools of a policy to encourage adoption of large commercial farming. As they shed traditional economic roles, the landed elites exchange communally centered, socioeconomic functions for market ones. With rising land values, the once paternalistic landlords are often anxious to evict tenant farmers. The employer and the newly salaried worker, their relationship reduced to a largely cash nexus, are more inclined to view each other as political as well as economic adversaries.

### Distributive Strategies

Strategies aimed at strengthening the capacity of the agricultural sector to expand production are the most pervasive in the region. Assistance policies make available needed inputs, transmit information to farmers, upgrade infrastructures, and in general, lower perceived risks in production. The public sector supports a wide range of specific programs, allocating fertilizers, seeds, pesticides, and so on at below market costs, subsidizing machinery purchases, and in some cases, discounting rates for electricity and fuel for farm use. A distributive strategy is reflected in construction of roads, dams, storage facilities, and other public works. A well-designed strategy also creates incentives for farmers to improve their land in order to increase crop yields. Public policies establishing low land and water taxes or permitting agricultural profits to escape taxation are part of a deliberate effort to support farm income and slow the flight of capital from the land. As much as any other action, the setting of official prices for crop procurement guides commercially oriented farmers in their cropping and investment choices. Although a distributive strategy often involves high-technology transfers, traditional inputs are rarely slighted. In the most successful assistance policies, the public sector is able to increase credit to farmers, particularly for the purchase of fertilizers, and to expand reliable water resources. Once these are assured, farmers are expected to be receptive to a wider range of inputs and more advanced farming methods. By and large, the strategy stresses mobilizing new resources rather than redistributing those in use.

Pursued alone, a distributive strategy is a conserving, system-supporting approach that may intensify inequalities. Agricultural programs may be highly innovative; they frequently shift resource allocations, substantially alter incentives, and introduce major technological advances. But policies intended to raise production levels are usually not designed to restructure production relations. Assistance is able to extend (as well as retard) social and economic gains for both small and large farmers. Additional public expenditures for farm subsidies and other preferential policies for agriculture have carried some previously marginal farmers into the class of surplus cultivators. In practice, however, these policies have not worked broadly in the region to meet demands for higher incomes or improved social conditions. Assistance programs have more often been means by which governments hoped to relieve pressures for more politically difficult agrarian reforms and changes in farm structure.

The actual mix of policies in a distributive strategy varies enormously across countries of the region. There exists no consensus of the "correct" combination of programs or sequence of assistance. There is considerable variation in existing infrastructural needs and the capacity to absorb investment. Within a single country the form of assistance is likely to vary for different crop-growing areas. Wide contrasts are found between assistance integrated with high government controls and that based on largely permissive market-oriented policies. The extent to which foreign aid and investment have been allowed to influence planning choices also shapes development assistance.

The highly touted Green Revolution in agriculture, essentially a distributive strategy, has been limited in its impact on economic growth in the Middle East, as indicated in Chapter 1. Application of its package of modern inputs was spotty and the information on their use incomplete. For a technology that is in theory value-free, its benefits have been most uneven where inequalities of power and income were already strong. As is found throughout the Third World, those who have profited most from technology's penetration of the countryside are the farmers and landed entrepreneurs with adequate land, cash, management skills, and political influence. Successful proprietor-cultivators and proprietor-investors, those aware of the availability and uses of the often handsome subsidies and other forms of government assistance, are best able to capitalize on programs and respond to incentives. Much of the conventional wisdom about why poorer farmers have failed to employ the more progressive practices stresses their natural suspicion and resistance to change. In the Middle East as elsewhere, however, many modern implements and practices have dubious economic value and are, in any case, not available to tenant farmers and smallholders.

No doubt the prime constraint on the access of the small farmer class to assistance programs, and specifically to a level of fertilizer consumption critical to increasing yields, is the frequent shortage of institutional, normally public, credits and their high cost in private channels. Christopher Brunner has described how, during the Daoud era in Afghanistan, the government was unable to broaden sufficiently the supply of institutional credits at reasonable rates. Small farmers, with heavy private indebtedness, had no real hope of raising themselves above subsistence-level farming. An embryonic cooperative system was incapable of assuming the job of reaching the small farmer with credits needed for small-scale modernization.[19] Nuba farmers in Sudan, introduced only recently to a money economy and exploited economically by Arab town merchants-cum-landowners, were unable to compete with politically influential townsmen for available credits and inputs.[20] Some notable progress had been made by the mid-1970s in bringing inputs within the reach of Pakistan's small farmers, especially in the more intensively cultivated irrigated areas. But these gains were not matched by credit facilities that would allow the majority of cultivators, most of whom lacked financial liquidity and collateral, to secure the available supplies. Cooperatives assigned the task of distributing credit never took more than 3 percent of the lands furnished to the farm sector.[21] As elsewhere in the region, credit in Pakistan remained largely in the private sector.

Mechanized agriculture offers a good example of how assistance policies can carry a clear class bias in distributing income, favoring those with ample resources or the means to obtain them. A distributive strategy enables tractors and other modern equipment to be made available to farmers for lower than market prices, often with generous credits for their purchase. Predictably, access to this credit is highly unequal. For most countries of the region, the import of equipment and the fuel it consumes represents a heavy burden on foreign exchange holdings. Many public credit institutions are thus anxious to make only safe loans, and the larger, commercially oriented farms are seen as the most acceptable risks. In Pakistan the top 2 percent of farmers, those with 20 hectares or more, obtained better than a quarter of the loans offered by the country's Agricultural Development Bank.[22] In 1969, the average tractor owner in Pakistan owned 91 hectares of land, and 69 percent of all tubewells were on farms covering more than 10 hectares.[23]

Using tractors, tubewells, and other modern instruments, commercially oriented farms often score impressive increments to production. The rental fees from tractors for cultivation and haulage offer another source of profit. With their increased earnings, middle farmers are often able to buy out small-scale farmers or, by offering them loans, to recreate former dependencies. Because the scale of farming normally influences the optimal use of mechanized equipment (some say that at least 10 hectares are required to make a tractor profitable), its introduction encourages greater concentration of landholdings. Rising land values also contribute to higher rents and the eviction of sharecroppers. While these changes may lead to more intensive use of land and thereby create, at least initially, the need for additional agricultural labor, more typically the introduction of tractors hastens the transformation to fuller commercial operations and avoids the problems associated with seasonal labor.[24] The results of technical change may thus be highly regressive, with unintended victims. Advantages accrue mainly to those already privileged while the hardships are borne by those farmers already deprived.[25]

Crop pricing policies are frequently a critical component in any distributive strategy and can be, at least over the short run, a powerful incentive for higher production. Market-oriented farmers naturally endeavor to bring about increases in official or guaranteed prices for major crops. But improved prices are not likely to work, directly or indirectly, to the benefit of the small farmer or wage laborer. Higher prices are largely irrelevant to the farmer who has little or no surplus to market for cash and who is already cultivating as intensively as his means allow. Although increased prices for commercial producers sometimes lead to higher agricultural wages, the gains registered frequently fail to keep pace with the rising costs of commodities wage laborers must buy. Not uncommonly, then, output subsidies only aggravate further economic disparities.

At the same time artificially low government-set prices can, besides creating disincentives, accentuate class differences. This is shown clearly in Egypt, where long periods of depressed prices for staple crops have encouraged the more successful farmers to evade government regulations and, even though they must forego assistance programs, to profit from shifting to uncontrolled crops. But the smaller farmer, unable to do without the subsidies and credits from cooperative membership, is tied to specific crop quotas and is largely unable to take advantage of open market opportunities. In any event, a price incentives policy is a debatable basis for agricultural growth as well as rural equity. For after the initial gains in output stimulated by higher prices, additional increments to production are likely to prove difficult in the absence of improvements in the productivity of the land.

Distributive strategies have failed to raise production and incomes for many other reasons, including adverse weather, unpredictable domestic and international market conditions, and ineffectual implementation. As a result assistance programs have not been fully able to win the confidence of middle farmers or to complete a transformation to large-scale commercialization from traditional tenant farming. Some programs have too sorely taxed a state's resources, and many lack sufficient political commitment. The most successful are government assistance programs of a comprehensive kind, delivering a broad set of integrated agricultural inputs and services. Yet very rarely have these policies been tailored to the requirements of small farmers. Even those governments that make a sincere effort to spread economic benefits and extend social progress through assistance policies are seldom able to accomplish much more than enabling peasants to maintain themselves at or near subsistence levels. Distributive strategies probably succeed most in propelling rural migration, although the perceived attractions of urban and foreign employment have been powerful magnets on their own. It is usually thought that assistance policies can offer security and economic well-being for the lower rural classes only within the context of legal and structural reforms.

### Reformative Strategies

A reformative strategy in agrarian development is conceived of as a major weapon against vestiges of feudalism and as a practical means to achieve sustained agricultural growth. Such policies as expanding land ownership, improving water rights for tillers, and revising tenure and tax laws can meaningfully serve distributive justice and help realize the productive capacity of the region's farmers. Attacks on concentrations of large private holdings, and efforts to lift tax burdens and adjust tenurial rights for smaller farmers, are expected to give the beneficiaries the capacity and motivation to use their talents and resources more fully. Underlying this view is the conviction that the division of larger, unproductive private holdings into smaller, individually operated units will result in more intensively cultivated land. Equitable and effective collection of taxes on land and on agricultural income should induce more productive use of the land by market-oriented farmers and extract increased revenues for the country's economy. Land redistribution and tenure and financial reforms are generally seen as preconditions, although not a sufficient basis, for creating the incentives and means for progressive (and certainly more socialized) agricultural systems.

Land policies are, of course, a time-honored means of dispensing rewards and punishments. The granting of land to faithful soldiers and bureaucrats and its confiscation from enemies of the state and the politically weak have a continous history in the region. Contemporary reform strategies, whatever their impact on the productivity and equity of landholding, are often submerged in political objectives. The transfer of land is, in the end, a transfer of wealth and power, and the readjustment of rights can be a reordering of economic and social advantages. Reform can serve, as Elias Tuma noted, as "a problem-solving mechanism" for ruling groups.[26] It has been used to legitimize and popularize postrevolutionary systems and has served the needs of conservative governments in dealing with real or potential rural discontent. With all its limitations, a reformative strategy can be an effective way to attack rural privilege as well as to adjust the boundaries and hierarchies of a class structure.

Nearly all countries in the Middle East have at one time or another proclaimed a basic program of agrarian reform. Egypt led the way in 1952, and subsequently all the self-pronounced socialist states in the region have embarked on ambitious land redistribution programs and tenure reforms. Such policies are predictably more limited in coverage and effect in the less radical states, although their prominence over two decades in Iran and Pakistan offers evidence that reform suits the needs of countries with very different economic and political systems. Impetus for change is found in different circumstances. It followed the fall of the Egyptian and Iraqi (in 1958) monarchies to radical military cliques, and Algeria's independence from France in 1962. Syria's unification with Egypt prompted reform legislation, and land redistribution occurred in Pakistan in the wake of a military coup in 1958 and again on the heels of the country's defeat by India in 1971 and the formation of a new, populist government. Iran's land reform was preventive rather than reactive, designed by the shah to free his government to accelerate the country's industrial growth. In Jordan land reform legislation came about in connection with U.S. financing of new public investment in agriculture.[27]

Land awarded to small farmers has been expropriated from rural elites or allocated from reclaimed or relinquished state lands. Changes in land tenure systems have frequently accompanied major development projects. In almost every case, the legal rights of the underprivileged are formally expanded and promises made of new social and economic benefits. The size of parcels given to farmers has varied — the smallest was in Egypt; the number of peasant families affected has differed widely — the largest was in Iran; and the economic advantages to the region's farmers have been unequal.[28]

Although some regimes have reconsolidated land in collectivist schemes, especially on estates recovered from foreigners, the prevailing mode of land reform has been to extend small-scale, private ownership, often encouraging cooperative activities. Almost everywhere, reform policies have failed to match their original blueprints and, in the end, have been shaped by particular domestic conditions.[29]

Programs adopted in Jordan and Syria illustrate often divergent goals and a contrasting scope of reform. Jordan's 1959 legislation was never more than a minimal approach to agrarian change. It was limited to a development area in the Jordan Valley created by the construction of the East Ghor Canal. The reform legislation that set ceilings on ownership sought to redistribute relinquished land in parcels patterned to optimize the newly irrigated cultivation. By also establishing a minimum size for holdings, the law was expected to prevent continuing land fragmentation and ensure a scale of production that would permit modern agricultural practices. Uppermost was the aim of using public funds to boost national agricultural output by expanding the number of modest-sized, owner-operated farms.[30] Although authorities sought to emulate some of the successes of Egypt's land reform and raise living standards in the valley, the Jordanian development left prevailing social relations untouched. Nothing was said about landlord-tenant relations in a country on whose East Bank roughly two-thirds of farmers rented all or part of their land. By contrast, the Syrian law of 1958 leaned heavily on the equity goals in Nasser's agrarian reforms. Over and above land ceilings and redistribution, the legislation provided for tenants' rights nationwide and new protections for agricultural workers. Evictions of tenants were restricted, and sharecroppers were authorized to receive a greater portion of their produce.[31] Later additions to the reform, decreed by Baathist socialist governments that came to power beginning in 1963, further reduced the allowable size of agricultural landholdings. Agrarian policy also assumed a distinctively doctrinal coloration in nationalization measures affecting agricultural trade.

In both Jordan and Syria, the consequences of reform deviated considerably from the stated objectives. Subsequent legislation in Jordan in effect dropped attempts in the 1959 law to reduce family ownership concentrations in the valley and to exclude already commercial farmers. Individual members of former landowning families acquired the right to hold newly distributed parcels in their own name. Moreover, as Jared Hazelton reported, 65 percent of the units were permitted to fall to less than the minimum authorized size; and rather than sharecropping and cash rental tenancies diminishing with the distribution of land, their number increased on the East Bank as new holders leased acquired land.[32] The expanded irrigation that succeeded in raising incomes among proprietor farmers also increased the need for landless wage laborers in the valley. The areas cropped failed to expand substantially, and the rising yields never reached the high projected levels. Far-reaching for the national economy was the shift in the project area from cereals to exportable fruit and vegetable crops.

Syria's 1958 reform was flawed in many respects. The law initially allowed landlords to retain extensive holdings and relinquish the least fertile parcels. It also placed the burden of indemnifying the expropriated landlords entirely on the peasants and failed to take full account of the different values of land in various regions, the amount of capital invested, and the kind of irrigation practiced.[33] In many instances landlords removed their water pumping equipment in order to qualify for larger parcels, no doubt a contributing factor in the decline in Syria's cultivation and irrigated land area in the decade after reform. A sustained drought and lowered productivity of the soil, as well as credit and input deficiencies and poor reform administration, left most of Syria's production and social objectives unfulfilled through the 1960s. No more than 50,000 families, by government admission, received titles to the confiscated land, and only a third of these had been distributed by 1975.

The great bulk of reformed agricultural land remained under state ownership of one form or another, most of it rented to farmers who preferred the government's nominal costs of leasing to land purchases that obliged them to join a cooperative. Meanwhile, through the 1970s the more pragmatic Assad regime looked the other way as older family units, broken up to avoid confiscation in the reforms, were reintegrated and private farms expanded beyond the legal size through the buying or leasing of reform created parcels from smallholders.[34]

Reform has seldom been able to satisfy the rural masses, who hoped through land redistribution to acquire economic independence and enhanced social status. The strategy has, on balance, intensified rather than ameliorated class differences in the region. This is an inescapable outcome of programs that in many countries have bypassed large segments of the peasantry. Although new lands brought under cultivation are sometimes divided among the landless, the more numerous beneficiaries in the redistribution of expropriated private holdings are normally only those who were tilling the land as tenants at the time of reform. In Iran, despite the wide scope of land redistribution, the large rural population of landless were virtually shut out of government programs.[35] The breaking up of large estates and promised legal changes can also succeed in reducing available agricultural employment for the landless. New recipients of land titles, farming as a family unit, have limited or no need for outside labor. Landlords seeking to avoid sharecropping and rent reforms are encouraged to replace tenancy systems with direct owner exploitation of the land and expand mechanization. A reformative strategy that is unaccompanied by institutional change leaves the landless in conditions of poverty and insecurity often worse than before reform.

Significant class differences and privileges have not disappeared under the reformative model, even in the region's most egalitarian systems. Long after independence in Algeria, large areas of the countryside were, in effect, unreformed. In the early 1970s, some 3 percent of Algeria's farmers owned 27 percent of all cultivated land.[36] The gap between the small cultivator and the rural rich was initially narrowed in Egypt as a result of the 1952 and 1961 laws. A substantial transfer of wealth and income to less affluent farmers took place, most of it at the expense of rich landowners and foreigners. By one estimate, the lowest 40 perent of the rural population saw their incomes increase to 25 percent of the total income earned. In general, living standards improved so that only 13 percent of the rural population (and 7.5 percent of the urban) fell below what was judged in 1975 to be an absolute poverty line.[37] Still, much of the cultivated land in Egypt has remained concentrated, especially in the hands of middle farmers. After the reforms, although the number of farm owners with between 5 and 50 feddans declined, their share of the cultivated surface rose to more than 40 percent of all holdings.[38]

The direct beneficiaries of land redistribution share much of the economic vulnerability of the landless. The parcels allocated are frequently too small to be economically viable. Recipient small farmers are consequently able neither to generate investment capital for land improvement nor even to employ fully the labor of their own families. The poor quality of the land parceled out ensures low crop yields. The subdivision into small uneconomic units can, as in Iraq, lead to the abandonment of land and help to exacerbate endemic problems of soil salinity and waterlogging. Large landowners who had once provided small farmers with water and other basic inputs may after reforms be under no contractual obligations to new owners and can charge for or even deny water use. Public programs expected to furnish credits to land recipients for the purchase of seeds, fertilizer, and irrigation equipment have been typically delayed, underfunded, or refused to small-scale farmers who resist participation in cooperative schemes. In areas where village practice had been to draw lots each year in order that no tenant farmers should be permanently tied to a piece of marginal land, the new owner-cultivators may actually have been better off before reform. In some countries of the Middle East, farmers have received parcels of land without payment; in others, they have been obliged to buy the land with the assistance of long-term government loans that allow compensation by the state for former owners. These farmers, as a result, find themselves in the same economic circumstances as before, although they are now in debt to a distant central bank no more sympathetic to their economic plight than a landlord or village moneylender.

The area's larger landlords have understandably resisted agrarian reforms that were perceived as a direct threat to their way of life. In several countries they were dispossessed or at least forced to reduce their holdings substantially. Egypt's reform laws of 1952 and 1961 managed, as already observed, to disinherit the country's wealthiest landlords and diminish the size of the prerevolutionary middle class.[39] Predictably, where they could, traditional landlords across the region have engaged in evasions and avoidance when faced with government efforts to recover land or impose legal restrictions on tenancies. The most common practice has been to legally divest themselves of land in advance of government action through the subdivision of titles and their distribution among family members. Large landholders could sometimes avoid accurate declarations or take advantage of special exceptions in the law. National legislation that sets high ceilings on the size of landholdings has permitted larger owners in several countries to retain the most fertile, economically valuable land. Some of the most blatant uses of legal loopholes as well as obfuscation took place under Pakistan's 1959 legislation. One estimate claims that 67 percent of the acquired property was later restored to landlords in one form or another. Among Iran's old aristocracy, about 1,300 landlords, each with 200 or more hectares, survived the land redistribution.[40]

Laws aimed at protecting small tenant farmers from evictions, regulating rental and sharecropping agreements, ensuring water rights, and shifting input and tax burdens are often poorly understood by the illiterate and socially oppressed. Many laws are simply not enforced. Even when small farmers become aware of their rights, there may be little opportunity to press for redress of grievances against landlords who are able to use the legal-administrative system to their advantage and are in a position to mobilize power informally through economic and derivative status resources.[41] Some laws, in fact, can be turned against small farmer interests. As suggested above, large landholders forced to cope with laws setting maximum rents or a division of crops find impelling reasons to evict tenants in favor of wage-based operations. Although the institution of a graduated land tax on landlords may seem a progressive policy on the face of it, it may result in new tax burdens simply being passed on to tenant farmers, bringing an increase in the already wide income disparity between the two classes.[42]

Nikki Keddie's observation about Iran, that reform has regularized rather than revolutionized the rural areas, has wider validity.[43] Redistribution of land and regulatory reform have for the most part succeeded in tying peasants to the same subsistence holdings they had been farming for generations. Reform can affirm the advantages of better-off peasants by legitimizing and giving legal protection to their property rights. It thus helps them to justify and at times disguise the retention of sizable parcels of land. In some rural areas those left with sufficient excess land have expanded rental arrangements and, with their higher incomes, have quit direct cultivation. Middle farmers may come to resemble traditional landlords as savings are increasingly channeled into consumption, typically for the construction of new houses. Wealthier middle farmers may move to the cities, recreating the kind of absentee landlordism that reformers had expected to abolish.[44] It is noteworthy that with the possible exception of Algeria, no regime in the region has even tried to outlaw the institution of tenancy. Despite stiff rent controls in Egypt, as much as 50 percent of the land is still under tenancy arrangements.[45]

Corrective strategies intended to meet strong political tests are evident in the cases of Iran and Pakistan. The shah's reforms had, according to Fred Halliday, imposed a political solution on the countryside.[46] A possible threat to the monarchy was removed with promises of a more egalitarian society and a landed elite that was politically, although not economically, emasculated. To the degree that land redistribution took place, it resulted in agricultural fragmentation rather than the hoped-for creation of a large body of prosperous, middle-sized farms that would serve as a solid rural political base for the shah's regime. Commercial farming was slow to materialize and a bureaucratic state filled the void left by a reform that failed to bring about the intended capitalist transformation in the countryside.[47] In Pakistan, all political forces beginning with the Muslim League government saw land reform as a tool for stabilizing the political system.[48] The 1959 land redistribution ceilings were imposed on the holdings of a landed gentry that easily evaded the legal provisions. The Ayub Khan government hoped to retain political and economic elite support while spurring the development of more productive farm enterprise. Z. A. Bhutto, author of the 1972 and 1977 reforms, without disavowing his populist support, willingly traded his initially far-reaching plans to modernize and transform agriculture for a political alliance with entrenched landlords and prosperous farmers. Regionwide, agrarian reforms progressed only so far as they continued to satisfy conscious, if also changing, political objectives.

Reform legislation in some systems is deliberately created to provide strong economic and political inducements for market-oriented farming. Special provisions allow the retention of large holdings by those farmers who can demonstrate progress in mechanized farming. In Iran, many larger farms remained in private hands after the 1962-63 reforms because they were exempted as productive modern enterprises, although to some degree, the extent of mechanization was only token. The case of Pakistan is especially illustrative. Lands served by tubewells and tractors were specifically exempt from acquisition in the 1959 law. Through a 1972 reform that imposed new controls over production, distribution, and pricing, government officials also hoped to foster larger, more efficient farms. Incentives to mechanize were expanded by again providing exemptions to farms with tubewells and tractors. A 1977 agrarian reform law prescribed a further surrender of land by larger owners. Introduced by Prime Minister Bhutto with a view toward improving his faded popular image prior to the 1977 elections, the legislation for the first time taxed farm income. Yet it also permitted deductions for the purchase of equipment, use of improved seeds, and land development. In basing the income to be taxed on average crop yields, planners expected the more productive farmer to profit and the less productive to be penalized. They were willing to gamble that a tax aimed at the income of commercial farmers and a lowered ceiling on ownership would not instead cause these holders to shift their investments away from the agricultural sector.[49]

Almost invariably, government planners in Middle East countries have been disappointed, if not entirely surprised, by the failure of reformative strategies to lead to higher crop production and yields. In some cases land redistribution resulted in the transfer from major food crops to cash crops. Marginally greater profitability for smaller farmers came at the expense of national economic planning. The threat posed by the uncertainty of government policies and fears of confiscation has sometimes caused commercial farmers to lose confidence and lowered marketable output. In the short run, government officials have usually accepted reduced production as the price of adjustment to change. Over the longer term, the productivity of reformed land is a matter of deep concern to planners. For many regimes, full-fledged agrarian reform is a less attractive strategy for the future than programs that broadly increase farm income in order to stimulate production and raise living standards.

The structural and legal changes in the reformative strategies have not, as some had hoped, provided in the region a shortened, cheaper way to pursue agricultural development. Legislative declarations of land reform are no substitute for sustained, well-financed support policies. The economic returns from laws distributing land titles or redefining rights and obligations appear minimal unless combined with improved infrastructures, substantial input assistance, and technical services to small and middle farmers. Even then, to be economically effective for the lower economic classes, agrarian reforms and agricultural development policies have had to include other strategies that seek to transcend fragmented, independent modes of production and to replace older rural institutions.

### Institutional Strategies—Cooperative Schemes

Attempts to reorganize agricultural systems and rural life in Middle East countries have engendered a third set of development policies. Qualitative changes are rarely entrusted to older rural institutions, and new or revamped ones are considered indispensable where policies envision the reordering of productive and social relations. An institutional strategy can take the form of creating cooperative or collective structures, organized along family, social group, or industrial lines. It often incorporates the means to deliver social services and new structures for research, extension, and marketing. Many new organizational forms are logical extensions or concomitants of programs of assistance and reform in the agrarian sector and are frequently a direct response to the shortcomings of these programs. Institution-building goes beyond distributive and reformative approaches, however, in the strong combination of political commitment, financial support, and administrative skills required. Because the reorganization of production relations can demand increased sectoral resource transfers and has greater potential impact on class interests, it is most likely to breed determined resistance.

Farm cooperatives are the region's most pervasive mode of reorganization. In the most comprehensive form, peasant farmers volunteer or are pressed to join state-managed units designed to provide them with credits, distribute a wide range of farm inputs, supervise input use, and purchase harvested crops. Farmers retain legal title to land, and the family is ordinarily kept intact as a labor unit. Cooperatives instituted on expropriated land may take on responsibility for the community social organization that replaced a system once dominated by large landlords or traditional institutions. The key to the success of the comprehensive cooperative form is the competence of its administrative and technical personnel. Through crop planning and the enforcement of quotas, these state-appointed officials are supposed to ensure both that the basic needs of farmers are met and that the unit implements the government's macroeconomic policies.

The cooperative offers an appealing means to overcome the patterns of land fragmentation created by laws that accede to peasant demands that they own the land they till. Without nullifying these gains in equity, the cooperative system introduces the economies of scale that are available through bulk purchases, the sharing of equipment, and the joint marketing of crops. Institutional support in helping to spread risks is supposed to make smallholders more willing to undertake innovative approaches to farming and to accept production planning. Doreen Warriner has captured the system's logic in observing that it "reconciles individual incentives and the growth of cooperative spirit with large scale operations."[50] Robert Springborg, describing the Egyptian cooperative movement, also found it able "to buy political support [among the peasantry] at a crucial time and to provide a substantial foothold for the state in the dominant sector of the economy."[51] Cooperatives offer, then, an approach to reorganization that promises to satisfy both the goal of greater efficiency in production and the desire for preserving the family labor unit. They also meet the state's concern that it be able to monitor and control the use of expropriated and new lands and mobilize, when needed, the rural population.

Egypt's cooperative societies have provided a model for many countries in the region. As they took shape in the 1950s and 1960s, first on reformed land and later in reclaimed areas, there was good reason to judge them a resounding success. Crop yields rose sharply on those lands under cooperatives' supervision, and farmers' incomes improved, often dramatically. Through more rational and careful use of the land, important conservation measures were enforced. Averaging a membership of 300 farmers, the cooperative seemed well designed to capture the spirit of mutual assistance. Members were allocated individually owned parcels of land in each of three blocks; they were, however, expected to farm collectively in such large-scale activities as ploughing, harvesting, and pest control, while retaining individual responsibility for such other activities as sowing and weeding. Equipment was shared by society members, whose essential inputs were supplied at subsidized prices. Marketing was put in the hands of the cooperative management for some crops and left to the farmers for others. Most important, the society's members received rewards based on the output of their own fields rather than on compensation for their collective labors.[52] The society also provided a mechanism that was supposed to ensure a cooperative basis for decision making. An elected administrative board was authorized to appoint a manager and agree on a common crop rotation plan and the unit's input requirements.

Popular acceptance of agrarian cooperatives on reformed and new lands rapidly dissipated during the 1970s as many of the operational problems that had been assumed to be temporary became permanent fixtures. Delayed shipments of inputs in insufficient quantities, shortages of equipment and its frequent disrepair, and weak extension services to go with crop rotation systems plagued the cooperative societies.[53] The sharpest criticisms were directed at official marketing and pricing policies and generally at the bureaucratization of agriculture. Whatever the theory, the locus of control has come to rest with the cooperative manager, an agronomist assigned by the Ministry of Agrarian Reform. The manager dictates critical cropping decisions, most of them geared to ensure quotas for exports and surpluses for urban markets. What had initially seemed essential to sound operations, the authoritarian, top-down approach, is increasingly resented by participating smallholders.[54]

Many farmers feel that they have, in effect, exchanged an earlier subordination to traditional landlords for the often overbearing, sometimes exploitative supervision of cooperative officials. These managers, even when viewed as competent, are often accused of identifying with the interests of higher-status, richer members of the cooperative. Observers note how official credit and subsidy arrangements, crop rotation schemes, and especially crop pricing have worked against those with smaller holdings.[55] The system's "kulaks"—families may legally own up to 100 feddans of land—are better able to circumvent regulations, including quotas, and to be the first to receive scarce inputs. The well-off farmers, according to Waterbury, have monopolized the cooperatives and are frequently delinquent in their repayments. With their larger holdings, they are able to produce surpluses above the government quotas and sell the excess on the free market.[56]

Yet middle farmers complain about delays in payments for crops, and many feel that cooperatives have added to their costs. In one survey the great majority of members were found to prefer freedom to deal directly with the private sector.[57] Ministry authorities fretted during the late 1970s that the actions of cooperative members had undermined national economic objectives. But officials seemed incapable of curbing individualism and were unwilling to confront directly problems of mismanagement. They were also ideologically unprepared under Sadat to mobilize poor peasants against corruption and rally stronger adherence to government directives.[58] There were instead pressures on the Egyptian government to loosen controls over the agricultural cooperatives and to grant concessions on prices in order to stimulate production of export crops and alleviate balance of payment difficulties.

Cooperative movements were also intended to complement agrarian reforms in Syria and Iraq. Any repetition of Egypt's early successes was improbable, however, given the political instability in both countries in the 1960s and national differences with Egypt in the quality of land and the skills of ordinary farmers. A reported 3,385 agrarian cooperatives were in place in Syria by the mid-1970s, with more than a quarter of a million members.[59] The number had risen sharply from earlier in the decade, in part because of the conversion of many state farms to cooperatives. But experiences with cooperatives were no more promising. They had made only modest headway in getting farmers to mechanize production and had had even less success in introducing new cropping practices. Most structures served, at best, as buying agents for farmers and then were usually unable to deliver seeds, fertilizer, and equipment to the largely uneconomical small farm units. Syrian cooperatives never received sufficient public financing, and most were administered by nonexpert party officials. Growing disillusionment by the late 1970s led to debate among officials over whether to back away from the cooperatives idea by quietly permitting independent private farming to expand or by radically restructuring cooperatives into, in effect, large, state-run, collectively owned farms.[60]

Only a small fraction of Iraq's farmers have been touched by institutional change. Most expropriated arable land was leased by the government to small farmers, and not until the 1970s was there a determined effort to push them into cooperatives and collective units. Inferences from scanty statistics indicate that the percentage of peasants who cultivated reformed land increased over the decade from 22.7 percent in 1973, while the proportion of farmers leasing land from the government declined from a figure believed to be 34.5 percent. By 1978 a total of 1,652 cooperatives, with about 240,000 members, were on the books.[61] Operationally, however, cooperatives, including basic credit facilities, had largely broken down by the late 1970s. The failure of cooperative activities was held responsible for the country's declining crop yields and its deteriorating soil resources. Iraq's planners announced their intention to reverse these trends by converting many cooperative units into a larger body of Soviet-style collective farms. Predictably, though, the country's party officials were expected to move cautiously in implementing radical agrarian reforms. Despite its socialist dogmas on agriculture, the Baath party hierarchy had been unwilling, over time, to offend conservative clan, ethnic, and tribal elements in the countryside. The leadership found it necessary, moreover, to be responsive to the competing demands of the urban professional and bureaucratic middle classes.[62] Financial stringencies arising out of the protracted conflict with Iran also acted to tone down the most ambitious, controversial plans.

Cooperatively organized farming has posed no serious doctrinal problems for the region's politically conservative regimes. Structures associated with redistributive and egalitarian policies can be easily accommodated by regimes committed to a large private sector for agriculture. Jordan, Iran, Tunisia, Morocco, and Pakistan have at one time or another all tried to organize farmers' associations as a means of dispensing credit and carrying on various cost-efficient production and marketing functions. Programs of agrarian reform and agricultural development in these countries have ordinarily reserved a role for cooperatives in implementing plans and monitoring results. Yet almost without exception, the state-guided cooperatives have proved a heavy drain financially and administratively, and most have become moribund or irrelevant to the great body of farmers. Cooperatives have failed to compete successfully with private interests, urban and rural, in the allocation of scarce national resources, and bureaucrats remain fearful of their becoming vehicles for popular expression. But most cooperatives atrophy in the face of farmers' resistance to participation. The economic payoffs are problematic both for families and the state, although cooperatives frequently have been denied a full test of their utility and potential.

Iran's cooperative societies were assigned a central place in the 1962 land reform. With the older elites supposedly removed, the cooperatives were expected to reorganize the reformed communities economically and socially. They were to furnish additional links to the urban centers and foster participation and confidence in other local institutions. By the mid-1970s, there were more than 5,700 societies, with an official total of more than 2.6 million members. In fact, Iran's cooperatives never assumed the role of multipurpose organizations and were, at most, inadequate credit societies.[63] Cooperatives were poorly funded and seldom received the promised extension services. Their credit terms were too restrictive, and loan policies generally favored the middle peasants. Services formally assigned to the cooperatives were sometimes assumed by enterprising richer farmers.[64] The pooling of resources for machinery rarely took place, and without adequate storage and transport, only a small fraction of the country's agricultural production ever moved through the rural cooperatives. To the extent that production and irrigation activities were cooperatively undertaken, the basis of organization was more often the kinship group than a government-sponsored society. These same ties of kinship and the pervasive factionalism of villages in Iran, as elsewhere, put strong limits on most forms of peasant cooperation.

Cooperatives have been conceived as a solution to fragmentation and inefficient farming, even in the absence of comprehensive reform programs. Those in Jordan were patterned on a familiar formula that calls for a cooperative approach to credit, input procurement, storage, and marketing. In no small part because the approach gave farmers little sense of participation in decisions and was unable to demonstrate economic advantages, it failed to gain the confidence of members. Late in the 1970s, the Amman government revived the Farmers' Association as a component of an expanded Jordan Valley development program. On government-purchased land, parcels of roughly 5 hectares were sold off as part of 200- to 250-hectare cooperative units. A total of thirty-two were planned for the valley. The association is supposed to encourage mechanized production, promote joint farming activities, and assume responsibility as well for comprehensive public services. Above all, reorganized farming in Jordan is intended to increase the bureaucracy's control over what is grown in this major export crop region. To date, however, the scheme has allowed for little alteration of social patterns in the valley; many parcels of land have been sold to well-off farmers, even to speculators in the urban middle class.

The Comilla Thana project in the former East Pakistan has been perhaps the best example of a successful integration of cooperative institutions with existing social groupings. The project was the offspring of the Academy for Rural Development, founded in 1959 to serve as a research laboratory for rural programs and administrative experiments. Planners sought to form self-sustaining village agricultural cooperatives of up to sixty members through which credit could be channeled and necessary inputs and extension services supplied from a cooperative federation at the thana (county) level.[65] The scheme gave government administrators the means to diffuse new technologies while leaving farmers a meaningful role in planning and local decision making. Villagers selected their own cooperative leaders, who received continuous training by an academy center. Public works and irrigation projects were vital components in this comprehensive approach. Studies have shown that the cooperatives substantially raised crop yields and that incomes in the thana increased markedly for the majority of farmers. Not surprisingly, fewest benefits went to the very smallest holders and the landless.[66] All the same, the Comilla system of rural organization did not permit traditionally dominant elements in the villages to co-opt the benefits of development.[67]

By 1971 there were 310 village cooperatives in Comilla Thana and 2,360 throughout the province. After the secession of East Pakistan in late 1971, the new government of Bangladesh officially adopted the Comilla model as the basis for future rural development. By contrast, the several attempts to introduce cooperatives to West Pakistan during the 1960s were quickly dropped. The transfer of the cooperative system was no doubt inhibited by the concentration of land ownership in the West. Structural features of the Comilla project were probably less critical than the traditionally small holdings in the area as a key to the largely successful economic and social organization of farmers. A financial commitment by the military regime to the Comilla experiment did not disguise the fact that the federal bureaucracy viewed the project with considerable suspicion. Even peasants in the West who were anxious to throw off their feudal yoke were fearful of a scheme that seemed to compromise their independence and land tenure in a government-administered program. The slogans that helped to elevate Bhutto to office following the loss of East Pakistan gave support to those more ideologically minded ministers and party officials who advocated cooperative organization of agriculture. Voluntary cooperatives, imbued with a social purpose, were promised in the Peoples Party's Manifesto to replace large estates that had been broken up. These units would allocate labor, provide machinery, and regulate water for irrigation. Farmers would also obtain their seeds and market their crops through the cooperatives.[68] The program was deemed imperative for the establishment of a just socioeconomic order among the neglected rural population. But although the Bhutto government moved quickly to expand land redistribution, inaugurated an integrated rural development plan, and eventually nationalized agricultural processing plants, it never imposed a system of comprehensive agricultural cooperatives on Pakistan's doubting peasants and hostile rural elites. Nor could authorities in a period of inflation attract private savings to an older system of rural credit cooperatives.

For countries anxious to provide land to peasant workers but faced with a highly unfavorable land-to-man ratio, Sudan's Gezira Scheme provides an instructive case.[69] Inaugurated in 1925, this reclamation project eventually came to encompass an area of more than 800,000 hectares, making it the largest agricultural unit under a single management in the world. Production of export cotton was contracted with farmers who were given individual leases of government land on a twenty-five-year basis and were allocated inputs, including irrigated water, by the Gezira Board. Although the scheme gives administrators powerful control over the use of modern inputs and cropping decisions, not unlike a vast state farm, it retains individual cultivation and cooperative members' attachment to the land. Gezira continues to be critical to a national economy in which cotton is responsible for 75 percent of Sudan's foreign exchange. Initially for the British administration and later for postindependence governments, the scheme maintains most farmers at subsistence levels while incorporating them into a system of commodity production and capital accumulation for the state.[70]

The performance of Gezira began to deteriorate badly during the 1960s and 1970s as problems inherent in the system surfaced. Yields of its cotton had dropped well below the world average, and farming practices and equipment had become outdated.[71] In 1963, low world cotton prices and rising production costs led to a strike at harvesttime by the Gezira Tenants Union, an almost unique example in the Middle East of small farmer organization. In spite of threats by the military junta, the union was able to force concessions from the government. During the 1970s, farmers diverted fertilizer and other inputs earmarked for cotton to other crops that could be sold through private channels for better returns. Difficulty in getting people to work unprofitable land even led to the distribution of some legal titles. Still other tenants had so prospered by Sudanese standards that they sublet Gezira land. At the urging of Sudan's international creditors, the Gezira Board sought to regain control of production and stimulate output by imposing charges on essential inputs. These actions were again met by the powerful opposition of tenants in a summer 1979 strike. The settlement agreed upon with the government of President Numeiri raised the average tenant's income substantially but also tried to ensure land improvement and greater mechanization. In all, the weak incentives, management problems, and emergent class differences among members leave strong doubts about the possible transfer of a Gezira-type approach to areas of rain-fed agriculture in Sudan or elsewhere in the Middle East.

### Institutional Strategies — Collectives

Centrally managed collectives and state farms appeal to many development planners in the region as alternatives to the individually oriented farmers' cooperatives. As structures in which cultivators are rewarded according to their labor inputs on communally owned land or as salaried employees in large-scale state enterprises, these collective models are found superior by advocates on both economic and ideological grounds. They are thought better designed to bring about rational production and land-use decisions and to ensure adequate investment in inputs. Collectives and state farms are considered more logical structures for vertical integration of production with marketing and food processing activities. The modes are also considered well suited to addressing the problems of landless peasants and the consequences of the continuous division of land through inheritance. The property rights of smallholders recognized in most cooperatives are believed to perpetuate traditional peasant attitudes about land and to inhibit acceptance of advances in agricultural technology.[72] For those on the left, the collective or state farm is a means to instill a socialist spirit and a vision of a transformed society among small farmers. It is expected to break down resistance to social progress among those with a "kulak mentality."[73] Yet the introduction of, in effect, state farms by several regimes in the region that are in no sense Marxist also suggests that they have rejected rural cooperatives on pragmatic grounds and that large publicly managed and owned agricultural units may be the only way to boost marketable surpluses, increase employment, and also extract surpluses for industry.

Regimes in the Middle East have usually moved very cautiously in introducing collective and agri-industrial approaches. Farmers in the region are most likely to resist changes that confuse the bases on which independent cost-benefit calculations can be made or that minimize opportunities to participate in decisions affecting profitability. Cultivators have not adapted easily to collective modes, particularly when they have previously tilled their own land or farmed under long-term tenancy agreements. Small farmers drawn into consolidation schemes seldom acquire a sense of personal accomplishment through working under collective conditions or develop a concern for the fate of large enterprises. Most continue to prefer those organizational modes that least violate traditional social groupings.

Reorganization of agricultural production in the form of large state-managed farms made an appearance in Egypt, Iraq, and Syria. Proposals for collectives to simultaneously deal with unemployed landless peasants and allow maximum government direction of agricultural development and productivity coincided with periods when socialist influences were in the ascendant. Egypt's Tahrir Province Reclamation Project was abandoned as a collective scheme when its technological and administrative problems and low productivity threatened the prestige of the Nasser regime.[74] President Sadat resisted efforts by leftists in the government to extend collectivization to other new land projects in his policy of distributing land to peasants, agronomists, and veterans, some of them middle-class investors. In playing down the transfer of reclaimed lands to landless peasants, the Sadat government instead set as its goal the exploitation of new lands by large, commercially oriented private firms capable of producing cash crops. Iraq seemed headed in its early revolutionary period toward total collectivization of land confiscated by the state from wealthy owners. But with the waning of communist influence by the early 1960s, few new state farms were created beyond the five founded by the Soviets in 1959, and there were only eighty-eight collective farms in the country in 1978.[75] Similarly, Syria's Baathist governments have not been able to muster the political courage or find the needed dedication to force small farmers into collective arrangements. The fifteen in operation in the mid-1970s contributed in only a very minor way to the country's marketed agricultural production.[76]

On land recovered by the Moroccan government, largely from foreigners, the state operated several farms in the late 1970s. As many as 880,000 hectares of land was being cultivated on some form of collectively or cooperatively held land by about 650,000 farm families in 1977.[77] But whereas King Hassan and his planners sought to attack the still dominant traditional system of subsistence agriculture through distributive strategies aimed at creating a class of middle farmers, in Tunisia more radical approaches won favor in high places. Farm collectives, known as *unités,* had been formed in the early 1960s and were expanded with the confiscation of the remaining foreign-held land in 1964. New units of 1,000 and 2,000 hectares were created to provide the management and capital that would cushion the collapse in agricultural production that was expected with the departure of French owners and managers.[78] Moreover, government officials envisioned the reorganization as a strategy of agricultural development that would advance the self-improvement and social security of the country's farm wage earners. Some progress was, in fact, made during the 1960s in rural health and education, and farm work methods were modernized. Greater mechanization on collective units contributed, however, to more farm unemployment. And with cumbersome bureaucracies and shortages of technical personnel, most collectives were economic liabilities.

Despite earlier mixed results with collective approaches, Tunisia embarked in January 1969 on a major socialist experiment. The Tunis government announced that all farms would be incorporated within state-run units, in effect nationalizing the country's cultivated land. The policy was met by the bitter resistance of many smallholders, and widespread violence erupted in reaction to government coercion. It was, however, the country's richest farmers who succeeded in convincing President Bourguiba of the error of trying to impose a system that, they argued, was inefficient and politically dangerous.[79] Within eight months the policy was dropped and its major exponent, the minister of planning, placed on trial for treason. The process of liquidating the units that were created allowed farmers to redeem their land, although it left some 250 voluntary, limited-purpose cooperatives and about fifty of the larger farms on state-owned land. At least some of the earlier collectivized area has been turned over in large and small parcels to independent farmers, some to wealthy leasees.[80] The return to an essentially private economy for Tunisia's agriculture worsened unemployment and the rural exodus; but it helped during the 1970s to stimulate handsome gains in overall agricultural production.

Algeria offers an ideologically more hospitable setting for an agricultural revolution. The performance of its socialist sector also raises doubts, however, about the economic soundness of large state-run farms. The Algerian experiences pose the question whether gains in social and economic equality are sufficient to create a dedicated agricultural work force. The sought-after institutional transformations, moreover, seem incompatible with the low priority accorded agricultural development in government planning. Over the decade following Algeria's independence in 1962, some 7.2 million hectares, the major part of the country's agricultural land, remained in private hands. An additional 2.3 million hectares once owned by French colonialists, much of it highly productive, was appropriated by peasant farmers in a popular nationalization that became the basis for Algeria's collectivist sector. Some 22,000 farms were grouped into nearly 1,900 so-called workers' cooperatives, which were actually state farms. Although intended to be rural showcases of Algeria's socialism, these farms, averaging 1,000 hectares each, were treated poorly by the government; the national investment that went to build industry was much greater than that in collective farms. However, state agriculture became every bit as centrally controlled. The system of *autogestion,* or worker's self-management, that initially characterized the country's collective approach was gradually ushered out after 1965 by directives from the Ministries of Agriculture and Interior, the actions of government-appointed farm managers, and national agencies charged with credit, input, and marketing decisions.[81]

The jurisdictional confusions, bureaucratization, and continual improvisation that had characterized the system through the era of President Ahmed Ben Bella (1962–1965) improved only slightly during the regime of his successor Houari Boumedienne. The large agricultural enterprises, despite seeming economies of scale, have proved too unwieldy for effective local management or intelligent central administration. Important goal conflicts have been observed at the two levels. The determination of central planners to maximize agricultural output and rural employment is often at odds with the goal of the local units to maximize farm profits. While low farm wages have been seen as necessary by officials concerned with capital accumulation for economic development, agricultural workers understandably strive for higher personal incomes.[82]

An absence of growth in farm output during the 1960s and the steady drift of peasants to the cities motivated Boumedienne to try to invigorate Algeria's private agrarian sector. The government decreed the Charter of the

Agricultural Revolution to remedy employment and production problems and simultaneously raise the income and social welfare of the rural population, while more fully integrating them into the country's political mainstream. The crucial phase of this reform involved plans to eliminate absentee landlordism and limit better-off farmers to no more than 5 hectares of land. Newly expropriated and previously leased state land was given to smallholders and the landless on a nontransferable basis. The beneficiaries were urged to form production cooperatives of from ten to twenty-five members and to work the land in common along the lines of Egypt's cooperative system. Officials guaranteed participants minimal incomes on the more than 6,000 units that were formally in existence by 1978. In all, although an estimated 800,000 hectares were slated to be distributed, the area was hardly large enough to absorb more than a small fraction of the rural unemployed and subsistence-level farmers.[83] Many who received land balked at joining cooperatives or quit unprofitable units for family farming or nonagricultural employment. Mismanaged field irrigation, soil erosion, and neglected orchards seriously reduced the country's agricultural potential; and because reorganization had replaced any modern commercial farms, the supply of agricultural goods failed to keep up with the increasing demands of Algeria's food markets and industry. In what seemed to be a reversal of priorities, a five-year plan published in 1980 also acknowledged disappointment with Algeria's large socialist farms (some 2,300 in number, still supplying 60 percent of all agricultural production), with indications that output in the future would be raised by permitting more private farming.[84]

Mounting pressures to raise agricultural production forced policymakers in Iran to look beyond the country's moribund cooperative societies. Determined to find appropriate structures for modern agriculture, they moved simultaneously in socialist and capitalist directions, to state farms as well as agribusinesses. Whatever the form of organization, it had to accommodate capital-intensive methods and national economic goals. Quickly forgotten was an earlier reform rhetoric that had stressed land-to-the-tiller slogans. Indeed, to realize the plans, the state dispossessed many peasant beneficiaries of earlier land redistribution programs.[85] Members of so-called farm corporations were forced to surrender tangible property rights for abstract shares in state-administered units, typically 2,000 hectares in size. The former smallholders received wages for their labor and dividends from any profits realized by the collectively farmed operations. Ten years after their creation in 1967, there were only eighty-five farm corporations in existence, and most were economic embarrassments to the regime and a cause of indignation to peasants. The corporations were furnished the same kind of poorly paid, poorly trained supervisory personnel and suffered from the same chronic underfinancing that had so long plagued the country's cooperative societies.[86] Because farmers felt little personal responsibility for the crops they worked or identity with the corporations, productivity was low. To rectify these problems government planners retreated in the early 1970s to another approach. The newly formed production cooperatives were expected to meet the same commercial objectives as the corporations and to continue crop specialization, machinery pools, and volume input purchases. They compromised the state farm model by allowing for somewhat looser management and, importantly, by permitting farmers to retain land titles. Only thirty were in place by 1977, and none had yet been tried in the country's more marginal agricultural regions.

Iran's consolidation policy for agriculture in the same period had as its centerpiece a set of agri-industrial farms. These agribusinesses put into practice laws inviting joint ventures between private foreign and domestic agricultural interests. In 1975 there were fourteen 5,000- to 25,000-hectare farms; the largest farms occupied 68,000 hectares in the southwest province of Khuzistan. The agribusinesses were intended to provide an important source of food for urban consumer markets and also to serve as models for crop experimentation and highly mechanized cultivation in all newly developed areas.

As in other attempts to reorganize production, agribusiness had serious shortcomings, and in Khuzistan the results were economically disastrous, socially disruptive, and politically costly for the regime. Land-leveling to permit field irrigation turned out to be far more difficult than had been anticipated. The private Iranian and foreign investors in Khuzistan's consortia, many of them American, had assumed that they would receive a reasonably early and substantial return on their investment. Instead, stockholders were asked repeatedly to bear increases in the capitalization of the projects. Government agencies were accused of defaulting on promised financial assistance. In the haste to see results, many commercially unsound decisions were made and unrealistic targets set. From the outset the agribusinesses lacked competent managers; a dearth of mechanics, tractor drivers, and skilled farm workers forced repeated delays in completion of projects.[87] As capital-intensive ventures, the agribusinesses could absorb only limited numbers of unskilled laborers from the local population. By one estimate, 17,000 people in Khuzistan had been forced to relocate to new towns.[88] Some returned to work as seasonal laborers on land they had once owned. Altered life styles created social tensions, and many landless peasants held the government responsible for misleading them into believing that, with the planned development of the province, they would become landowners.

A direct consequence of the regime's experimentation with state farms, collectives, and agribusinesses was to frighten off Iran's innovative peasant farmers. The possibility of incorporation into government-managed corporations or eviction by larger capitalists constantly discouraged land improvement and initiative. Official support for market-oriented farms and the article of faith among planners that private and public enterprise could work together were never able to dispel doubts about the government's interventionist policies or to stem the movement of private savings away from the agricultural sector. In the end, institutional changes gave the shah's regime neither the hoped-for production gains to relieve the heavy requirements of food imports nor the politically valued gratitude of the small peasant or middle elements in the countryside.

Any discussion of the institution of cooperative and collective farming in the Middle East calls for at least some comment on the kibbutzim and moshavim of Jewish Palestine and later Israel. The kibbutz is surely the region's most authentic planned communal settlement. Common ownership of the means of production, largely communal property, and collective work and consumption patterns make the kibbutz the realization of Zionist-socialist beliefs in social equality and economic contribution based on individual abilities. A conscious aim exists to balance group interests with individual autonomy.[89] With the economic success of kibutzim, an earlier stress on providing for basic community needs has given way to greater concern with profitability and collective success, although the kibbutz continues to coordinate its economic role with the larger goals of the Jewish state. These largely self-sufficient settlements on slightly more than a third of all cultivated land account for a roughly similar share of all agricultural output and a high proportion of export crops.[90] Kibbutz members amount, however, to less than 3 percent of the total population.

The moshav is a far looser organizational form, with goals that are often similar to those of the kibbutz but with fewer ideological antecedents. Its members are village-grouped smallholders on land that is privately owned or leased from the government on a long-term basis and designed for integrated rural development. These communities carry on varying degrees of mutual assistance and joint enterprise, mainly cooperating in purchasing and marketing activities. More than 40 percent of Israel's agricultural production comes from the country's 350 moshavim. Private farming in Israel accounts for less than one-quarter of agricultural production, the bulk of it from Jewish settlements cultivating about 55,000 hectares. The far larger Arab farm population in the private sector worked only 79,000 hectares in 1976, and by contrast to Jewish farmers, on largely unimproved and nonirrigated land. By themselves the Israeli Arabs contributed less than 6 percent of the country's total agricultural output.[91] The kibbutzim and moshavim are hence the leading institutions of Israel's agricultural economy. The kibbutz, in particular, has set an example for the country's highly mechanized modern agricultural sector.[92]

Israel's kibbutzim and moshavim are not sui generis and would seem to provide development models for the region. They matured in a system of government committed to economic planning and controls and had to compete for public investment. Most were linked initially to programs of land improvement. The role of the kibbutz and moshav as leading institutions in the absorption of immigrants may also contain lessons for those societies trying to transplant and transform culturally large numbers of people. The experiences, both successes and failures, of the moshav movement in integrated rural development can be especially instructive; they are studied widely in the Third World. But for obvious political reasons, Jewish rural institutions, if not their technologies, are shunned as guides to policy in Arab countries.

They may, in any case, be of limited applicability for those states in the region seeking to overcome structural obstacles to reform and social attitudes resistant to change. The Jewish settlements absorbed people largely shorn of earlier class identifications who were, besides, seldom agrarian. In trying to build cohesive, productive units, planners were not forced to challenge prevailing social and economic institutions; there were no classes to suppress, older antagonisms to dissolve, or attachments to ancestral land to satisfy. Compared to the rest of the region, the disparities in income between urban and rural dwellers throughout the country have been relatively small. The kibbutz founders were sensitive to the possibilities of introducing class exploitation, and at least until it became economically inconvenient, they resisted as a matter of principle the hiring of wage labor. Although the kibbutz and moshav have adjusted to what is now a capitalist economy, their values largely survive. Even in a highly industrialized society, the preference for small-scale farming still prevails over the huge state or private agricultural enterprise. The kibbutzim and moshavim remain nonexclusive, voluntary communities. Their ties to political parties and the national labor federation notwithstanding, these settlements are free of government-imposed management and have avoided permanent local bureaucracy. Also, in obvious contrast to cooperatives and collectives elsewhere in the Middle East, they allow for a wide degree of member participation in their affairs.

Plainly, no consensus exists regionwide over the forms most appropriate for organizing agricultural production and, indeed, no modes have been anywhere continuously successful in meeting a country's economic, social, and political objectives. Some planners insist that small, family-operated farms, provided that they are aided with overhead costs and technical services, are ceteris paribus the most efficient and productive units and the best able to absorb excess supplies of rural labor. Given the incentives, small groups of self-managed farms will engage in joint activities, including purchases of inputs and machinery sharing. Advocates of farm cooperatives assume that more direct government supervision of production and greater responsibility for services capture the advantages of scale and ensure cropping decisions that are compatible with national goals. While providing joint access to water, modern inputs, and marketing facilities, cooperatives avoid violating traditional feelings in the Middle East about land ownership. A third approach argues the need to apply a quasi-industrial model to the agricultural sector. Despite obvious doctrinal differences between state enterprises and private agribusinesses, the two are in agreement on how best to introduce capital-intensive agriculture. Large-scale operations and planning, it is contended, offer the basis for feeding a country and providing critical export crops. Carrying the logic of bigness one step further, some governments advocate creating agricultural development areas or poles where concentrated rural populations can be provided with agricultural assistance, public services, and nonagricultural employment.

In practice, the organization of agricultural production in the Middle East is multi-patterned. Scarce financial and human resources, hesitation to take political risks, and conscious experimentation have precluded national uniformity in public policy. Each approach has, moreover, revealed disturbing, if not unique, drawbacks. The family-run unit is not easily reached with the required information and material inputs; nor do small farmers in the region voluntarily associate to permit the use of modern methods. Cooperative farms have usually failed to dispense sufficient credit or to discourage individualistic responses to market signals. Whatever the gains over traditionally farmed estates, collectives do not compare well with middle-sized private farms in managerial capabilities or incentives. Agri-industrial-modeled farms, either state or private, are usually scaled too large for effective management. Most suffer from underfinancing and low productivity of land and capital.

## Basic Needs and Class Interests

Policies that allow countries to meet demands for the improved economic well-being of rural majorities and that also establish the basis for a modern agricultural system have, for the most part, eluded the region's planners. An approach that emphasizes increasing the productivity and incomes of the poor as a means to more equitable sharing of economic growth could obviate a redistribution of national wealth that is potentially more politically difficult. Such an approach often fails of solution, however, because of the inability of governments to accurately direct public investment or ensure peasants access to sufficient land through legal and institutional changes. Tensions between equity and growth regularly turn up in such basic issues as food imports and crop pricing policies. Economic planners in the Middle

East have not, moreover, adapted very successfully to the regular intrusions of nonmarket, politically motivated choices. Unstable political rule and the need to satisfy influential classes and groups result in policy discontinuities and choices that often defy economic rationality. Very rarely resolved, for example, is the dilemma of squaring farmers' organized economic demands with the insistence of public authorities that agricultural sector activities be centrally orchestrated and politically safe.

Programs to deal simultaneously with agricultural growth and equity goals did increase, nonetheless, during the 1970s. At least by comparison with the two previous decades, there was, over most of the region, less tendency to divorce production aims from social consequences in national development planning. As policymakers in Middle East states have set plans for rapid expansion in food production, they have increasingly acknowledged that the benefits of aggregate increases do not always accrue to rural underclasses. They concede that the kinds of technologies introduced will determine whether the poor can profit from higher productivity and raise their consumption. However, few signs appeared in the 1970s to indicate that regimes were willing to take the necessary political risks to implement what they understood.

Empirical indicators to show a trend toward more balanced objectives are not directly available. There exist for the Middle East few recent, reliable cross-national data on land concentration and income differentials or good comparative measures of rural social improvement. Table 3.1 relies on two national indicators, adult literacy and primary school attendance, as measures of the distributed social product. These figures are compared with average annual agricultural growth rates for those twelve countries in the region with more important agricultural sectors, those averaging at least 10 percent of GDP over the two decades examined. The aggregate data lend some credence to the impression that countries in the region are increasingly committed to improved social gains and balancing of equity and growth aspirations; the regional averages for the two periods increased nearly 100 percent for adult literacy and just over 50 percent for enrollment in primary schools. There were six countries in the 1960–1970 period with strong agricultural expansion rates (4.4 percent or better), but only two, Syria and Jordan, could show a relatively high level of social investment, far better than the regional averages on the two measures. By the 1970–1978 period, however, of the five countries most successful in improving their agricultural growth rates, all but Sudan were well above the national averages in both literacy and primary schooling.

The data can also shed light on the question of whether gains in social programs or improved output offers a better basis for public investment in development. There are opposing views, of course. Some insist that the best

TABLE 3.1
Comparative Social Investment and Agricultural Growth for Middle East Countries Where Agriculture Is At Least 10 Percent of GDP

| Country | Adult Literacy Rate* | | | | Primary School Enrollment*** | | | | Average Annual Agricultural Growth Rate (Percentage) | |
|---|---|---|---|---|---|---|---|---|---|---|
| | (Percentage) | | Deviation from Regional Average | | (Percentage) | | Deviation from Regional Average | | | |
| | 1960 | 1970 | 1960 | 1975 | 1960 | 1977 | 1960 | 1977 | 1960-70 | 1970-78 |
| Syria | 30 | 53 | +10 | +14 | 65 | 103 | +14 | +26 | 4.4 | 7.4 |
| Tunisia | 16 | 55 | -4 | +16 | 66 | 100 | +15 | +23 | 2.0 | 5.5 |
| Turkey | 38 | 60 | +18 | +21 | 75 | 98 | +24 | +21 | 2.5 | 3.9 |
| Algeria | 10 | 35 | -10 | -4 | 46 | 90 | -5 | +13 | 0.4 | 0.2 |
| Iran | 16 | 50 | -4 | +11 | 41 | 98 | -10 | +21 | 4.4 | 5.2 |
| Iraq | 18 | 26 | -2 | -13 | 65 | 100 | +14 | +23 | 5.7 | -1.5 |
| Jordan | 32 | 59 | +12 | +20 | 77 | 83 | +26 | +6 | 5.0 | 2.6 |
| Afghanistan | 8 | 12 | -12 | -27 | 9 | 20 | -42 | -57 | -- | 3.5 |
| Egypt | 26 | 44 | -5 | +5 | 66 | 72 | +5 | -5 | 2.9 | 3.1 |
| Morocco | 14 | 28 | -6 | -11 | 47 | 68 | -4 | -9 | 4.7 | 0.1 |
| Pakistan | 15 | 21 | -5 | -18 | 30 | 51 | -21 | -26 | 4.9 | 1.9 |
| Sudan | 13 | 20 | -7 | -19 | 25 | 41 | -26 | -36 | 3.3 | 8.8 |
| Regional Average** | 20 | 39 | | | 51 | 77 | | | 3.6 | 3.4 |

SOURCES: World Bank, World Development Report, 1979 (New York: Oxford University Press, 1979), 126-127, 170-171; and Report, 1980, 112-113, 154-155.

*Some national statistics are for years or periods that vary slightly from those indicated here.

**Averages are only for the twelve countries with agriculture at least 10 percent of G.D.P.

***These figures are based on people enrolled in primary school as a percentage of age group. For countries with universal primary education the ratio enrolled may exceed 100 percent since some students are above or below official primary school age.

national returns come from investment in human capital, especially education, that improves human capabilities; others, that expenditures to raise
production levels (urban and agricultural) result in broad economic gains
eventually benefiting poor majorities.[93] Of those countries in Table 3.1 with
relatively satisfactory rates of agricultural expansion during the 1960s,
namely Iraq, Jordan, Pakistan, Morocco, Iran, and Syria, only two were able
to sustain a high output during the following decade. But among the four
countries with the highest levels of social achievement in literacy and school
enrollment in 1960, Syria, Turkey, Jordan, and Egypt, the averages for
agricultural growth in the 1970s dropped only in Jordan which may, because
of its dismemberment in 1967, be a special case. The average annual rate of
growth for these four more socially advanced countries, at 4.25 percent in
the 1970–1978 period, compares with a regional average of 3.4 percent and
is up from 3.7 percent in the 1960–1970 period. Meanwhile, of the five
countries with the lowest social investment in 1960, Algeria, Iran, Morocco,
Pakistan, and Sudan (for which we have comparative agricultural growth
rate figures), the average growth dropped sharply in three between the two
periods, and only Sudan recorded an impressive gain in output from one
decade to the other. It is reasonable to suggest, then, that countries in the
Middle East that accelerated their social investment may have created better
conditions for agricultural gains than countries that were more indifferent to
basic needs.

Choices of agrarian development strategies and goals continue to have, as
this chapter shows, considerable bearing on class interests and contribute to
strains in rural class relations. Although distributive programs are broadly
endorsed, their application and impact are conspicuously uneven. Subsidy
and incentives policies have accentuated economic disparities between the
haves and the have nots and helped to undermine social values among those
active in agriculture. Reformative approaches have improved the security
and status of many middle peasants only to underline their differences with
the large number who fail to share the benefits of reform. Laws altering the
rights and obligations of farmers also raise aspirations beyond the capacity or
will of national leadership to fulfill them. Institutional changes, expected to
liberate economically oppressed farmers in new production relations, have
generally been seen by affected farmers as designed to deny their promised
economic independence and force them to relinquish control to class-biased
lower-level administrators. Although growth-oriented policies, in the
absence of other goals, most satisfy the interests of an entrepreneurial class,
and equity objectives by themselves are likely to benefit only the lower
agrarian classes, middle farmers profit from policies that have tried to recon-
cile or maximize the two goals.

The use of middle farmers as central actors in agricultural planning throughout much of the Middle East can thus be understood in terms of their role in helping to meld the several norms in development. Public investment directed to assist the vast majority of farmers has at best long-term economic payoffs; resources distributed to the market-conscious middle farmers offer more immediate and substantial returns in agricultural efficiency and output. Distributive and reformative strategies weighted in favor of the wealthier peasants can also help to satisfy equity, at least to the extent that improved income and status for this class narrow social and economic differences with traditional rural elites and often come directly at the latter's expense. And with heavy dependence on national programs, middle farmers provide for many regimes their most reliable and active political allies. The well-off peasant farmer has emerged as a force for rural stability, able to assume from the older landlord class many of the economic levers needed to control the rural poor.

The state is, as has been described, seldom neutral in rural class relations. Development strategies can be used consciously as instruments in reinforcing or altering property relations. Government bureaucracies, particularly local ones, are commonly viewed as defenders of economic and social privilege and direct beneficiaries of policies of change. Politically conservative regimes have pursued radical means in trying to preserve established interests, and revolutionary governments have often settled for far less than sweeping changes in order to avoid confrontations with entrenched groups or to keep from alienating those recently arrived elites who have begun to prosper from a new status quo. Both conservative and radical regimes in the Middle East have employed reform policies to transform or eliminate landed aristocracies. Assistance programs that have enabled some governments to solidify the economic advantages of large commercial farmers have been the means for others to try to reduce the influence of these entrepreneurs. The class attachments of regimes are frequently bound up with their foreign policies and degrees of integration within international capitalist and socialist economic spheres. Class-oriented policies can be obvious consequences of trade dependencies created by a monocultural export economy and severe food deficits.

National policy elites in the Middle East are, all the same, not inevitably the captives or trustees of particular class interests. Ruling groups have shown themselves remarkably capable of shunning former allies and cultivating new ones as the price of political survival. Conservative leaders who have refrained from tampering with economic relations have seized the opportunity, through rural programs, to help legitimize a regime by broadening its popular appeal. Radical regimes have tolerated interests whose contributions to agriculture were thought to improve the chances for political stability and economic growth. Although leftists governments across the region view the capitalist farmer as an ideological enemy, none yet has felt politically secure enough to employ coercive force against its wealthier peasants. Winning the loyalties of the rural poor may warrant curtailing the power of the middle farmers, but this goal cannot motivate destroying a class that most peasants still aspire to join. No regime to date has approached rural income equality, eliminated all private agricultural property, or attempted the kind of class transformation necessary for a communal agricultural system on the Chinese model. Above all, the Middle East's commercially minded, independent farmers are not expendable in view of the limited success of collective modes of production in reducing national food deficits.

## Notes

1. A somewhat different threefold classification to describe strategies in rural development is found in Keith Griffin, *The Political Economy of Agrarian Change* (Cambridge, Mass.: Harvard University Press, 1974), pp. 199–200. Griffin located three strategies, technocratic, reformist, and radical, as points on a continuum from conservative to radical policies. The categories used in this chapter recognize, along with Griffin, the beneficiaries of agrarian policies in class and group terms, and their associated ideologies. But the analytic emphasis here is on the eclectic approaches to development followed by governments of varying ideological coloration in the Middle East and the pursuit of nonmonopolistic strategies.

2. World Bank, *Land Reform* (Washington, D.C., May 1975), pp. 60–63. Statistics are from International Labour Office, *Yearbook of Labour Statistics, 1971,* and *Yearbook of Labour Statistics, 1972* (Geneva: International Labour Office, 1971 and 1972).

3. Fred Halliday, "Revolution in Afghanistan," *New Left Review,* no. 112, (November-December 1978), p. 33.

4. International Labour Office, *Yearbook of Labour Statistics, 1979* (Geneva: International Labour Office, 1979), p. 102.

5. Samir Radwan, *The Impact of Agrarian Reform on Rural Egypt, 1952–75* (Geneva: International Labour Office, January 1977), p. 42. Also, Alan Richards, "Egypt's Agriculture in Trouble," *MERIP Reports,* no. 84 (January 1980), p. 7. Another source noted by Richards estimated the rural proletariat at between 30 and 45 percent. Leonard Binder cited a 1959 study reporting that, of Egypt's total rural population of about 19 million persons, 10 million were landless laborers available for employment when there were no more than 3 million jobs. *In a Moment of Enthusiasm* (Chicago: University of Chicago Press, 1978), p. 71.

6. See discussion in M. G. Weinbaum, "The March 1977 Elections in Pakistan: Where Everyone Lost," *Asian Survey* 17, no. 7. (July 1977):603–604.

7. *Middle East,* September 1979, p. 79. See "Torn Between Food and Energy," *Arab Economist* 13 (April 1981):44, for the percentages of cash and sharecropping

farm tenancies in selected countries.

8. Ervand Abrahamian, "Structural Causes of the Iranian Revolution," *MERIP Reports,* no. 87 (May 1980), p. 23.

9. The 71 percent represented merely 20 percent of the cultivable area of Jordan. Richard N. Nyrop, ed., *Area Handbook for the Hashemite Kingdom of Jordan,* Foreign Area Handbook Series (Washington, D.C.: American University, 1974), p. 207.

10. Harold D. Nelson, *Morocco: A Country Study,* Foreign Area Handbook Series (Washington, D.C.: American University, 1978), p. 172.

11. Halliday, "Revolution in Afghanistan," p. 33. *Viewpoint* (Lahore), September 19, 1977, p. 18. In another estimate for Pakistan, the percentage who till less than 7.5 acres (3 hectares) was put at 44 percent of all Pakistan's farmers. Ronald J. Herring and Charles R. Kennedy, Jr., "The Political Economy of Farm Mechanization Policy: Tractors in Pakistan," in Raymond F. Hopkins, Donald J. Puchala, and Ross B. Talbot, eds., *Food, Politics, and Agricultural Development: Case Studies in the Public Policy of Rural Modernization* (Boulder, Colo.: Westview Press, 1979), p. 219.

12. Griffin, *The Political Economy of Agrarian Change,* pp. 184–186. Also, Norman L. Nicholson, "The Political Economy of Agricultural Research in Developing Countries: The Case for the Farming Systems Approach," an unpublished paper presented to a U.S. Department of Agriculture–sponsored conference, "Farm Structures and Rural Policy," Iowa State University, Ames, Iowa, October 20–22, 1980, pp. 12–16.

13. Oddvar Aresvik, *Agricultural Development of Iran* (New York: Praeger Publishers, 1976), p. 101. These figures are for 1972.

14. "Holiday Is Over," *Pakistan Economist* (Karachi), January 15, 1977, p. 13.

15. Nelson, *Morocco,* p. 172.

16. Hamza Alavi, "The Rural Elite and Agricultural Development in Pakistan," in Robert D. Stevens, Hamza Alavi, and Peter J. Bertocci (eds.), *Rural Development in Bangladesh and Pakistan* (Honolulu: University Press of Hawaii, 1976), pp. 317–333.

17. John Waterbury, "Egyptian Agriculture Adrift," *American Universities Field Staff Reports,* Africa Series, no. 47 (October 1978), p. 4. Iliya Harik, "Mobilization Policy and Political Change in Rural Egypt," in Richard Antoun and Iliya Harik, eds., *Rural Policy and Social Change in the Middle East* (Bloomington: Indiana University Press, 1972), pp. 304–306.

18. Marvin G. Weinbaum, "Structure and Performance of Mediating Elites," in I. William Zartman, ed., *Elites in the Middle East* (New York: Praeger Publishers, 1980), pp. 154–195.

19. Christopher J. Brunner, "Afghanistan's Agrarian Policy," an unpublished paper presented at a conference, "Rural Life in Afghanistan: The Prospects for Development," under the auspices of the Center for Afghanistan Studies, University of Nebraska at Omaha, September 23–26, 1976, pp. 9–10.

20. Richard Critchfield, "The Changing Peasant: Part I: The Magician," *American Universities Field Staff Reports,* Africa Series, no. 28 (March 1979), p. 2.

21. A. S. Haider and D. A. Khan, "Agricultural Policy Reconsidered," an un-published paper, U.S. Agency for International Development, Islamabad, Pakistan, March 1976, p. 6.

22. A. Malik, "A Quarter Century of Agricultural Development in Pakistan," paper presented at a meeting of the Western Economic Association, Anaheim, Calif., June 1977, p. 41.

23. Herring and Kennedy, "The Political Economy of Farm Mechanization Policy," p. 219. See also, Griffin, *The Political Economy of Agrarian Change,* p. 221.

24. Mechanized agriculture can, of course, create its own headaches in the form of shortages of spare parts and competent mechanics. For a discussion of the Egyptian case, see Sarah P. Voll, "Egyptian Land Reclamation Since the Revolution," *Middle East Journal* 34, no. 2 (Spring 1980):143.

25. Herring and Kennedy, "The Political Economy of Farm Mechanization Policy," p. 221.

26. Elias H. Tuma, "Agrarian Reform in Historical Perspective Revisited," *Comparative Studies in Society and History* 21, no. 1 (January 1979):3.

27. Jared E. Hazelton, "Land Reform in Jordan: The East Ghor Canal Project," *Middle Eastern Studies* 15, no. 2 (May 1979):268.

28. Hossein Askari, John Thomas Cummings and James Toth, "Land Reform in the Middle East: A Note on Its Redistributive Effects," *Iranian Studies* 10, no. 4 (Autumn 1977):267–279.

29. A useful typology of programs is found in Tuma, "Agrarian Reform in Historical Perspective Revisited," pp. 12–15.

30. Hazelton, "Land Reform in Jordan," p. 260.

31. Richard E. Nyrop, ed., *Syria: A Country Study,* Foreign Area Handbook Series (Washington, D.C.: American University, 1979), p. 118.

32. Hazelton, "Land Reform in Jordan," p. 264–65. Also see Oddvar Aresvik, *The Agricultural Development of Jordan* (New York: Praeger Publishers, 1976), p. 311.

33. "The Agrarian Reform (2): Syria," *Arab World File* (Beirut), no. 137 (November 27, 1974), p. I-S11.

34. Nyrop, *Syria,* pp. 119–122. Robert Springborg has described Syrian land tenure policies and the government's willingness to put aside ideology in order to raise production in "Baathism in Practice: Agricultural Politics and Political Culture in Syria and Iraq," paper presented at the annual meetings of the Middle East Studies Association, Washington, D.C., November 1980, pp. 11–15.

35. Eric J. Hooglund, "The Khwushnishin Population of Iran," *Iranian Studies* 6, no. 4 (Autumn 1973):236.

36. John Waterbury, "Land, Man, and Development in Algeria; Part I; Problems of Trained Manpower," *American Universities Field Staff Reports* North Africa Series 17, no. 1 (March 1973), p. 12.

37. U.S. Agency for International Development, "U.S. Economic Assistance to Egypt," A Report of a Special Interagency Task Force, February 15, 1978, p. 42.

38. Waterbury, "Egyptian Agriculture Adrift," p. 3.

39. Disagreement exists over whether the rural middle class in Egypt has been

declining in numbers and influence. Binder relied primarily on Hasan Riad, *L'Egypte nasserienne* (Paris: Les Editions de Minuit, 1964) who contended that the share of holders with 5 to 20 feddans had not declined over several decades, and conceivably since the late nineteenth century, despite Islamic inheritance laws. *In a Moment of Enthusiasm*, pp. 104, 344. Binder concluded that most of the rural middle class, and even many larger landowners, were unaffected by the land reforms, except as they gained politically with the ousting of the great absentee landowners (p. 26). Iliya Harik, drawing on his own field research (see the *Political Mobilization of Peasants: A Study of an Egyptian Community* [Bloomington: Indiana University Press, 1974] and recent (unspecified) data in a review of the Binder volume in the *International Journal of Middle East Studies* (11, no. 4 [July 1980]:564), argued that the rural middle class were major losers in the reforms. He reported that holders of 10 or more feddans exploited 44 percent of the cultivated area in 1961 but only 17 percent in 1975, and their numbers dropped from 90,000 to 65,000 over the same period. Other observers of rural Egyptian society have suggested that many of the real holdings of middle farmers have been disguised and that they wield undiminished local economic and political power, whatever their numbers.

40. "Economic Causes of Our Political Crisis II," *Viewpoint* (Lahore), September 25, 1977, p. 18. Also, Abrahamian, "Structural Causes of the Iranian Revolution," p. 23.

41. Ronald J. Herring, "The Rationality of Tenant Quiescence in Tenure Reform," unpublished paper presented at the annual meetings of the American Political Science Association, Washington, D.C., September 1, 1979, pp. 4–10. Also, Ronald J. Herring and M. G. Chaudhry, "Land Reforms in Pakistan and Their Economic Implications: A Preliminary Analysis, *Pakistan Development Review Quarterly* 13, no. 3 (Autumn 1974):272.

42. Christopher J. Brunner pointed to this possible outcome in "New Afghan Laws Respecting Agriculture," unpublished paper, March 1976, p. 6.

43. See Nikki R. Keddie, "Stratification, Social Control and Capitalism in Iranian Villages, Before and After Land Reform," in Richard Antoun and Iliya Harik, eds., *Rural Politics and Social Change in the Middle East* (Bloomington: Indiana University Press, 1972), pp. 364–402.

44. Daniel Craig, "The Impact of Land Reform on an Iranian Village," *Middle East Journal* 32, no. 2 (Spring 1978):146, describes this absentee pattern in an Iranian context.

45. John Waterbury, "The Balance of People, Land and Water in Egypt," *American Universities Field Staff Reports* Northeast Africa Series 19, no. 1 (January 1974), p. 4.

46. Fred Halliday, *Iran: Dictatorship and Development* (New York: Penguin Books, 1979), p. 134.

47. Ibid., p. 103. Also see Nikki R. Keddie, "The Iranian Village Before and After Land Reform," *Journal of Contemporary History* 3 (1968):69–91; and Ann T. Schulz, "Food in Iran; The Politics of Insufficiency," in Hopkins et al., *Food, Politics, and Agricultural Development*, pp. 171–191.

48. Sigemochi Hirashim, "Interaction Between Institutions and Technology in

Developing Agriculture: A Case Study of the Disparity Problems in Pakistan Agriculture," Ph.D. dissertation, Cornell University, 1974, p. 176.

49. Marvin G. Weinbaum, "Agricultural Development and Bureaucratic Politics in Pakistan," *Journal of South Asian and Middle Eastern Studies* 2, no. 2 (Winter 1978):57–58.

50. Doreen Warriner, *Land Reform and Development in the Middle East: A Study of Egypt, Syria and Iraq*, 2nd ed. (London: Royal Institute of International Affairs, 1962), p. 203.

51. Robert Springborg, "New Patterns of Agrarian Reform in the Middle East and North Africa," *Middle East Journal* 31, no. 2 (Spring 1977):130.

52. See discussion in Hung-Chao Tai, *Land Reform and Politics: A Comparative Analysis* (Berkeley: University of California Press, 1974), pp. 248–251.

53. Voll, "Egyptian Land Reclamation Since the Revolution," pp. 145–147.

54. Russell King, *Land Reform: A World Survey* (Boulder, Colo.: Westview Press, 1977), p. 386.

55. Alan Richards, "The Agricultural Crisis in Egypt," *Journal of Development Studies* 16, no. 3 (April 1980):307–308.

56. Waterbury, "Egyptian Agriculture Adrift," p. 7.

57. Ibid., p. 8.,

58. Richards, "The Agricultural Crisis in Egypt," p. 308.

59. Hossein Askari and John T. Cummings, *Middle East Economies in the 1970s* (New York: Praeger Publishers, 1976), p. 153.

60. Springborg, "Baathism in Practice," pp. 13–14. See also, Nyrop, *Syria*, p. 122.

61. Joe Stork, "The War in the Gulf," *MERIP Reports*, no. 97 (June 1981), p. 13. Also see Springborg, "Baathism in Practice," p. 16.

62. See discussion in Phebe A. Marr, "The Political Elite in Iraq," in George Lenczowski, ed., *Political Elites in the Middle East* (Washington, D.C.: American Enterprise Institute, 1975), pp. 148–149.

63. Nikki R. Keddie, "Oil Economic Policy and Social Conflict in Iran," *Race and Class* 21, no. 1 (Summer 1979):24. See also A. K. Lambton, *The Persian Land Reform 1962–66* (Oxford: Clarendon Press, 1969), pp. 36–65.

64. Daniel Craig, "The Impact of Land Reform on an Iranian Village," *Middle East Journal* 32, no. 2 (Spring 1978):148.

65. Robert D. Stevens, "Comilla Rural Development Programs to 1971," in Robert D. Stevens, Hamza Alavi, and Peter J. Bertocci, eds., *Rural Development in Bangladesh and Pakistan* (Honolulu: University Press of Hawaii, 1976), p. 100.

66. Ibid., pp. 103–104.

67. Peter J. Bertocci, "Social Organization and Agricultural Organization in Bangladesh," in Stevens et al., *Rural Development in Bangladesh and Pakistan*, p. 167.

68. Bruce J. Esposito, "Agrarian Reform in Pakistan," *Asian Survey* 14, no. 5 (May 1974):430–431.

69. Springborg, "New Patterns of Agrarian Reform," p. 136.

70. Carole Collins, "Sudan: Colonialism and Class Struggle," *MERIP Reports* 46 (April 1976):10.

71. *Middle East,* April 1980, p. 56.

72. Elias Tuma, "Agrarian Reform and Urbanization in the Middle East," *Middle East Journal* 24, no. 2 (Spring 1970):166.

73. Springborg, "New Patterns of Agrarian Reform," p. 133.

74. Ibid., pp. 130–131.

75. Springborg, "Baathism in Practice," p. 16.

76. Springborg, "New Patterns of Agrarian Reform," pp. 131–132.

77. Nelson, *Morocco,* p. 172.

78. King, *Land Reform,* p. 421.

79. Ibid., p. 422.

80. "Releasing Fair Weather Hold on Crops," *Middle East,* August 1979, pp. 105–106.

81. For extensive treatment of the topic see Waterbury, "Land, Man and Development in Algeria," pp. 6–14, and Nico Kielstra, "The Algerian Revolution and Algerian Socialism," *MERIP Reports* 8, no. 4 (May 1978):6–7.

82. P. Foster, "Land Reform in Algeria," *Spring Review of Land Reform* 8 (1970):10–11. See also King, *Land Reform,* p. 430.

83. Kielstra, "The Agrarian Revolution and Algerian Socialism," pp. 7–8.

84. Harold D. Nelson, ed., *Algeria: A Country Study,* Foreign Area Handbook Series (Washington, D.C.: American University, 1979), p. 169. Also *New York Times,* November 18, 1980.

85. Halliday, *Iran: Dictatorship and Development,* pp. 114, 125.

86. M. G. Weinbaum, "Agricultural Policy and Development Politics in Iran," *Middle East Journal* 31, no. 4 (Autumn 1977):438.

87. Ibid., p. 429.

88. Halliday, *Iran: Dictatorship and Development,* p. 115.

89. Michael Curtis, "Utopia and the Kibbutz," in M. Curtis and Mordecai Chertoff, eds., *Israel: Social Structure and Change* (New Brunswick, N.J.: Transaction Books, 1973), p. 111.

90. Since the 1940s, kibbutzim have also assumed about 7 percent of industrial production in the country. Ibid., p. 109. More than 20 percent of the labor force is involved in nonagricultural occupations. Also, see Richard F. Nyrop, ed., *Israel: A Country Study,* Foreign Area Handbook Series (Washington, D.C.: American University, 1979), pp. 195–196.

91. Nyrop, *Israel,* p. 197.

92. For treatment of agricultural settlements and the economy in Israel see Eliyahu Kanovsky, *The Economy of the Israeli Kibbutz* (Cambridge, Mass.: Harvard University Press, 1966); Haim Barkai, *Growth Patterns in the Kibbutz Economy* (Amsterdam: North-Holland Publishing, 1977); and Alex Weingrod, *Reluctant Pioneers: Village Development in Israel* (Ithaca, N.Y.: Cornell University Press, 1966).

93. See arguments and a cross-national analysis of the evidence in Norman L. Hicks, "Is There a Tradeoff Between Growth and Basic Needs?" *Finance and Development,* June 1980, pp. 17–20.

# 4
# Bureaucratic Values, Structures, and Decisions

Without effective administrative structures—more specifically, the competence, dedication, and resources available in national and local bureaucracies—programs for the development of agricultural systems are at best symbolic. Nearly everywhere in the Middle East, the failure of small-scale traditional farming to meet the demands of urban populations, industry, and export markets had led typically to government intervention to modernize agriculture and better conditions of rural life. All states in the region, to be sure, exercise less than full control over the behavior of producers and markets and depend on nonpublic resources and shared concerns. Policies of permissiveness, partnership, or domination in relation to the private sector may grow out of principle or practicality or both. But with the accelerating integration of agriculture into national economies, governments in the region are prime movers in transforming market relations and altering incentives for agricultural producers. Ministries that were once engaged in setting only the broadest economic parameters now regularly manipulate commodity and financial markets, help to modify conditions of production, and most important, guide almost every aspect of development planning and implementation. The degree of public sector involvement is revealed, as it is throughout the Third World, by the substitution of public agencies and receipts for private institutions and savings.[1] It is also marked by the imposition of bureaucratically enforced rules and expectations on individual motives and aspirations.

It is hardly surprising that so much of the blame for the poor record of regimes in the Middle East in coping effectively with their food requirements and development needs is laid on public ministries. These bodies additionally stand accused of inability to realize promised rural social justice and demands for increased economic equality. Bureaucracies are regularly criticized as administratively cumbersome and inefficient, incapable of formulating workable programs and guiding rural change. The skills and personal interests of officials are often viewed as major obstacles to the implementation of policy decisions. Institutional capability and individual motives cannot be understood fully, however, without reference to normative expectations or apart from the processes of competing interests, ideals, and ambitions within and outside the public bureaucracies. Any examination of agricultural and rural development policies in the Middle East must, then, consider the values and styles of administrators and the broader institutional and societal context for their decisions and actions.

Agriculturally related bureaucracies are unmistakably political. They offer an instructive setting in which to observe the ascendance of particular elites and the penetration of demand-bearing groups. Ministries are themselves participants in struggles for resources and power among units and levels of government. Few agricultural bureaucracies are insulated, moreover, from a country's major cleavages and controversies. The imprints of center-periphery tensions, competing economic doctrines, and class and ethnic conflicts are easily discernible. Because agricultural ministries and departments are normally service-oriented, their programs administratively intensive, they are distinguishable from many other agencies by their mass clientele and high public exposure. Gross mistakes are registered, sometimes in a short time span, in human suffering and dashed hopes. Policies are hence capable of generating suspicion, cynicism, and resistance and figure prominently in the erosion of confidence in government authority. At the same time, regimes are increasingly judged by their performance in the agricultural sector. The principal officials of agricultural bureaucracies are, as a result, politically vulnerable, among the first to be replaced in changes of government priorities and leadership.

### The Patrimonial System

Judging from appearances, Middle East bureaucracies are in the process of an administrative revolution. New units have proliferated, while older, restructured ones have been assigned more explicit functional responsibilities, their procedures made more streamlined and defensible. Bureaucratic communications and coordination are a conscious concern, to which interagency working groups and conferences are a visible response. Computer technology is increasingly available to aid policymakers, both for long-range planning and practical problem solving. Efforts are being undertaken to recruit better-trained personnel from a wider population pool, through less ascriptive means. Younger, foreign-educated personnel, now in the middle and even upper echelons, are expected to be the carriers of a new ethos of efficiency, honesty, and dedication.

These changes are not, of course, characteristic of agricultural bureaucracies alone. Nor are they peculiar to the Middle East, where they are found, in any event, unevenly across the region. Yet the widely observed elaboration of decision structures, the rationalization of procedures, and the officially revised norms in agricultural bureaucracies from Morocco to Pakistan illustrate well how newer modes have, in fact, overlaid rather than displaced older attitudes and practices. More important, adherence by administrators to more traditional patterns and the failure to harmonize these with newer ideas and institutions remain significant impediments to modernizing agricultural systems and establishing adequate food policies.

Agricultural ministries and agencies in most of the Islamic Middle East continue to labor under a time-honored patrimonial system. It is a system of administrative authority in which power emanates from a single political leader and the influence of others is derivative in rough proportion to their perceived access to him or their share in his largesse. The system relies on informal relations in which institutional roles and formal organizations matter far less than personal networks and reputations. The informal decision process offers a sometimes necessary antidote to the rigidities of formal bureaucratic structures. Tensions from rivalries and jealousies endemic to the system are mediated, if at all, by the security offered by family and friendship cliques, and clientele relationships.[2]

In general, bureaucratic behavior is marked by defensiveness, both individual and institutional. Officials are careful not to offend superiors or to identify themselves with decisions and programs that might fail to realize expectations. Ministries are typically engaged in a competition for funds with other units of government, not so much as a means of pursuing particular programs as an ongoing test of their standing in the bureaucratic pecking order. The measure of institutional success often seems to be in the growth of personnel and scope of operations rather than in their contributions to development. High officials are otherwise preoccupied with such symbols of recognition as upgrading existing posts, adding new staff and cars, and securing choice residential accommodations.

Bureaucracies are wedded to a rigid seniority system that does little to improve the motivation or professional self-esteem of middle-level officials. There are seldom any systematic means of recognizing merit as the basis for promotion and other rewards, financial and nonfinancial. Without agreed-upon achievement criteria, ambiguity prevails over whether one will be judged by performance standards, paper credentials, or family and friendship ties. Opportunities for personal gain are expected very often to offset low salaries and poor working conditions, especially in the rural areas. The elaborate, often redundant procedures designed to thwart administrative wrongdoing may create obstacles to many forms of petty corruption but are typically ill designed to prevent serious conflicts of interest. In some countries at least, profit from or permissiveness in corrupt practices gives administrators a personal stake in the prevailing political order and regime leaders a powerful lever against possible political deviation. On a more regular basis, political and personal loyalties are injected into bureaucratic personnel policies, resulting in the outright dismissal of some officials and the regular intimidation of many others.

Like other bureaucracies in the Middle East, agricultural ministries are usually subject to a policy of frequent and unpredictable transfers of personnel. Shifting people around is a continuous reminder that those in superior positions can intervene on a whim and at will.[3] The transfer of higher officials usually has direct implications for agricultural programs. Much of the considerable time required for project identification and approval, as well as the high attrition rate of officials, results from the unavoidable personalization of policy. A strategically placed official's willingness to champion an idea or to intervene on behalf of a project is normally essential to its survival. Yet many officials hesitate to be closely associated with a policy whose failure can be used to discredit them and impede their career advancement. Conversly, a project's identification with specific individuals may increase its vulnerability. Transfers are likely to remove a program's original defenders and replace them with political rivals or officials with different priorities who are anxious to put their own stamp on policies. The frequent use in higher posts of generalists, known to be politically reliable, rather than agricultural specialists increases the likelihood of divergent approaches. Some development projects are sensibly allowed to stagnate or die because, as personal vehicles of previous officials, they were poorly conceived. More often, programs are prematurely dropped lest someone else earn the credit for a possible success.

In a manner not peculiar to agriculture or the Middle East, new administrative units are formed in the comforting belief that, somehow, by the creation of an agency, a problem has been addressed and is on its way to being solved.[4] Some units are thus disbanded or bypassed while newer ones are formed with almost identical goals and with no more authority or commitment of resources than the structures they replaced. The purpose of parallel agencies is as often as not to break up concentrations of power that threaten to upset the balance of rivalry and conflict that reinforces the leaders' sense of control and policy dominance. At other times, however, the creation of single-purpose agencies can conceivably reduce managerial demands. Erection of units that are in theory independent of the traditional bureaucracy may be a conscious decision by leaders to overcome known bottlenecks and to advance more quickly better qualified people. Rural development and new-lands agencies have in several countries been established to circumvent old-line ministries and to group logically related activities. But unless these newer agencies continue to attract the special patronage of high political authority, their funds will in time be diverted to and their powers sapped by traditional departments. In any case, once bureaucratic relations become firmly established in the new units, the latter are likely to assume most of the same patterns of patrimonial behavior as are found elsewhere in the bureaucracy.

Relations are frequently formal and strained between senior officials and their subordinates, especially when they are also divided by social class origins. In several countries, higher-echelon bureaucrats retain an identity with older landed elites and the advantages of better education and family connections. The advice of middle-level officials, mainly technocrats, may be sought on a regular basis and comprehensive policy recommendations submitted. But although the ideas and analyses of specialists are often used to support or rationalize decisions, top officials rarely give credit to subordinates or, for that matter, involve them in final decisions. Middle-level technocrats are regularly ignored when their views fail to fit the policy preconceptions of ministry superiors.

Few agricultural development proposals advance very far in the region's low-income countries in the absence of a prospective foreign donor. Aside from the financial resources promised and the special expertise of foreign nationals, foreign assistance is expected to provide coveted rewards to government officials in the form of travel and study. Foreigners can be useful, moreover, in sharing with government officials responsibility for projects. Unlike colleagues in the bureaucracy, the foreign adviser is not a claimant for credit in any successes and presents a convenient scapegoat in the event of failure. It is not uncommon for foreign experts to become involved, inadvertently, as allies in bureaucratic struggles. Predictably, the foreign adviser is resented by many in the administrative structure, especially those at the middle levels, who feel that their own advice is ignored. There are others who understandably fear that they would be unable to carry out a scheme should the foreign patrons withdraw.

Agricultural research and planning units tend to focus on technological concerns rather than broad agricultural policy issues and alternatives. Research is often unrelated to macro development strategies. Much of it offers little practical advice to decision makers, aside from conventional wisdom. Data-generated research may reach agencies only after a long time lag, and information collection processes tend to be notoriously outmoded and poorly organized and supervised. Serviceable raw data are often unsystematized or presented in unusable form. Aside from questions of data reliability, there are also cases of deliberately exaggerated and falsified results, especially agricultural output figures, presented both to enhance the reputation of departments and to please the national leadership. Information feedback mechanisms capable, for example, of indicating the appropriateness of a new technology for small farmers, are rarely built into research activities.

Because principal policymakers are not disposed to delegate real authority any more than their subordinates are to seek direct responsibility, important policy choices are often at the discretion of a single individual. In several Middle East bureaucracies, for example, a senior official has the power to determine whether a particular commodity is to be imported and at what level. But unless motivated by strong personal interest, administrators often consider it wiser to reach no decision than to make one that they may later regret. Because of officials' reluctance to act, many decisions involving food and rural development eventually find their way to top political levels where they come under the purview of personal advisers to prime ministers, presidents, and monarchs. These nonexperts typically have few inhibitions about giving advice; in fact, throughout the region, people in public life feel competent to give their opinions on agricultural matters by virtue of belonging to landowning families. More generally, the elevation of decisions to the highest political levels is encouraged by leaders known to have an almost obsessive desire to demonstrate their indispensability by having all policy choices, often routine ones, appear to emanate from their offices.

A patrimonial style in the Middle East normally follows a strategy of divide and rule. To ensure a high level of competition among a leader's subordinates, they are endowed with roughly equal power and given overlapping areas of authority.[5] An absence of defined responsibility fits well the system's informal modes and enhances the leader's flexibility to choose among personnel and policies. Yet many administrative problems besetting agricultural policymaking are readily traceable to uncertain jurisdictional lines and competing bureaucracies. Different ministries and departments are often responsibile for related aspects of the same problem. In Iran the government monopoly over the import of wheat, sugar, and dried milk was vested in one department, while another arranged for the purchase of meat and poultry from abroad. Both were beyond the control of the Ministry of Agriculture, which was authorized to set the guaranteed prices for domestic procurement of these items. For many years, separate Iranian administrative structures assisted farmer cooperatives, managed public farm corporations, and dealt with agribusinesses.[6] The effectiveness of Egyptian cooperatives has been impaired by the highly complex national administrative structure. Lines of authority are frequently unclear among the many diverse intermediary units that lie between the Ministry of Agriculture and the five thousand or so local cooperatives. The Egyptian Ministries of Agriculture and Irrigation were both allowed to compete for control over reclaimed lands, and in Pakistan, several government departments were expected to cooperate with an independent federal agency to administer waterlogging and salinity control programs, without clear agreement over the division of tasks.

Predictably, rural development and food policies are confounded as different bureaucratic sectors work at cross-purposes. Even at the sacrifice of overall planning and broader economic policy, senior administrators, after showing the proper fealty to the top political leadership, are allowed to pursue strategies that may vary widely in goals and philosophy. One ministry may stress the primacy of monetary inducements to larger producers, while another prefers to see increased public resources for agriculture go mainly for grants, subsidies, and easier credits to small farmers. The conservative land policies of public development banks frequently have little in common with agricultural development strategies advocated elsewhere in the bureaucracy. Administrative structures hence come to represent largely disparate economic interests, institutionalized at the national level but also manifested through clientele relationships that reach down to the lower rungs of the bureaucracy. The conflicts and struggles that exist horizontally among national administrative units can thus be carried to the local level. But as the lines extend from the center and become more remote from the highest political leadership, vertical administrative authority, basically informal and personalized, is strained. The kinds of friendships and family networks that give bureaucracies necessary information and direction are impossible. The consequences for the execution of policy decisions are manifest.

## Policy Implementation: Center and Periphery

A wide gap is normally found between those who formulate and promulgate policies and those who implement decisions. The former have little capacity to monitor performance or ensure compliance. The latter, in turn, are never certain of their superiors' full commitment in resources, personnel, and materials. In either case, development plans often bear little correspondence to their application in the fields and villages. Only a modest overlap exists between an official's supposed realm of authority and his actual scope of effectiveness. Poor communications between personnel in the capital's bureaucracies and those at the provincial level are largely to blame. The failure of intermediary structures to transmit information up to policymakers and down to farmers is frequently noted. A fundamental problem nearly everywhere is the small base of skilled and motivated fieldworkers. But the ambivalence of top political leaders and senior officials toward their own policies, and their lack of sustained attention to them, are no less important. It is rare that the same energies that go into starting up a program are also devoted to seeing it through.

Announcements of new agricultural projects or food production targets are designed to give the impression that the government is both concerned about and capable of inducing desired change. These activities are, however, less directives than exhortations to those who in fact can shape outcomes. It is almost as though the approval of an undertaking is synonymous with its realization. This distance between prescription and execution means that aspirations and weak gestures usually substitute for carefully designed blueprints. And what decisions are made somehow fail to filter down through the top-heavy agricultural bureaucracy, least of all to the operational level. When they do, they are as often as not misunderstood, ignored, or deliberately flouted.

Higher-ranking officials typically have an unrealistic set of expectations about the feasibility of policies or the prevailing conditions in the countryside. Desk-bound, they seldom venture into the field and then rarely for more than token visits. This does little to rectify the preconceptions of decision makers based on faulty data and inappropriately applied notions of development and rural life. Although higher officials are generally competent in economics and well versed through foreign travel and conferences in the latest technical advances, most remain unfamiliar with or insensitive to the day-to-day problems of the cultivator and the social implications of policy. In the climate of expectation and change of the 1970s, ministries and other government agencies were eager to fashion new policies, too often with insufficient consideration of what was required for their successful implementation. Not a few agricultural schemes, including some well-publicized ventures with foreign governments, were conveniently dropped when the full dimensions of the necessary commitment were appreciated.

The success of any agricultural development policy ultimately rests on the cooperation, capabilities, and resources available at the district and field levels. It is there that the most formidable obstacles to the implementation of service activities, public works, and agrarian reform are encountered. Inadequate public funding accounts in part for the observed shortcomings, but they are most often identified as problems of grassroots management and organization. Staffs at the provincial level are composed in many countries of party loyalists rather than trained managers and agronomists. Agricultural extension activities, which are designed to attract small and large farms alike to modern methods and enable them to apply farm inputs correctly, offer perhaps the most obvious illustration.

Extension services in most Middle East countries are conducted by badly understaffed organizations that are only minimally active or are concentrated in selected areas. Many exist only on paper. For all of Iran's 60,000 villages, there were fewer than 1,000 full-time agricultural extension officers during the mid-1970s. A field extension worker in Pakistan looked after, on the average, 2,000 hectares of cultivated land, and even then, about a third of the total farm area and the bulk of Pakistan's farmers were left without extension services. It was estimated that in 1970, Algeria had less than 2,500 agricultural technicians at a time when there was need for at least 78,000 employees.[7] Assigned personnel are, in any case, often neither well trained nor highly motivated. Few receive sufficient technical educations, and their salaries reflect their low status. Regular communications between extension organizations and research units are uncommon, making it impossible for workers to be informed of the latest findings and techniques and for research groups to obtain sufficient field data. Because extension workers are frequently assigned away from their areas of residence, they may be unfamiliar with local conditions and liable to promote inappropriate solutions to farmers' problems. Even if capable of conveying technical information, the government agent may be the wrong person to try to educate farmers about the logic of cooperation. Aside from their lack of credibility among farmers, they are frequently apt to be rejected as intruders by village influentials who tolerate no alternate authority figures. The more competent extension workers are, in any case, likely to attach themselves to or be enlisted by already progressive farmers, becoming, in effect, their field assistants.

Dedicated and skilled local workers are especially essential to the task of educating farmers and peasants in the social and technological aspects of rural development. On the assumption that most aspects of rural life are interrelated, governments have been increasingly attracted to the idea of bringing together all efforts in a more or less formalized rural development policy. Typically, the programs have been built around the concept of rural centers that are expected to improve the accessibility of services and supplies, local self-reliance, and community leadership and to decentralize administration down to the village level. The goals of these integrated programs are not entirely new; indeed, some have been tried and many abandoned. But with the creation of more comprehensive development structures and an approach that calls for less "prescription from the top," it has been thought possible to overcome the familiar resistance to rural change.

Many of the problems faced in implementing rural development are attested to by experiences in Pakistan, where one of the more ambitious programs was attempted during the Bhutto regime. Initially, plans envisioned nearly 700 provincial centers designed to provide rural populations with basic goods and services. Claims were made for 130 in existence in the late

1970s, but in fact no more than 34 centers were active, and merely 3 of these had taken on significant development activities. Although the program had survived its identification with Bhutto, plans for expansion were unrealistic in the absence of trained personnel to staff even those in place.[8]

Rural development in Pakistan suffered still more from weak links between the federal government's market and incentives strategies and the province-directed delivery of material and technical assistance to the farmer.[9] Provincial planners found themselves hampered by federal commodity-purchasing policies that failed to entice farmers to alter prevailing cultivation practices. Increased yields in the nonirrigated areas were also unlikely without complementary policies from Islamabad providing sufficient farm credits and fertilizer. Not unexpectedly, nearly everywhere that programs were established, they became prey to local political pressures and the captive of provincial influentials. Still more, little was done to change the attitudes and practices of local functionaries. The programs were soon subject to the same kind of administrative bottlenecks the scheme was supposed to overcome.

Public credit institutions have assumed a critical place in furthering government agricultural strategies. Without loans, small and medium farmers have little opportunity to purchase the necessary fertilizers, seeds, pesticides, and machinery necessary to farm intensively. Nearly all governments in the region have established cooperative loan societies and agricultural development banks to meet this need. Yet these institutions, typically underfinanced, have in many countries never fully resolved whether their principal mission is to uplift the poor farmer or to make commercially sound loans. Not surprisingly, and despite often strong egalitarian rhetoric, credit goes disproportionately to those successful farm operators who are able to demonstrate sufficient collateral and reasonable returns on their investments. Even in the few countries where farm credit is sufficient and a system exists to reach farmers with necessary financial assistance, the aid may not always be timely and is often too restrictive. Once credit is allocated, public organizations often have little or no way to ensure that the loans—usually given in kind—are in fact used for the declared purposes. Hence, subsidized fertilizer is not infrequently resold on the black market or diverted to more profitable cash crops. Moreover, it may be more economic to rent out a tractor or have it used for haulage than to employ it on its owner's lands. In any case, most farmers are regularly in debt, either to public agencies or to private moneylenders who typically demand exorbitant rates of interest.

Problems of administration are nowhere more apparent than in the operations of state farms and cooperatives. Both have acute needs for qualified agronomists, accountants, and technicians, irrespective of the peasants' enthusiasm and dedication. Many units are scaled too large for efficient management and too great a drain on the available pool of national talent. Supervisory personnel, even when they are capable professionals, are viewed suspiciously by peasants as the government's monitors of farm production and as its tax collectors. Most government-run units are plagued by bureaucratic delays affecting the delivery of fertilizer, machinery, and other basic inputs, which may force farmers to seek them at higher prices from private sources. Widespread corruption by managers, often in connivance with cooperative board members and better-off farmers, creates cynicism. In Egypt, factionalism in cooperative society boards, often carried over from local rivalries, adds to administrative difficulties.[10] Yet government officials at high levels in Egypt have little interest in altering administrative patterns and personnel. As elsewhere, they have devoted years to building personal clientage networks within the cooperatives' administrative structures.[11]

### Reform and Administrative Decentralization

Continuous administrative intervention and supervision is a prerequisite for the enforcement of agrarian reform programs. In what can be, as Ronald Herring and M. G. Chaudhry observed, "a severe drain on administrative energies," provincial and local bureaucracies carry much of the burden of seeing that reform is fully and justly implemented.[12] The inefficiency and abuses often found to characterize the activities of these agencies can be used, then, to explain the failure of governments across much of the region to follow through on their designs for agrarian change. Weak political commitment from the top, as signaled by faulty legislation and contradictory directives, is not lost on provincial officials. More important, local functionaries are likely to be guided in their actions by class-based perceptions that are disdainful of poorer peasants. Even with a commitment to reform in principle, many officials come to identify with the more socially compatible farm and village middle classes. Tenants and other beneficiaries of change would also seem to bear some responsibility for the limited success of programs. Farmers must assert their rights and report illegal actions if programs are to work. But their acquiescence may be entirely rational in those countries in which reforms do not alter fundamental economic forces or offer security. Aggrieved farmers and the landless may logically fail to take any initiative on their own behalf when they are obliged to seek relief from local officials they feel are neither impartial nor capable of protecting small farmers' rights.[13]

The administrative machinery required to enforce ceilings on landholdings is found especially wanting. Both inertia and unreliable data allow many landlords to avoid having to declare land in excess of legal limits. Landlords have been most successful in concealing their full holdings where these are spread over several villages. Officially abetted misclassifications of soil, forgeries, and illegal evictions of tenants are not uncommon. Opportunities for administrative corruption increase when land is to be redistributed. Unscrupulous reform officials sometimes sell land to the highest bidder or indirectly purchase it themselves. Expropriated land is at times turned over to local people with good party credentials. In Iran much of the promising new development tracts went to individuals with sizable capital and personal access to the bureaucracy rather than to qualified peasants. New tenancies were created in Pakistan on expropriated land in order to provide additional income for provincial governments. At a minimum, rural influentials have been able to use their influence with key functionaries to soften the blows of reform and even to turn it to financial advantage. Local elites have usually fathomed the corruptibility and ineffectuality of the bureaucracy and have learned that they can often outlast reformers.

Events in the Middle East appear to confirm that nothing short of major transformations of social and economic power in the countryside is likely to prevent landlords from frustrating reform, and only the displacement of traditional political authority, including an entrenched bureaucracy, will allow peasants to claim and retain new legal rights. Of the region's larger land redistribution programs, all but those in Iran, Sudan, and Pakistan were accompanied or preceded by major political upheavals and noteworthy shifts in the distribution of power.[14] Even then, a more privileged group of farmers has survived in virtually every country. Moreover, as agrarian reforms in Afghanistan indicate, radical changes can create administrative problems of another sort.

In the determination of the shaky Afghan government to win over the sympathies of the rural masses to the April 1978 Revolution, the Marxist leadership initiated rural reform by waiving all debts and mortgages hanging over the heads of small farmers. The new regime followed up this largely popular move with the inauguration of a massive program to redistribute the property of larger estates throughout the country. Rather than entrust the administration of this program to provincial civil servants or create a land reform bureaucracy, the Khalqi leadership detailed more than a thousand of their party faithful to the countryside. By mid-1979, these workers, most of them young urban ideologues, had directed the distribution of land to some 180,000 families.[15] But in their haste to bring revolutionary change to the rural areas, they produced a program that quickly courted economic disaster and proved to be a dubious way to win popular loyalties. Uncertain which land would be confiscated, the more prosperous farmers refused to fully cultivate their fields or provide the accustomed credits to smaller farmers. In the absence of adequate land surveys, undemarcated seized land, perhaps as much as 15 percent of the cultivable area, went unsown.[16] Those peasants who benefited from the changes were awarded hardly economical plots of 1 hectare of first-grade land or its equivalent in larger, poorer-quality parcels. Despite promises to form cooperatives to assist these farmers, little thought was given to cooperative organization or funding. With no institutional means to obtain seed and fertilizer, many new landowners felt deserted and cheated by the government.

For all its mistakes, the Afghan reform effort had idealistically sought to use local committees to involve peasants in the land redistribution process. Decidedly less radical regimes also claim to champion popular participation. Opportunities for peasants to gain an awareness of government plans and to participate in decisions affecting them are now supposedly built into most rural development programs. Institutionally, local involvement takes the form of councils where farmers or their representatives are, in theory at least, able to initiate and shape projects. Farmers are expected to feel greater incentives to cooperate and to be less suspicious of new technologies. Ideally, participation should also help in making more informed planning decisions at higher government levels and in improving field personnel supervision through local accountability. Expanded local initiative could help settle the question of whether the benefits of development can come only from a national bureaucracy or whether administrators sometimes are not themselves major constraints on change.

Reversal of a top-down approach, all the same, runs counter to the historical trend in most countries of the region. As a rule, central governments have struggled over time against local and provincial elements to create more economically and politically integrated systems. Just as central planners distrust local bureaucracies and their allied elites, they fear that, if peasants are delegated real authority, they may be in a better position to resist innovations. In particular, self-management on state-operated farms is thought impossible for inexperienced, illiterate workers. In practice, then, higher administrators almost everywhere continue to monopolize agricultural development decisions. These officials view almost any increase in the role of popular bodies or, for that matter, in subnational departments, as a net loss of power in resources and possibly jobs. Ministry officials are seldom willing to provide the taxing power or to transfer the planning authority that would allow locals to make their own mistakes and learn through trial and error. There is particular concern that if decentralized, participating structures flourish, they will undoubtedly demand the right to assume still more ministry functions. Attempts to widen participation and control are also vitiated by those people, in and outside of government, whose vested interests depend on the concentration of policymaking discretion in the capital.

At most, farmers are invited to engage in forms of pseudo-participation. Local structures lose their credibility among peasants as they are found to be essentially a means for government functionaries to legitimize development decisions reached elsewhere or are used primarily to monitor local criticism of the regime. Policy spokesmen across the region continue to acknowledge the need for a better balance between ministry control and local initiative in development policies. Poor coordination between central decision-making institutions and local production units is understood to be at the bottom of many problems in program implementation. But the region's mainly authoritarian regimes, always fearful of loosening their grip on power or yielding valuable political currency, are hesitant to accept any devolution and deconcentration of authority, even when it might help them to win popular support for change and gear bureaucratic directives more accurately to local conditions.

### Bureaucratic Decision Styles

If a public policy consists of a defined body of coherent objectives from which are derived a set of strategies, then few governments in the Middle East can be said to have a policy for food and agricultural development. In place of comprehensive policy analyses that identify targets and propose activities designed to realize goals, projects are likely to be assembled ad hoc and specific budgetary allocations are likely to be arrived at without reference to the consequences of various plans or their consistency with national economic objectives. Agriculturally related bureaucracies must make highly complex decisions, necessarily based on objectively analyzed, adequate information. Yet decisions very often take place within a process that lacks such information, either because it is unavailable or because bureaucratic competition or poor coordination precludes its sharing. In the absence of timely, reliable, and relevant data, attention given to administrative detail and policy planning may be based on pure guesswork. Still more, the informal nature of decision making often removes policy from those agencies and officials who are responsible and best qualified. As a consequence, the criteria for policy choices can be extraneous by professional standards and irrelevant to the problems faced. Analyses are constrained by a shortage of qualified economists and others, either because too few have been trained or because the best are drawn off by employment in the region's oil-producing states and international organizations. For the most part, then, bureaucracies are incapable of the kind of policy-relevant research and analysis required for long-term, consistent development strategies and rational food planning.

The means or the inclination to monitor and evaluate the impact of programs in a way that would aid top officials in making adjustments in policies is found in few bureaucracies in the region. Indeed, the very design of programs often makes it difficult to gauge their progress. But without regular assessment of, for example, the economic returns to farmers of increased mechanization or irrigation, or the impact on producer incentives of higher food price supports and tenure reforms, no firm bases exist for setting future policies. In part because it is so much easier for decision makers to point to progress in quantitative increases in agricultural production than to measure improvements in the sector's productivity capacity, nearly all the region's governments stress the former in their development planning. Investment strategies place demonstrable gains in inputs and outputs ahead of longer-term dividends from strengthening rural infrastructures and institutions or motivating farmers to adopt new farming practices. Although this ordering of priorities is understandable in countries faced with immediate and serious food shortages, it becomes a continuing justification for delaying confrontation with more intractable problems.

One of the more characteristic features of policy style among the region's planners and political leaders is an impatience with, even an intolerance for, planned incremental change. For reasons that may be as much cultural and psychological as political, decision makers typically seek out policies that promise quick, dramatic results. In this search for easy panaceas, projects are likely to be dropped prematurely in favor of new, often imported solutions. Program failures seldom serve as learning experiences in which workable ideas are retained and others discarded. Even conscious trial-and-error procedures may not be additive. A good argument can be made that this tendency toward abrupt turns in policy is increased by the lack of meaningful participation by affected publics.[17] In the absence of public accountability, which would bring a continuous questioning of decisions and require a grassroots test of results, officials are not prevented from making sudden new departures in approach and emphasis. Many discontinuities in distributive policies can be explained in this fashion.

The disinclination to improve rather than displace programs is illustrated on a grand scale in Egypt's Open Door policies, begun in the mid-1970s. Instead of dealing with the shortcomings of existing policies, including the strengthening of institutions long in place, the Sadat government turned its back on much of Nasser's socialist legacy. In the hope of gaining an illusive economic miracle, policymakers sought to introduce a set of market-oriented investment and production priorities, encouraging private, profit-maximizing firms to compete with the publicly managed agricultural sector.[18]

Ideology has seldom served as a good guide to government decisions involving agriculture. If it had, no doubt a more consistent set of policies would have emerged in most countries. A frankly capitalist agricultural strategy would provide for a maximization of incentives for producers by eliminating government intervention in the form of price controls, non-competitive procurements, export constraints, import subsidizations, and restrictions on farm size and land tenure. Through the lure of higher prices for crops, the most enterprising farmers would be stimulated to increase their output. These policies would be expected to encourage modernizing rural elites to increase private investment and, in the process, buy out smaller producers, introduce modern management, fully mechanize their operations, and in general take advantage of economies of scale. Private-sector distribution of inputs would be stepped up in a supportive climate. The"trickle down" mechanism that is supposed eventually to increase the national well-being would unavoidably lead to wider disparities in income. It would, however, reduce urban-rural sector differences, and the possible expansion of production could employ more people in the countryside, even with increased mechanization. The consumer, although paying more for food in the short run, would be expected over time to be a beneficiary of more plentiful domestic production and higher national growth rates.

Alternatively, an uncompromising socialist strategy would require full state control of planning and agricultural investment, as well as buying and selling by the state of farm output at fixed prices. A socialist system would stress the removal of economic privileges through radical agrarian reform that would destroy the traditional class structure. Along with tenancy and sharecropping, there would be no place for the small independent farm, which would be phased out in favor of government-managed cooperatives and — more likely — collectives and state farms. The strategy would aim for a more equitable distribution of rewards and would expect to attain higher levels of agricultural output through rationalization of the modes of production, the introduction of advanced technologies, and the release of previously untapped human resources.

Both systems have their advocates in the region, but no regime has consistently followed one set of agricultural development strategies or the other. Rather than a socialist or capitalist model, ruling elites have almost everywhere adopted policies that contain bits and pieces of both. Thus, countries with large private sectors regularly intervene to control selected crop prices and consumer food costs, and countries with bulging public sectors decline to monopolize production or relations of exchange. National leaders in the Middle East and elsewhere are apt to insist that theirs is a "third" or "middle" way. As described by John Osgood Field, the middle way "rejects the evolutionary progress of Western societies at the same time as it seeks a viable alternative to the disruptive, revolutionary prescriptions of the Communist model. It seeks an immediate, focused response to a particular program without waiting for development to trickle down and without requiring a wholesale transformation of the nature of society."[19]

Historical experiences with Western imperialism as well as a continuing aversion to the anti-Islamic doctrines associated with the Soviet system have naturally left regimes reluctant to try to impose foreign blueprints without modification. Policies that reject the wholesale incorporation of economic theories and practices of the West or communist countries ideally should allow countries of the Middle East to avoid unnecessary doctrinal binds and enhance their chances of policy flexibility and adjustments suited to national and subnational differences. Yet, as described above, bureaucratic decision styles militate against an incremental approach that experiments with various schemes inspired by one or the other model. In the willingness of policymakers to accept the utility of elements of both the capitalist and socialist systems, they have not so much created a synthesis as impetuously picked piecemeal from or oscillated between largely contradictory or incompatible approaches.

The anomalies in agricultural and development policy are plainly visible, helping to account, at least in part, for half-hearted, self-defeating national efforts. These outcomes are a predictable consequence, in some countries, of trying to reserve a critical role for the private sector while following an interventionist path that encourages severe distortions of the free market. Despite the biases of some governments toward more successful, private agricultural enterprise, their policy instruments are often blunted by uncoordinated and uncertain actions. Even among regimes concerned with the income of smaller producers, strategies designed to provide the strong incentives necessary to stimulate output break down through ineffectual delivery of farm inputs or through deference to urban consumerism. Guaranteed prices that are supposed to make a farmer's livelihood more secure manage only to stifle what initiative exists. A new class of private holders may be created in countries committed to agrarian reform only to be allowed to succumb economically because governments fail to allocate the necessary resources or prove unwilling to incur the political costs of enforcing participation in cooperative projects. For governments that otherwise are committed to managed economies, there is surprisingly little consideration for the behavioral effects on farmers of the price relationships among crops or price differences between domestic and international markets. In their failure to find coherent mixed strategies, these regimes often ignore the logic of both the capitalist and socialist models and deny themselves the presumed advantages of each.

Patrimonial patterns of administration account for much of the ambivalence in design and faulty implementation of agricultural and food policies for the region. But policymakers' unwillingness to employ fully or consistently the available material resources, information, and skills is sometimes more conscious and purposeful. What is termed weak political will may be policymakers' reluctance to assume risks if the political costs of programs are more probable and calculable than the promised benefits. Natural constraints make even the best-intentioned efforts in agricultural development problematic. Unpredictable global commodity market and foreign credit conditions and other factors beyond the control of government upset even well-conceived plans. More predictable are the need to placate entrenched domestic interests fearful of policies that could alter the distribution of income and wealth and the suspicions of rural majorities about development prescriptions that too often seem to increase economic uncertainty. The very people expected to gain most from new policies are often too cynical, impotent, or uninformed to welcome reforms or to make dependable, effective political allies. A low-risk strategy leading to bureaucratic inertia and delay may be optimal for policymakers, as the social and economic gains from change are likely to be cumulative and diffuse, while the political costs always seem to be immediate and specific.

## Notes

An earlier version of part of this chapter appeared in Marvin G. Weinbaum, "Agricultural Constraints and Bureaucratic Politics in the Middle East," Chapter 7 in David N. Balaam and Michael Carey, eds., *Food Politics: The Regional Conflict* (Montclair, N.J.: Allanheld, Osmun and Co., 1981).

1. Raymond F. Hopkins, "The Politics of Agricultural Modernization," in Raymond F. Hopkins, Donald J. Puchala, and Ross B. Talbot, *Food, Politics, and Agricultural Development: Case Studies in the Public Policy of Rural Modernization* (Boulder, Colo.: Westview Press, 1979), p. 10.

2. An extensive and valuable discussion of patrimonialism in the Middle East is found in James A. Bill and Carl Leiden, *The Middle East: Politics and Power* (Boston: Little, Brown and Company, 1979), pp. 150–177.

3. Ibid., p. 167.

4. Richard M. Fraenkel, "Introduction," in Richard M. Fraenkel, Don F. Hadwiger, and William P. Browne, eds., *The Role of U.S. Agriculture in Foreign Policy* (New York: Praeger Publishers, 1979), p. 13.

5. See Robert Springborg, "New Patterns of Agrarian Reform in the Middle East

and North Africa," *Middle East Journal* 31, no. 2 (Spring 1977):140.

6. For a full discussion see M. G. Weinbaum, "Agricultural Policy and Development Politics in Iran," *Middle East Journal* 31, no. 4 (Autumn 1977):438–441.

7. Nico Kielstra, "The Agrarian Revolution and Algerian Socialism," *MERIP Reports* 8, no. 4 (May 1978):9.

8. Robert LaPorte, Jr., "The Public Sector and Economic Development in Pakistan" (mimeographed), American Institute of Pakistan Studies, Pakistan Report Series no. 1, May 1980, p. 26.

9. See Norman K. Nicholson and Dilawar Ali Khan, *Basic Democracies and Rural Development in Pakistan* (Ithaca: Center for International Studies, Cornell University, 1974), p. 38.

10. A highly revealing examination of Egypt's cooperative system is found in John Waterbury, "Egyptian Agriculture Adrift," *American Universities Field Staff Reports,* African Series, no. 47, October 1978, pp. 6–8. Also see Iliya Harik, "Mobilization Policy and Political Change in Rural Egypt," in Richard Antoun and Iliya Harik, eds., *Rural Politics and Social Change in the Middle East* (Bloomington: Indiana University Press, 1972), pp. 298–301.

11. Springborg, "New Patterns of Agrarian Reform," p. 141.

12. Ronald J. Herring and M. G. Chaudhry, "The 1972 Land Reform in Pakistan and Its Economic Implications," *Pakistan Development Review Quarterly* 13, no. 3 (Autumn 1974):272–273.

13. These points are more fully argued in Ronald J. Herring, "The Rationality of Tenant Quiescence in Tenure Reform: Production Relations and the Liberal State," paper delivered at the annual meeting of the American Political Science Association, Washington, D.C., September 1, 1979, pp. 4–10.

14. For descriptions of developments in most of these countries, see Hossein Askari and John T. Cummings, *Middle East Economies in the 1970s* (New York: Praeger Publishers, 1976), pp. 119–177.

15. *Washington Post,* June 11, 1979.

16. "Afghanistan's Marxists Face Many Problems," *Middle East Economic Digest,* May 4, 1979, p. 3.

17. See *Pakistan Economist,* May 13, 1978, p. 11.

18. For an extended treatment of the Open Door policy, see John Waterbury, "The Opening, Part I: Egypt's Economic New Look," *American Universities Field Staff Reports,* Northeast Africa Series no. 20 (June 1975). Richards has traced the crisis in Egypt's economy to policies that fall between the stools of socialism and capitalism. Alan Richards, "The Agricultural Crisis in Egypt," *Journal of Development Studies* 16, no. 3 (April 1980):303–304.

19. John Osgood Field, "Needed: Nutritional Planning and Development," in Ross B. Talbot, ed., *The World Food Problem and U.S. Food Politics and Policies: 1977* (Ames: Iowa State University Press, 1978), p. 33.

# 5
# Food Aid, Trade, and Development Assistance

Few, if any, countries in the Middle East are destined to meet their food requirements domestically during the 1980s. Earnest and intelligent national efforts may be better able to exploit available land and water resources, assure farmers of modern inputs and services, and offer adequate economic incentives. New modes of organizing farmers can help optimize agricultural production while dedicated agrarian reform, if linked to comprehensive rural development, could stimulate productivity. Prospects for these programs can be expected to improve with more effective administrative structures and personnel. But even with progress on these fronts, reliable sources of foreign food trade and assistance will continue to be indispensable over most of the region. Imports of farm commodities, equipment, and expertise are likely to loom large for the foreseeable future. The goal of self-sufficiency, still frequently asserted by government spokesmen, symbolizes more a yearning for increased economic independence than a serious economic blueprint.

Just as most Middle East states have been unable to escape cultural penetration from the West or to avoid falling under the political sway of superpower patrons, so, too, countries in the region are not very well insulated from the world economy and its food markets. At present about 80 percent of all exports from countries of the Middle East go to highly industrialized nations, and the West provides roughly the same proportion of the region's agricultural and industrial imports. Because of the colonial economic heritage or a conscious economic strategy, or both, most nonoil-exporting countries in the Middle East are integrated into an international system involving them in trade-offs: They earn foreign currency through sales of agricultural crops in exchange for cereals to feed their populations and for finished goods to satisfy domestic consumer demand. Along with other Third World low-income countries, they are normally subject to fluctuating markets for their raw materials while they are forced to cope with the steadily rising prices of manufactured products from developed countries.

Unplanned food imports, frequently unavoidable in financially strapped countries lacking contingency reserves, ensure that the commercial prices they pay for food commodities are high.

Both affluent and low-income states in the region are increasingly uneasy about the extent of their dependence for expensive foodstuffs on foreign sources, particularly those outside the Middle East. Neither foreign trade nor aid is viewed as entirely reliable, and both have carried from time to time implicit political expectations and, in the case of poorer countries, explicit economic preconditions. For several countries, the United States has over at least two decades served as the principal creditor in programs of food aid and development assistance. By the late 1970s, U.S. commercial sales of agricultural commodities also bulked large in the region's trade. Although the United States represents for many Middle East governments their best hope for food security, it is also identified as the country most equipped and inclined to use its food and credits for political ends.

The political motives in U.S. food aid and trade with the Middle East have never been very far from the surface. Since the 1950s, the sale of food commodities has served U.S. foreign policy objectives in the region. Designed also to satisfy domestic economic needs and humanitarian aims, food assistance figured prominently in efforts to strengthen the Middle East against Soviet penetration and to isolate radical Arab nationalism. Aid policies were additionally supposed to bring protection for U.S. corporate investments in the region. Many nations earned U.S. economic assistance, including food and agricultural development aid, as a reward for their resistance to destabilizing forces. Others qualified in the expectation that they could be dissuaded from pursuing disruptive roles in the region.

The geopolitical and economic stakes rose dramatically after the 1973 Middle East war left oil-exporting countries in fuller control of oil production and prices. The continuing access of the West and Japan to reliable, affordable sources of oil came into question. A growing U.S. dependence on Middle East oil imports underscored the massive transfer of dollar reserves to the region. These rapid changes created, however, offsetting commercial opportunities. The rising income and ambitious development plans of the oil-producing countries, along with high population growth rates and altered consumption patterns over most of the region, opened lucrative export markets for the developed countries. As the number of Middle East nations unable to meet their food requirements with domestic production increased, the United States and other food-surplus countries obligingly filled the gap. The potential political leverage that they held over the region's poorer countries was extended to the wealthiest. At the same time, inherent constraints on the use of food as a forceful, discriminating instrument of political power have become more apparent. So too has the possibility that food and development policies may at times be counterproductive for those nations they are designed to assist.

## U.S. Food Aid and Trade

More than a quarter century of U.S. food aid illustrates how political, economic, developmental, and humanitarian goals, although not always consistent, can be pursued simultaneously. The principal vehicle for this assistance has been the 1954 Trade and Development Act (Public Law 480). Under its Title II, the legislation provides for food shipments on a grant basis for emergency relief to be administered by approved private voluntary organizations. Table 5.1 indicates that during the period FY 1954 through FY 1977, almost $2 billion in food relief found its way to seventeen Middle East nations. Gratis allotments of wheat to Afghanistan, Egypt, Morocco, Pakistan, and elsewhere helped to fill a critical need in national efforts to overcome perennial malnutrition and avoid famine. But the larger dollar value of P.L. 480 aid has come under Title I in the form of concessional sales

TABLE 5.1
Loans and Grants to the Middle East Under Titles I and II of
Public Law 480, FY 1954-77

| | (In millions of dollars) | | |
|---|---|---|---|
| | P.L. 480 Aid | | |
| Country | Total | Title I | Title II |
| Afghanistan | 158.1 | 20.9 | 137.2 |
| Algeria | 194.7 | 11.6 | 183.1 |
| Egypt | 974.9 | 752.9 | 222.0 |
| Iran | 71.5 | 15.8 | 55.7 |
| Iraq | 14.8 | 2.5 | 12.3 |
| Israel | 307.0 | 244.6 | 62.4 |
| Jordan | 167.7 | 40.1 | 127.6 |
| Libya | 35.3 | 00.0 | 35.3 |
| Lebanon | 65.0 | 14.4 | 50.6 |
| Morocco | 522.0 | 155.7 | 366.3 |
| Pakistan | 1,762.5 | 1,528.7 | 233.8 |
| Sudan | 45.6 | 27.4 | 18.2 |
| Syria | 102.1 | 60.8 | 41.3 |
| Tunisia | 436.1 | 156.0 | 279.1 |
| Turkey | 386.7 | 244.8 | 141.9 |
| Yemen (North) | 20.7 | 00.0 | 20.7 |
| Yemen (South) | 4.5 | 00.0 | 4.5 |
| Total | 5.269.2 | 3.276.2 | 1.992.0 |

Source:  U.S. Agency for International Development, U.S. Overseas
Loans and Grants, 1978.

by private U.S. businesses responding to invitations by importing countries. During much of the history of the program, repayment of Title I loans was permitted in local nonconvertible currencies that, by agreement with the recipient countries, could be used only for U.S. diplomatic operations and to support U.S. education programs in the assisted countries. Title I also indirectly provided general budgetary support to aided countries by making possible import substitutions and local sales of import-assisted commodities.

The legislative language of P.L. 480 left no doubt that the program was intended to cater to specific U.S. domestic interests and to further broad foreign policy objectives. The foreign sale of U.S. farm products, even on bargain terms, gave assurance to U.S. farmers of higher market prices for crops. At the same time it reduced heavy government expenses for grain storage. Government-financed purchases offered hefty benefits as well to private commodity dealers and the domestic transportation industry, particularly an ailing U.S. maritime fleet. Even traditional critics of U.S. foreign assistance could be mollified by prospects that food aid would help foster future commercial markets for U.S. agricultural products. Congressional proponents of P.L. 480 took for granted that U.S. assistance would win the gratitude of food-deficient nations and thereby enhance U.S. influence abroad.

Changes in the basic parameters of food aid policy during the mid-1960s resulted in major revisions of P.L. 480. With U.S. grain reserves eroded and an unsatisfactory U.S. trade balance, Congress enacted amendments to P.L. 480 that widened both its economic and political uses. Commodities to be disposed of through food assistance were no longer limited to U.S. surpluses. U.S. crops could not, however, be designated for P.L. 480 purposes if they were needed for domestic requirements, an adequate reserve, or foreign commercial sales. Thus, grants and concessional agreements were given low priority in any competition for available resources. By December 1971, Congress also put a halt to the accumulation of local currencies. After this date the United States would accept only enough to finance its obligations and operations in the recipient countries. Concessional loans were otherwise repayable in dollars or other convertible currencies. To be sure, the terms were exceedingly favorable. As much as forty years was allowed for repayment, and a grace period of ten years was given before payments had to begin. Interest on loans was set at 2 percent during the grace period and 3 percent thereafter. Yet the shift to hard currency sales unmistakably signaled the intention to put food aid on a more businesslike footing.

The siphoning off of food aid for U.S. allies in Indochina under the Nixon administration at the same time revealed a strong determination to establish strategic priorities in the use of P.L. 480. Moreover, as the Vietnam War became increasingly unpopular in the United States, congressional restrictions placed on other forms of economic assistance to South Vietnam encouraged government officials to shift U.S. support to food relief and concessional sales to the Saigon regime. It was recognized that it would be far easier to overcome domestic critics with a program ostensibly intended for humanitarian purposes. This kind of flexibility, used to circumvent congressional sentiment, had been demonstrated earlier in the P.L. 480 program. Food deliveries to nonaligned Egypt and India during the 1950s and 1960s would never have been tolerated by Congress had authorization been sought for more conventional modes of foreign aid.[1]

It took the massive wheat sales to the Soviet Union during 1972 and 1973 to highlight the full incompatibilities in U.S. food policy goals. Where once U.S. concessional agreements accounted for better than 40 percent of agricultural exports worldwide, they dropped to only 21 percent in 1972 and 5 percent in 1973. P.L. 480 sales to traditional recipients in the Middle East came to a virtual halt. The Soviet wheat deals indicated how readily the United States, in its anxiety over a worsening trade picture, would ignore its international food obligations in favor of commercial markets. The sudden, if temporary, unavailability of wheat revealed the vulnerability of those nations that had taken for granted P.L. 480 deliveries, especially in years of generally poor harvests.

To quiet complaints of these food-client nations, Congress legislated in the 1973 Foreign Assistance Act a provision that reasserted the U.S. sense of obligation to respond to emergency situations and provide aid on humanitarian grounds. The secretary of agriculture was given discretion to determine the level of agricultural commodities that could be diverted to meet P.L. 480 requirements. And in a clear post-Vietnam congressional reaction, legislation that became effective in 1975 limited P.L. 480 aid going to countries not demonstrably needy. Congress stipulated that at least 70 percent of Title I sales be earmarked for nations included among those on the United Nations list of "most seriously affected countries."[2] While legislators continued to debate other possible criteria to define nonpolitical aid, much of the controversy raised by P.L. 480 was overshadowed by commercial U.S. sales and other forms of assistance undertaken during the 1970s.

Until the 1970s, U.S. farm exports to the Middle East went almost exclusively to the region's populous, poorer nations and were financed largely by concessional loans and outright grants. In 1972, total U.S. exports to Middle East countries stood at less than $600 million, and the U.S. share of agricultural imports by the region was only slightly more than 8 percent. By the end of the decade, the value of U.S. exports to the Middle East had jumped to more than $2.5 billion. Although the U.S. share of the market in these countries in no single year exceeded 16 percent, the United States had become a major supplier for a large number of countries, and the strong potential for further growth exists. Table 5.2 indicates the level of agricultural trade with twenty-three countries in the late 1970s and underscores the growing overall value of exports resulting from increased demand as well as rising farm commodity prices. Although a large share of the exports is absorbed by traditional recipients, namely Egypt, Pakistan, and Israel, a strong trade has developed with Algeria and Morocco. Much of the expansion of U.S. exports is accounted for, however, by the entry into the market of Iran and Saudi Arabia, beginning in 1974. Together they purchased over $800 million in farm exports in FY 1979 (July 1978–June 1979). Iran's revolution brought a sharp reversal in U.S. imports, first registered in FY 1980, but the dollar value of sales to Saudi Arabia has continued to rise

TABLE 5.2

Total Value of U.S. Agricultural Exports to the Middle East, FY 1977-79

| (in thousands of dollars) | | | |
|---|---|---|---|
| Country | 1977 | 1978 | 1979 |
| Afghanistan | 818 | 4,721 | 3,892 |
| Algeria | 105,823 | 152,312 | 114,306 |
| Bahrain | 4,689 | 4,983 | 5,757 |
| Egypt | 563,464 | 552,164 | 567,737 |
| Iran | 441,882 | 452,092 | 489,946 |
| Iraq | 61,648 | 125,142 | 123,335 |
| Israel | 313,194 | 270,817 | 312,514 |
| Jordan | 24,774 | 27,020 | 28,634 |
| Kuwait | 13,908 | 17,597 | 24,983 |
| Libya | 12,736 | 22,239 | 12,154 |
| Lebanon | 19,957 | 32,510 | 44,649 |
| Morocco | 70,131 | 114,716 | 68,469 |
| Oman | 1,989 | 3,693 | 2,149 |
| Pakistan | 116,137 | 218,439 | 246,957 |
| Qatar | 1,684 | 5,025 | 2,689 |
| Saudi Arabia | 145,729 | 283,508 | 311,740 |
| Sudan | 14,548 | 35,811 | 43,683 |
| Syria | 22,902 | 13,529 | 44,772 |
| Tunisia | 29,765 | 40,011 | 53,218 |
| Turkey | 3,666 | 3,817 | 900 |
| United Arab Emirates | 12,413 | 21,995 | 44,785 |
| Yemen (North) | 4,419 | 3,869 | 10,278 |
| Yemen (South) | 147 | 16,178 | 6,832 |
| Total | 1,986,423 | 2,422,188 | 2,564,379 |

Source: U.S. Department of Agriculture, U.S. Foreign Agricultural Trade Statistical Report, Fiscal Year 1978, p. 25; Fiscal Year 1979, p. 26.

steeply and was believed to have reached $500 million in FY 1980, up from $145 million in FY 1977.[3]

The trade figures in Table 5.2 are less revealing, however, of the dominant position of the United States in certain commodities, especially cereal sales to the Middle East. To make up for the region's shortfall, U.S. rice exports grew from 350,000 tons in 1969 to 1.7 million tons in 1979. Countries that had formerly had a modest share of the region's agricultural trade with the United States had become greatly dependent on wheat sales by the late 1970s. The total imports by Tunisia from the United States, only $53 million in 1979, included wheat purchases that made up 60 percent of the country's imports of the grain.[4] Even without formal diplomatic ties, Iraq bought from the United States 689,000 tons of wheat during 1978, giving U.S. sellers a 46 percent share of that market.[5]

The balance in U.S. trade between concessional and commercial sales worldwide shifted considerably during the 1970s in favor of the latter. Behind this change was the breakdown of a system of stable world grain prices resulting from increased international demand and the disappearance of once ample U.S. reserves. Table 5.3 shows that almost everywhere in the Middle East the value of commercial sales during FY 1979, including those to low-income countries, exceeded the value of those programs providing agricultural commodities on highly favorable credit terms. Countries short of foreign exchange, such as Pakistan, Morocco, Jordan, and Tunisia, although they were recipients of P.L. 480 credits, were obliged to buy a high proportion of their food commodity purchases from the United States at the going commercial rates. Running against this trend are Egypt and Israel. With a combined total of $881 million in support in FY 1979, they were able to capture the major portion of P.L. 480 concessionary aid as well as agricultural commodity credits under a Security Supporting Assistance (SSA) program, an impressive share of U.S. food aid, not only to the region but to the entire developing world. Of a total of $784 million in commodity assistance under Title I of P.L. 480 slated in 1980 for the world's poorest countries, $275 million alone was allocated to Egypt. Nearly one-third of the roughly $1 billion in P.L. 480 assistance slated to go to all countries in FY 1981 was budgeted to cover a Camp David–related concession that assured Egypt a specific wheat tonnage rather than, as is customary, a credit limit.

## U.S. Food Aid and Foreign Policy

Despite a period in the late 1970s of budget cutting and general disillusionment in the Congress with foreign aid, the Middle East was a conspicuously favored region for economic assistance. The overriding motive

TABLE 5.3
U.S. Agricultural Exports:   Concessional Government-Financed Programs and
Commercial Sales in FY 1979

| | | | | Commercial as |
|---|---|---|---|---|
| | | | (In thousands of dollars) | |
| | | Mutual | | Percentage of |
| Country | P.L. 480 | Security | Commercial | Total Exports |
| Afghanistan | 4,460 | 0 | -568 | 0 |
| Algeria | 0 | 0 | 114,306 | 100 |
| Bahrain | 0 | 0 | 5,757 | 100 |
| Egypt | 239,722 | 81,446 | 246,569 | 43 |
| Iran | 0 | 0 | 489,946 | 100 |
| Iraq | 0 | 0 | 123,335 | 100 |
| Israel | 5,373 | 217,464 | 89,677 | 29 |
| Jordan | 7,656 | 0 | 20,978 | 73 |
| Kuwait | 0 | 0 | 24,983 | 100 |
| Libya | 0 | 0 | 12,154 | 100 |
| Lebanon | 4,682 | 0 | 39,967 | 89 |
| Morocco | 18,470 | 0 | 49,999 | 73 |
| Oman | 0 | 0 | 2,149 | 100 |
| Pakistan | 40,481 | 0 | 206,476 | 83 |
| Qatar | 0 | 0 | 2,689 | 100 |
| Saudi Arabia | 0 | 0 | 311,740 | 100 |
| Sudan | 21,147 | 0 | 22,536 | 52 |
| Syria | 19,375 | 0 | 25,397 | 56 |
| Tunisia | 16,213 | 0 | 37,005 | 69 |
| Turkey | 71 | 0 | 829 | 92 |
| United Arab Emirates | 0 | 0 | 44,785 | 100 |
| Yemen (North) | 337 | 0 | 9,941 | 96 |
| Yemen (South) | 0 | 0 | 6,832 | 100 |

Source:   U.S. Department of Agriculture, FATUS (May–June 1980), pp. 104–105.

was of course political, involving U.S. efforts to obtain a negotiated peace in
the Middle East. Of the total of $3.5 billion appropriated by Congress for
bilateral economic assistance programs in FY 1979, more than $1.9 billion
of it was designated as Security Supporting Assistance. Of this, better than
90 percent of the cash grants, budgetary supports, capital assistance projects,
and, in particular, commodity exports under SSA funding, were promised
to four countries: $875 million to Israel, $750 million to Egypt, $93 million
to Jordan, and $90 million to Syria, all directly sought as participants in a
peace settlement. Similar amounts, adjusted for inflation, were requested
by the Carter administration for Israel and Egypt in FY 1980 and FY 1981.[6]
The undisguisedly political allocation of financial aid to Israel and Egypt of
course left very little to be divided among some sixty other countries of the
world in need of development assistance for their underprivileged majorities.

Food aid to the Middle East serves more broadly as a basis for U.S. bilateral relations. Credit sales and relief offer Middle East countries a benign form of involvement with the United States requiring a minimum of foreign administrative personnel in the recipient country. The disposition of commodity aid is ordinarily left to the recipient government's discretion. There are seldom obvious ideological or partisan tests for assistance. As shown above, even radical socialist regimes in the region, namely Algeria, Syria, and South Yemen, have at one time or another been recipients of P.L. 480 credits. Cash agreements for U.S. agricultural exports to Libya and Iraq gained approval while these countries' support of terrorist activities was being loudly condemned in Washington.[7] Aid to Afghanistan was cut back to just $13 million in protest against the Kabul regime's actions in the February 1979 killing of the abducted U.S. ambassador, Adolph Dubs. But P.L. 480 arrangements were not immediately ended, and the long-standing commitment to solve the salinity problem in the Helmand-Arghandab Valley agricultural project also survived for a time. While the U.S. Agency for International Development (USAID) mission remained, it gave the Americans what little leverage they had on the Marxist government.

Undisguised attempts to use food aid as a blunt instrument of U.S. foreign policy are rare and have never fully succeeded. One of the better-documented efforts to force a quid pro quo involved support to Egypt during the period 1964–1966.[8] Economic assistance to the Cairo government began in 1953. Aid ceased following the Suez War of 1956 but was resumed with a $25-million P.L. 480 wheat agreement in December 1958. In subsequent years, concessional food sales and other forms of economic aid grew, reflecting in part Egypt's cooling relations with the Soviet Union. By 1964, deliveries to Egypt accounted for better than 10 percent of all U.S. foreign wheat and wheat flour sales. Under the Kennedy and Johnson administrations, food aid matured into a conscious tool with which President Gamal Abdul Nasser was to be persuaded to temper the more radical aspects of his foreign policy, most of all Egypt's agitation against the region's more conservative regimes. This policy did not, however, restrain Egypt from stepped-up support for revolutionary forces in Yemen during 1964 and 1965. The Nasser government's denunciation of U.S. policies in the Congo and its toleration of anti-American demonstrations in Cairo were further testimony that the Egyptian government would not be easily influenced.

These events, along with new contacts between President Nasser and Soviet and Chinese leaders, prompted Washington's decision to curtail future P.L. 480 sales and to halt entirely other forms of assistance. In late 1964, talks on extending a food agreement were conspicuously postponed. A rider to an appropriations bill to cut $37 million from food aid to Egypt, which passed the House of Representatives in early 1965, was dropped from a final House-Senate version, but only after Johnson administration spokesmen insisted that the president needed the funds to provide meaningful leverage against Nasser. Even when Egypt balked at removing its troops from Yemen, the United States left open the door to food aid. This reluctance by the administration to sever the aid connection was in no small way a measure of Nasser's stature in the Arab world and Egypt's acknowledged geopolitical importance.

A short-term P.L. 480 agreement was reached with Egypt in January 1966. President Nasser had made some efforts to placate U.S. opinion but was constrained by his personal pride and an Egyptian public that applauded his tough stand against the United States.[9] The U.S. refusal to negotiate a wheat agreement in 1967 resulted finally in the withdrawal of a request for assistance and Nasser's belligerent declaration of Egypt's independence from U.S. aid. Egyptian-backed moves to cut off oil supplies to the United States and Britain during the subsequent June 1967 war with Israel would have, in any case, ended food aid. But until then, U.S. policymakers continued to believe that Egypt, unable to substitute fully for lost U.S. wheat, would eventually reach for an accommodation. The use of food aid as a strategy was in the end ill conceived to the extent that it served to confirm Nasser's suspicions of U.S. economic designs in the region and toward his regime. But the application of political sanctions was probably unavoidable in view of the hostility toward the Egyptian president on Capitol Hill. In spite of the more obvious setbacks, U.S. policy to 1967 probably did have some moderating effects on the Nasser regime.[10]

More typically, U.S. food and development assistance is characterized by subtle exchanges and unstated expectations. There is nothing in these arrangements that immunizes the United States against criticism by recipient nations or prevents them from following independent policies. As Richard Fraenkel has observed, the United States has normally not spelled out specifically the kind of reciprocal behavior it expects from those receiving aid.[11] Support programs appear to buy for the United States a hearing for its views and an appreciation of the boundaries beyond which the United States feels obliged to retaliate. These understandings are frequently so valuable to the United States that it may seem more anxious than the recipient countries to sustain programs. To the extent that the United States holds any trump cards, they tend to be accumulated over long periods and are most effective when played quietly. Aid to Pakistan offers a good case in point.

Over much of the period since the mid-1950s, U.S. relations with Pakistan have been strained, in part as a result of U.S. refusals to back Pakistan with material support in its periodic conflicts with India. In 1965, the United States instead used food aid to both combatants to induce a quick end to their war.[12] The Pakistan government tried to widen its options during the 1960s by agreements with the Soviet Union and China, receiving from the latter economic and arms aid as well as the psychological comfort of their mutual hostility to India. But despite Pakistan's international maneuvering, U.S. economic aid provided a strong basis for continuity in relations. Between 1952 and 1976, the United States gave Pakistan a total of $4.8 billion in various forms of assistance. The more than $2 billion received through 1979 in P.L. 480 assistance alone was indispensable to Pakistan's economy and the nation's ability to feed itself. For all Pakistan's flirting with the Chinese, its generals heeded U.S. advice to avoid overly close military entanglements. The Ayub Khan government accepted the presence of U.S. electronic listening posts, considered vital to U.S. defense plans, until their functions could be assumed by satellite reconnaissance. And Pakistan maintained its formal, U.S.-sponsored treaty obligations, unwilling to sever this nominal but highly symbolic tie to the United States.

This understanding of policy boundaries carried over to the leadership of Z. A. Bhutto (1971–1977). Notwithstanding the prime minister's often strident rhetoric and his ambitions for leadership of the nonaligned Third World, Bhutto refused to take Pakistan out of the Central Treaty Organization and refrained from frontal attacks on U.S. policy in Asia. In 1973, he acceded, moreover, to the United States's quiet advice that Pakistan limit its role in the Middle East war.[13] When Pakistan later balked at strenuous U.S. efforts to have it drop plans to acquire from France a nuclear reprocessing facility, the United States used its economic assistance to pressure the government of General Zia ul-Haq, Bhutto's successor.

Intelligence reports confirming that Pakistan was making headway in constructing facilities to produce weapon-grade enriched uranium prompted the Carter administration in 1979 to invoke provisions of federal law forbidding aid to countries embarked on nuclear proliferation. But although the United States withdrew some $40 million in approved economic assistance for Pakistan, it did not deny Pakistan P.L. 480 and commercial wheat sales. And within a year, in the wake of the Soviet invasion of neighboring Afghanistan and fears in Washington that Pakistan could fall under Soviet influence or before its military, a USAID mission was reestablished in Islamabad. In mid-1981 the Reagan administration negotiated a multi-year economic assistance package worth $100 million for FY 1982 that no longer pressed hard on Pakistan to renounce its nuclear program and that promised to obtain an exemption from congressional prohibitions.

Most recipients of U.S. food in the Middle East share common purposes with U.S. policies and require as much reinforcement as persuasion. Economic and commodity assistance to Morocco and Tunisia were plainly intended to keep in power those leadership elements committed to moderate regional policies. Assurances of commercial sales to Saudi Arabia and, until

1979, to the shah's Iran, had a similar rationale. Sudan, moderate in Arab politics, was encouraged by $20 to $30 million in credits for P.L. 480 wheat, as well as $30 million for U.S. military equipment. Financial aid to Jordan that included funds for a major dam project to benefit small farmers continued more than two decades of U.S.-assisted economic development. The aid took on special significance in 1979, however, in the campaign to revive King Hussein's interest in participating in the future of the West Bank and to help him resist the courting of more uncompromising Arab states. Economic assistance has similarly become a fixed component in planning in Israel, roughly half of whose food imports come from U.S. sources. Assistance also required a new urgency in the face of Israel's severe inflation, budgetary difficulties, and unemployment through 1981. Without financial inducements, Israel was unlikely to gamble on a U.S.-conceived peace treaty that jeopardized its access to oil and began a process that could lay the basis for a Palestinian entity.

U.S. aid policies in Egypt after 1973 perhaps best illustrate the use of economic assistance to bolster a government's resources and its determination to follow a course complementary to U.S. strategic designs. The resumption of economic aid to Egypt accompanied the reestablishment of diplomatic relations and President Anwar Sadat's decision following the October War to turn to the United States in hopes of prying territorial concessions from Israel. Not coincidentally, renewed assistance agreements accompanied Sadat's 1974 announcement of Egypt's Open Door economic policy. This approach was intended to rejuvenate Egypt's economy by attracting foreign capital along with technology and expertise from the West.[14] President Sadat's policies promised an expansion of opportunities in the private industrial and agricultural sectors that would better mobilize Egypt's resources. Where public-sector institutions, such as state-managed farms, could not be made more efficient, they would be de-emphasized and, conceivably, dismantled. The Egyptian leader also made his government more palatable to U.S. policymakers with plans for increased political liberalization through a more participatory and plural political system. A corresponding decentralization in the economic sphere was supposed to allow farmers more self-determination in cropping and marketing decisions.

The Cairo government's claims on the United States for generous aid were strongly enhanced by President Sadat's peace initiative in 1977–1978. It was quickly appreciated in Washington that Sadat's actions had increased the vulnerability of his government to domestic and external enemies. If Sadat was to be expected to withstand his Arab critics abroad and gain wide public acceptance at home for his peace policies and new economic orientation, an early improvement in Egypt's economic well-being would have to assume the highest priority.

The stated strategy in U.S. assistance to Egypt has been to provide benefits to the economy as a whole rather than to any specific target areas.[15] Even so, with political considerations in mind, U.S. assistance is directed to where it will have the most visible impact on the largest number of people. The urban areas, with almost half of Egypt's population, have an obvious claim, especially as public dissatisfaction and unrest are most likely to be sparked in the cities. The filling of critical agricultural and industrial commodity needs is considered the most politically expedient approach. This form of aid has immediate measurable impact on citizens' living standards, especially those of the poor majority. Commodity assistance also requires minimal planning, with Egyptian officials expected to identify those items in shortest supply. By the end of the 1970s, U.S.-supported imports for mass consumption, including P.L. 480 credit sales, made up the largest functional category, accounting for about 30 percent of all economic aid. In addition, a high proportion of the roughly 20 percent set aside for infrastructural improvements in 1979 was intended to increase domestic food production and included funds for grain storage, farm mechanization, pipe drainage, and irrigation pumps. Aid slated directly for agricultural development projects constituted barely 10 percent of U.S. assistance.[16]

More thoughtful U.S. officials worry about promising results that could raise elite and popular expectations in Egypt too high. A wide yearning for rapid material progress in the country should not be allowed to cloud the fact that Egypt's economic problems, whether agricultural or industrial, are unlikely to yield to easy or early solution. To the extent that massive foreign exports to Egypt or any other aided nation create the illusion that food problems are manageable, crises of supply may only be deferred to a time when the United States—providing more than 40 percent of all Egypt's food imports—or other suppliers cannot or will not provide the needed commodities.

Unqualified U.S. political support through food aid and trade can be shortsighted. Assistance intended to shore up individual political leaders unavoidably links the United States to the uncertain fate of a regime.[17] The decision of three U.S. administrations to provide the shah of Iran with both "guns and butter," at almost any level he requested, were reached with little thought for their economic impact on Iran or for popular acceptance of the shah's visions of a "Great Civilization." U.S. policymakers, in their concern for the monarch's cooperation in moderating oil prices and their desire for continued access to Iran's lucrative markets for agricultural and industrial goods, failed to consider whether the assurance of U.S. sales and technical assistance might have emboldened the shah to ignore legitimate criticism of his regime. Perhaps because food and development aid to Egypt requires heavy financing, the United States has been somewhat more sensitive to the possible domestic consequences. Its importance in carrying the country over immediate economic hurdles is not doubted, but there are questions about the amount of economic assistance that Egypt can absorb intelligently and smoothly. Some U.S. aid officials have wondered whether the United States, in an aid program that is potentially greater than either the Marshall Plan or wartime aid to Vietnam, had not identified too closely with President Sadat's often controversial economic policies.

The ascendance of political objectives in the contemporary Middle East has sometimes meant that U.S. policymakers supported aid programs and development schemes that were thought marginal or even unwise. It has also on occasion resulted, for reasons found in the recipient country's politics, in a U.S. failure to press for the extensive economic and political reforms believed necessary for more equitable food policies and higher agricultural productivity. The increasingly tactical use by the United States of its assistance no doubt reflects a preference for policies readily able to express pleasure or displeasure with a nation's support for U.S. vital interests. Because food aid and program assistance are highly valued in the region, both bear the marks of political strategists. But rather than signifying the variety of options available to policymakers, the political use of U.S. assistance programs and food aid is probably a better token of the absence or inappropriateness of other more direct and effective pressures.

### Assistance Programs and Trade:
### Europe and the Communist States

At the same time that U.S. contributions of food aid and development assistance have been declining globally, Western European countries have sought to strengthen economic ties with the oil-rich Middle East by assuming new regional responsibilities. The activities of the nine states of the European Economic Community (EEC) have grown substantially in the region's poorer states.[18] The motivation for food aid also comes, as earlier in the United States, from a program of surplus agricultural commodity disposal. During the late 1970s, Egypt was the major beneficiary in the Middle East of EEC commodity assistance. The community has supplied more than 100,000 tons of cereals annually and dairy products valued at $131 million per year.[19] The EEC was also most deeply committed to Egypt in the provision of financial and technical cooperation. A $230-million three-year agreement to the end of 1981 singled out specific projects to finance, some of them agricultural. In Egypt, EEC officials have themselves assumed the task of identifying projects. More commonly, bilateral investments of Western European countries must, in the absence of aid missions abroad, be prepared by multilateral organizations like the Food and Agriculture Organization. Prior colonial relations and surviving political, economic, and cultural ties in many instances explain the concentrated contributions of donor countries. France has been active in supporting programs in the Maghreb countries. Pre–World War II economic ties between Germany and Afghanistan created a foundation for the Bonn government's long postwar involvement in development projects in that country. Predictably, Sudan has attracted wide Western European development assistance. Loans to Sudan have been furnished by its former colonial administrator, Great Britain, but they have also been obtained in recent years from Denmark, Sweden, the Netherlands, and Italy. A willingness by France and several other European countries to assist with the financing, research, and excavation work for the Jangali Canal project helped to keep that scheme alive.

The European Community's heavy reliance on Middle East oil provides ample motive for an expanding trade with the region. About 44 percent of Arab countries' imports are from Western Europe, and exports to those countries from the EEC are greater than community sales to Japan and the United States combined.[20] Although less than 20 percent of the community's exports to Arab countries of the region were nonindustrial, agriculture has become important in the recycling of oil revenues. In this trade, the Western European countries have some clear advantages. Most obvious are their geographic proximity to Middle East markets and trade ties to traditional markets. For a number of agricultural products, notably poultry, processed food, and wheat, the EEC furnishes generous export subsidies designed to foster sales to the Middle East. The result is to undercut the United States and others, depressing prices and driving some suppliers out of the Middle East market.[21]

Europe's agricultural trade with the Middle East is highly diverse, featuring dairy products, meat, vegetables, barley, and refined sugar. In favorable crop years, France and other European countries become strongly competitive in the commercial sales of wheat and wheat flour to the region. The overall level of trade between the EEC and the wealthier countries in the Middle East soared after the 1974 oil price hikes spurred plans for domestic economic expansion and furnished the region's major producers—Algeria, Iran, Iraq, Kuwait, Libya, Qatar, Saudi Arabia, and the United Arab Emirates—the resources for higher food consumption. The value of agricultural trade with these countries in the Organization of Petroleum Exporting Countries (OPEC) rose from $508 million in 1973 to $1.2 billion in 1975 and 1.9 billion in 1978.[22] In 1978 Saudi Arabia and Algeria, with trade valued at $552 and $390 million respectively, provided the EEC's principal customers. Only in sales to Iran did the United States claim a larger share of the agricultural trade to a Middle East OPEC country.[23] Europe and the United States were also in competition in trying to capture markets for sales of agricultural equipment. Arab countries, led by Iraq, have repeatedly

threatened to make assured deliveries of oil to Western Europe and the level
of consumer trade, including food trade, contingent on the EEC's curtailing
trade and other contacts with Israel.

With development assistance and trade frequently meant to complement
efforts to win friends through political and economic strategies, the Soviet
Union and its Eastern European allies have not been far behind in
agreements with the Middle East; and for several countries they have been
well ahead of the West. Most aid agreements with the Soviets and Eastern
bloc countries create a framework of cooperation; often they set no specific
credit limits. Areas of assistance are identified, and in some cases, joint projects are designated. Many of the aid agreements combine trade and credit
transactions. Where possible, the Soviets have used assistance to the region
to establish long-term supply relationships for raw materials and strategic
goods.

A few Gulf States have shied away from any economic relations with the
Soviets and their allies, and communist economic assistance to Jordan and
Lebanon has been relatively modest. A once flourishing trade and assistance
program between the communist states and Egypt had virtually disappeared
by the late 1970s, and aid to Sudan also declined. But the great majority of
Middle East countries had, between 1954 and 1978, received substantial
economic aid from communist donors and had welcomed technical
assistance. Over a quarter century, economic credits and grants extended to
the traditional Middle East, North Africa, Sudan, Afghanistan, and
Pakistan from the Soviet Union totaled $13.1 billion, and from Eastern
Europe, $5.3 billion.[24] The signing in 1978 of a framework agreement with
the Soviets extending $2 billion in credits to Morocco for development of
phosphate deposits added to a balanced citrus-for-oil trade, and a 1975 plan
pledged $1.2 billion in development aid for Turkey. As a result, both of
these normally pro-Western countries had by far the largest share of promised Soviet nonmilitary assistance to the region in the late 1970s.

Although heavy industry, energy, and mineral exploitation projects have
generally predominated in communist aid, agriculture and water development, with related infrastructural improvements, have not been inconse-
quential or uncommon. During 1977, for example, irrigation and water
projects were the focus of aid by the Soviet Union and Eastern European
countries to Algeria, Iraq, Syria, Turkey, and Afghanistan. Credits for
agricultural development were offered by Hungary to Tunisia and Jordan,
and by Romania to Egypt and Syria. The Czechs agreed to help build a grain
silo for Syria and a fertilizer plant for Turkey, and Poland offered to set up a
tractor-assembly factory in Pakistan.[25] Bulgaria pledged to provide technical
assistance in agriculture to Libya the following year, when work was also
completed on the Euphrates River dam for which the Soviet Union had pro-

vided Syria $185 million. In South Yemen the Soviets were active during the late 1970s in agricultural development and agrarian reform programs. Obviously, not all these activities were successful. Cuban involvement in a poultry project in South Yemen was apparently a disaster.[26]

Continuous large and close economic support and trade ties were a prominent feature of Soviet relations with Afghanistan. Over the quarter century before the 1978 Marxist coup, between $1.3 and $1.5 billion in economic assistance, roughly three times the U.S. support, was committed to the Kabul government. The Soviet Union and Eastern Europe accounted, moreover, for 40 percent of Afghanistan's export-import trade. Aside from shipments of natural gas, the Afghans sent to the Soviet Union under barter agreements olives, citrus fruits, and raisins and received from them refined sugar and fertilizer. Soviet aid made possible the Ningrahar Development Project, whose irrigation opened for cultivation large sections of an eastern province and brought into being four state farms worked by military conscripts.[27] To repay the Soviets for the project, the Afghans agreed to a fruit export arrangement highly favorable to the Soviet Union.[28] When, prior to the December 1979 Soviet invasion, the Afghans found themselves short some 300,000 tons of wheat, the Soviets promised to reduce the deficit with 100,000 tons from their own limited stocks. As many as 5,000 Soviet economic and military advisors had been assigned to Afghanistan's ministries even before the arrival of Soviet troops, and the two economies were further integrated during 1980 with the signing of new agreements to furnish financial support for the hard-pressed Kabul government.

Chinese economic and technical assistance to the Middle East has been in direct competition with that of the Soviet Union and a prime instrument of Peking's foreign policy. Although it was at a level far below that of the Soviets and their Eastern European allies—$1.5 billion between 1954 and 1978—the aid was carefully targeted for maximum effect. Much assistance went for highly visible but small labor-intensive projects, many in the agricultural and food sector. During 1977, Chinese agricultural advisors were at work in Algeria, and Peking had offered to help Kuwait with a land reclamation project. Aid agreements were promised to Egypt when Soviet trade and aid diminished during the 1970s. Over the same period, the Chinese lost interest in South Yemen, where the Soviets stepped up their activities, and the Peking government shifted its aid to the Sana government in North Yemen. By far the largest recipient over time was Pakistan, which received more than one-third of all credits and grants in the region. Among several projects in the late 1970s, the Chinese were helping the Islamabad government to build a fertilizer plant. They were also willing contributors to agricultural and food projects in Afghanistan. Technical assistance was provided in poultry and fish production, and they had set up an experimental tea farm. Assistance for an irrigation and power project was also scheduled in a package of development projects for the late 1970s. A barter agreement, signed in 1975, called for the export to China of a wide variety of Afghan fruits. The expanded Soviet presence in Afghanistan after the fall of the Daoud regime and the virtual Soviet administration of the government beginning in 1980 foreclosed a Chinese role.

## Multilateral Development and Financial Assistance

Multilateral approaches to economic and development assistance presumably dilute the political benefits to participating countries and remove their direct control over the allocation of funds. Distributions of loans, credits, and grants, given without political distinction, can leave donor countries in the position of aiding regimes with which they would not normally deal bilaterally. Even so, a large part of general economic and project aid received by less developed, lower-income countries, including those in the Middle East, is funneled through international agencies. The United States and the other larger industrial, noncommunist states that dominate the largest of these funds go along with criteria that require sound banking practices rather than political tests. This depoliticization, all the same, has not precluded assistance from serving the foreign policy interests of the donor countries. International support shores up established regimes in their struggles with domestic opposition groups and, through most of its history, this aid has helped to perpetuate a preferred economic and social order. By its terms, multilateral aid also draws recipient countries into the prevailing world economic system.

The World Bank and its institutional affiliate, the International Development Association (IDA), are the most prominent of the multinational sources for development assistance to the region. A quasi-autonomous constituent organization of the United Nations, the bank's membership includes virtually the full community of countries, save for most of the communist states. Financial assistance is offered for projects in every sector through favorable long-term loans. IDA credits go exclusively to countries with the lowest per-capita incomes and carry no interest; recipients have a ten-year grace period and up to fifty years to repay. The IDA fund, raised mainly from special contributions from wealthier countries and projected at $12 billion for 1981–1983, includes three Middle East donors, Saudi Arabia, Kuwait, and the United Arab Emirates. In all, during FY 1980, the bank and IDA were responsible for $1.95 billion in loans and credits to Middle East countries, or 17 percent of the value of all projects approved. This compares with $1.7 billion for the previous year and $1.2 billion in FY 1978, when comparable proportions of funds and credits went to the region.[29]

TABLE 5.4
World Bank and International Development Association Project Assistance to the Middle East in FY 1978-80

| | Agriculture and Development | | | | | | All Projects | | | | | |
| | Number | | | Value (in million dollars) | | | Number | | | Value (in million dollars) | | |
| Country | 1978 | 1979 | 1980 | 1978 | 1979 | 1980 | 1978 | 1979 | 1980 | 1978 | 1979 | 1980 |
|---|---|---|---|---|---|---|---|---|---|---|---|---|
| Afghanistan | 2* | 1* | 0 | 40.0 | 16.5 | -- | 2 | 1 | 0 | 40.0 | 16.5 | -- |
| Algeria | 0 | 1 | 1 | -- | 42.0 | 8.0 | 2 | 2 | 4 | 172.0 | 168.0 | 120.0 |
| Egypt | 1* | 0 | 1* | 32.0 | -- | 45.0 | 6 | 6 | 7 | 241.0 | 322.5 | 421.0 |
| Jordan | 0 | 0 | 0 | -- | -- | -- | 1 | 2 | 2 | 14.0 | 50.0 | 29.0 |
| Lebanon | 0 | 0 | 0 | -- | -- | -- | 1 | 0 | 0 | 50.0 | -- | -- |
| Morocco | 1 | 1 | 2 | 65.0 | 70.0 | 92.0 | 3 | 6 | 4 | 84.5 | 349.0 | 204.0 |
| Oman | 0 | 0 | 0 | -- | -- | -- | 0 | 0 | 1 | -- | -- | 22.0 |
| Pakistan | 5* | 2* | 1* | 122.0 | 69.0 | 30.0 | 5 | 5 | 4 | 122.0 | 164.0 | 165.0 |
| Sudan | 3* | 1* | 1* | 56.0 | 15.0 | 10.0 | 4 | 2 | 3 | 78.0 | 56.0 | 170.0 |
| Syria | 0 | 2 | 0 | -- | 51.0 | -- | 3 | 2 | 0 | 118.0 | 51.0 | -- |
| Tunisia | 1 | 1 | 2 | -- | 28.5 | 55.0 | 2 | 4 | 5 | 67.0 | 99.0 | 171.0 |
| Turkey | 2 | 1 | 1 | 100.0 | 85.0 | 51.0 | 3 | 4 | 7 | 205.0 | 312.5 | 600.0 |
| Yemen (North) | 1* | 1* | 2* | 10.5 | 15.0 | 22.0 | 3 | 3 | 3 | 29.0 | 35.0 | 34.0 |
| Yemen (South) | 1* | 1* | 0 | 5.5 | 10.0 | -- | 3 | 2 | 2 | 11.4 | 14.0 | 22.2 |
| Total | 16 | 12 | 11 | 431.0 | 402.0 | 313.0 | 38 | 39 | 42 | 1,231.9 | 1,637.5 | 1,958.2 |

Source: World Bank, Annual Report 1978, pp. 28-29; Report 1979, pp. 97-98; Report 1980, pp. 121-122.

*IDA credits.

As is shown in Table 5.4, a total of thirty-eight separate projects for thirteen Middle East states were approved in FY 1978, of which sixteen agreements, worth $431 million, were for agriculture and rural development; of these, thirteen qualified for IDA credits. The number of projects assisted in the region rose over the next two years, although agricultural and rural development's share of loans and credits dropped in number and value after several years of increases. Three countries, Egypt, Morocco, and Turkey, absorbed most of the development aid in the region during all three years examined in the table, accounting for between 43 and 63 percent of all loans and credits from the bank and IDA to the Middle East.

Disbursements are another matter. As elsewhere, not all the funds made available through bank agreements are drawn upon, largely because of the poor absorptive capacity of borrowing countries. It is estimated, for example, that Algeria had actually borrowed only one-third of the loans and credits approved through FY 1979, and that roughly the same proportion had been disbursed to Egypt. Syria drew 37.5 percent and Morocco 59 percent of total approved borrowing. Despite the gap, these countries and others continued to request new support from the bank.[30]

Since 1973, the World Bank has paralleled the United States in its announced support for projects aimed at the rural sector and its poorer farmers. This strategy, directly attributable to the leadership of bank President Robert McNamara, had resulted in a quadrupling of worldwide lending for agriculture and rural development between 1973 and 1978. Attacks on rural poverty and provision for the basic needs of the masses in the countryside, although considered worthy goals in themselves, are also assumed to be a means to raise per-capita food output. The largest number of projects approved in this sector in FY 1980 for the Middle East, specifically ones in Algeria, Morocco, Sudan, Tunisia, and North Yemen, were directly targeted to reach small farmers and agricultural laborers. Increased productivity was expected to result from loans for the rehabilitation of irrigation infrastructures, soil production, increased agricultural credit, and better service cooperatives, among other investments. In FY 1979, by way of illustration, a $16.5-million credit to Afghanistan was to support a program to reach 62,000 farm families through agricultural expansion, irrigation systems, veterinary services, and the establishment of 150 cooperatives. The financing was also intended to assist in upgrading minor roads and installing a water system in about a hundred villages. A $70 million loan to Morocco the same year was designed to increase agricultural productivity among 475,000 farm families, and another loan to South Yemen would, if successful, improve living standards of 10,000 people directly and 60,000 more indirectly.[31] There has been greater interest of late in projects to aid rain-fed agriculture, on which most small farmers depend. This concern for the lot of the landless peasant and for increasing rural incomes unavoidably leads the bank into policy areas guarded by entrenched political interests.[32]

A recent entry among the multilateral, concessional loan institutions, the International Fund for Agricultural Development (IFAD), was given the mission of assisting in raising farm production and generating higher incomes and better nutrition among small farmers and the landless. Established at the suggestion of OPEC countries at the 1974 World Food Conference in Rome, IFAD was empowered to supplement the efforts of other sources through grants and loans, a special category of the latter allowing repayment over fifty years with a service charge of only 1 percent. Despite its seeming redundancy, the fund was the first to promise support exclusively for agriculture. IFAD offered as well a unique formula for voting in an international agency. Rather than the familiar mode of one country, one vote in U.N. political bodies, or the weighted voting by contribution size in most financial institutions, the IFAD formula divides equally the votes of three categories of members: the traditional developed-country donors, OPEC donors, and recipient developing countries.

Not until early 1978 were IFAD's first loans authorized. Disagreement between Western and OPEC countries over the relative size of the voluntary pledges in a prescribed capitalization of $1 billion persisted until agreement was reached on a division of 56 percent from the Western countries and 42 percent from OPEC. The United States was the largest single contributor, pledging $200 million, with the next highest donations from Iran and Saudi Arabia, at $124.7 million and $105.5 million respectively. IFAD was also nearly stillborn because of an argument over whether Israel would be entitled to assistance. An Afro-Arab effort to deny loans to countries that were said to practice racism, apartheid, or colonialism drew threats from the United States and West Germany to withdraw support for the agency. The issue was resolved with Israel's announcement that it did not expect to receive assistance from IFAD and would, in fact, make a modest contribution to the fund. By the end of 1980, some sixty projects had been aided and $900 million of the fund's resources committed.[33] Just three Middle East states had benefited, however: North Yemen for a project to construct an irrigation network, roads, and water supply for 103 villages; Morocco for loans to small farmers to purchase equipment; and Sudan for further development of cash crops. Future projects in the Middle East, as elsewhere, were of course contingent on another compromise between the Western community and OPEC members on a replenishment of IFAD resources.

Lacking a large bureaucracy, IFAD is obliged to work closely with sister international agencies, regional development banks, and others. At least one-third of its assistance through 1980 went to projects prepared by other bodies. Even for its own projects, IFAD turned to the Food and Agriculture

Organization (FAO) for identification and preparation. For that matter, as many as half of the prospective projects for the World Bank/IDA financing are first identified by the FAO. This U.N.-affiliated agency has few funds of its own for financing assistance to agriculture. Many of the projects it finds worthy in the Middle East are supported by the United Nations Development Programme (UNDP), by special contributions from European countries, and through a new fund sponsored by the region's oil-producing countries. Technical assistance activities have often come through agreements to assist private and state-owned agricultural development banks in forming their investment programs. Agricultural planning seminars and reports stand out as the FAO's most notable contributions to several Middle East countries.

Outside the U.N. community of agencies, the Ford Foundation has been the region's most continuously visible source of aid for agriculture. Ford-sponsored research on wheat in Mexico and rice in the Philippines led to the high-yielding varieties that set off the Green Revolution. Among several foci, the foundation continues to direct its efforts at increasing food production in less developed countries. It works through project grants and restricts its direct operations to specific countries and selected fields. Much of this assistance goes to the development of new institutions and expertise and provides for consultants from the United States and elsewhere. Over two decades, grants to the Middle East have gone mainly to the areas of research, planning, and training programs. Egypt and the Maghreb countries were assisted by the Ford-sponsored International Wheat Program. The foundation aided, moreover, the establishment in Egypt of the Institute for Land Reclamation, an agency created to train personnel for the new lands expected to be opened by the completion of the Aswan Dam. Jordan was supported in developing agricultural resources in the Jordan River Valley. A Ford-backed Arid Lands Agricultural Development Program, intended to benefit the entire region, was set up in Beirut. In Pakistan a Ford country mission channeled aid to the Agricultural Research Council and acted as a major booster of programs aimed at protecting and better utilizing the agricultural potential of the Indus River basin. As a nongovernment organization, Ford often had more leeway in its operations and fewer constraints in its choice of projects than countries or even international groups. The grant nature of its support makes its contributions especially sought after. But Ford's resources are small in comparison with other aid sources. Its full independence on U.S. interests is sometimes doubted, and the need of foundation personnel to work cooperatively with country aid representatives and missions, especially USAID, has meant that when U.S. stock in a country drops, Ford's activities are also adversely affected.

Pressures on the World Bank and others to furnish loans not tied to specific projects but intended to support the budgets of poorer countries have increased with the impact of surging oil costs and balance of payments deficits. In recent years, the bank has earmarked ever larger sums for non-project assistance, and it expected to put aside as much as $800 million for that purpose annually in the early 1980s.[34] But those countries faced with balance of payments deficits have more regularly turned to the International Monetary Fund (IMF) for short-term loans when commercial bank credits were impossible to obtain. Although borrowing from the IMF does not directly entail development assistance, the decisions of the fund often influence public-sector allocations for agriculture and the prices people pay for food commodities. IMF support is normally contingent on government acceptance of economic stabilization policies that may include the lowering of public spending, monetary devaluation, trimming or eliminating consumer subsidies, higher taxes, and tighter credit policies. Measures to slow the pace of economic growth force a reduction in imports and for many low-income countries, encompass limiting commercial agricultural imports. The usually stringent conditions typically carry increased economic hardship for already struggling populations and, consequently, raise political difficulties for borrowing countries.

It was on the advice of the IMF that food subsidies were reduced by the Egyptian government, thus sparking urban riots in January 1977. In subsequent years, there was still no agreement between Cairo and the IMF over the generous consumer subsidies or the size of Egypt's budgetary deficit. Yet a somewhat more flexible stance by the IMF in the late 1970s allowed the Sadat government to continue to apply to the IMF for new credits. At mid-1980, Egypt's indebtedness to the fund stood at more than half a billion dollars.

A more pragmatic orientation at the IMF, giving "due regard to the domestic and political objectives of borrowers," enabled Turkey to finally reach terms with the IMF late in 1979.[35] In protracted negotiations, the Ankara government had balked at the kind of economic guidelines insisted on by the IMF, but Turkey received $330 million when the fund finally made allowances for the country's still high inflation rate and tolerated other conditions that violated its usual economic dogmas. Most important, the agreement cleared the way for an additional aid package of $1.5 billion put together by the United States and other Western industrialized countries. In Turkey the economic problems that brought shortages in many consumer items, including certain foodstuffs, no doubt helped to erode confidence in successive governments. More basically, a decade of political instability was responsible for depriving the country of guidance and direction from the top that could enable Turkey to deal with its economic ills.

Negotiations between Sudan and the IMF in 1978 illustrate the possible

impact of loan agreements on agricultural development and the likelihood
of domestic political fallout. Sudan had steadfastly resisted the conditions
set down initially by the fund. Although the country was hard-pressed for
financial relief, an expected lowering of government spending, among other
measures, would force cuts in the protected defense budget.[36] The Numeiri
government was also concerned about the IMF's demand that Sudan reduce
sharply its multimillion dollar development expenditures, mainly those in
the agricultural sector. These public allocations had expanded after 1973
when, as will be described below, there was a sudden and heavy influx of
Arab funds for special projects. Most of the undertakings required a contribution from the Sudanese treasury, and these resource transfers to the
development sector escalated over time with higher overhead costs, especially in labor and fuel.[37] By 1976, foreign aid, including that from the Arab
states, had leveled off, and cotton, the country's major source of foreign exchange, was down in price. The government's mounting public debt virtually destroyed its creditworthiness abroad. Still, after years of praise for new
investments in rural projects and the raising of popular expectations over
Sudan's agricultural future, the Numeiri government was understandably
reluctant to cast doubt on the wisdom of its development plans.

Any economic belt-tightening also promised to have an adverse effect on
the price of imported goods at a time when the inflation rate was running at
25 percent. At stake, however, was more than $800 million in balance of
payments support, with Saudi Arabia promising to cover $700 million of
this in concessionary loans. The terms set by the IMF were not simply those
of a hard-nosed Western financier. For despite pleas from President
Numeiri, Saudi financial experts insisted that the Sudan go along with the
IMF's advice. In an agreement reached in June 1978, the IMF settled for
somewhat less than it had demanded, but Sudan also received less than it
had sought in loans. Although the effects of the infusion of fresh funds did
not have any immediate overall impact on the economy, the loan did bolster
the government's financial standing at a critical moment. The avoidance of
full austerity was critical while tensions were again rising between the
government and opposition elements in the country's southern region.
Belated implementation of some IMF recommendations also enabled the
Numeiri government to weather a Gezira farmers' strike. More broadly, the
Sudan case raised the familiar question about whether the IMF's role in dealing with the symptoms of a country's economic difficulties rather than the
structural problems that have produced them reduced the fund's construc-
tiveness and very possibly makes it an unwitting catalyst for political instability.

Few major economic assistance programs or larger aid projects are financed without the participation of both national and multinational

organizations. Funding is in fact often contingent on receiving aid from additional sources. Assistance to the Sudan for an irrigation scheme to increase production of export crops in FY 1980 was undertaken jointly by the IDA, the IFAD, and the African Development Fund (ADF). Other World Bank–sponsored projects in agriculture and rural development attracted cofinancing from Danish and Dutch development funds and the Kuwait Fund for Arab Economic Development.[38] IMF recommendations may involve, as they did in Sudan in 1979, a World Bank plan to implement them. Some twenty-one countries and institutions were involved in economic assistance to Egypt from 1974 through 1977, totaling $12 billion worth of aid. In 1977, nearly all of these donors formed a Consultative Group with the Egyptian government under World Bank auspices. Aside from its principal task of coordinating assistance to the country, the group has prodded Egypt on economic policy reform and advised it on how to proceed with long-term planning. A similar World Bank–led consortium of countries oversees general economic assistance to Pakistan. For at least two decades, the bank and the IMF have held considerable sway over Pakistan's monetary and fiscal programs. Without consortium support, which was held up during the political turmoil of 1977, no Pakistan government can hope to meet its international debt obligations, sustain development programs and food imports, or very likely, survive politically. The cooperation of the Middle East's wealthier states with the bank and the IMF is now expected and indispensable. OPEC countries agreed in 1980 to lend roughly $4.2 billion to the IMF for its Supplementary Financial Facility. Their contributions stem in the main from a sharing of much the same economic philosophy found in Western-led institutions and from their high stake in the health of the international monetary system.

**Intraregional Economic Assistance**

The Middle East's oil-exporting countries, in the eyes of their less affluent neighbors, have an obligation to assist the region's low-income states. Brotherly Muslim countries should be more flexible and understanding of domestic constraints, economic and political, than international financial institutions and Western or Eastern donor countries. With cultural obstacles removed, regular leader-to-leader contacts, so much a feature of the region's diplomatic scene, should facilitate appeals by the needy countries, allowing them to make a better case for the urgency of their requests. The wealthier Middle East states would presumably put aside national differences and personal animosities to take advantage of good investment opportunities within the region, including those in proximate sources of food. With Islamic strictures on usury, most loans would be made available on highly favorable terms. In fact, experiences during the 1970s gave financially weak countries in the Middle East reason to be both pleased and sorely disappointed.

Predictably, low-income states turned during the 1970s to regional donors for much of their economic and development aid. At the beginning of the decade, there had been only the Kuwait Fund for Arab Economic Development, founded in 1961. After 1973, a number of region-based institutions offered concessional loans and grants. The most important of the country funds were those created in Saudi Arabia, Abu Dhabi, Iraq, and Libya, all financing development activities. Additionally, several multinational organizations, led by the Arab Fund for Economic Development in Africa and the Arab Petroleum Investment Company, furnished concessional loans and project aid. In 1976, an OPEC special fund was founded both to cofinance development projects in the Third World and to provide balance of payments loans to needy countries. Together, the region's six major lending institutions handed out nearly $4.2 billion between 1975 and 1977. During the next two years, the eight largest Arab development funds extended an additional $1.3 billion yearly.[39] Middle East financial institutions gave development aid that included outright grants, interest-free loans, and low-interest loans with generous repayment provisions. Financing at commercial rates was also available from individual governments, quasi-public organizations, banks, and wholly private companies and individuals. Although most sources claimed an interest in extending help throughout the developing world, Arab financial assistance was largely reserved until recently for sister Arab states. Even now it goes disproportionately to other Islamic countries.

Despite these preferences, the region's recipient countries have not always obtained assistance on the desired terms, free of additional obligations. As already pointed out, some concessional funds establish criteria for financing similar to those set by the international organizations of which they are contributing members. An absence of coordination among Middle East–based donors frequently results, moreover, in delayed assistance. If the amount of aid promised is usually generous and the conditions, on the whole, less stringent than those on aid from extraregional sources, the aid seldom meets the expectations of recipient governments. A prevailing view holds that Saudi Arabia and others are rich enough to solve any problem, overcome any hardship. In practice, very little development aid or budgetary support, especially in bilateral agreements, has been given without consideration of how loans might bolster a friendly regime or buy a conservative donor country security from the region's more radical states. Recipient countries sometimes find themselves, willingly or not, caught up in the donor's economic orbit and strategic plans. Because of poorly disguised political objectives, long-term commitments have been less than reliable. Egypt's $7.2 billion in Arab financial assistance between 1974 and 1977 made it the most important focus of intraregional aid.[40] The aid, largely from Persian Gulf states and mainly in the form of foreign exchange financing, was quickly suspended after Sadat shunned Arab advice against signing the Camp David accords with Israel.

Although aid to agriculture, intended to expand food production, did take on increased priority among Arab donors and investors over the 1970s, the sector received directly a relatively small share of region-based financial support. When available, this assistance went in large measure to finance large capital projects and agribusiness ventures. The Saudi Development Fund, for example, which funneled $100 million yearly during 1977–1979 to North Yemen, allocated support for irrigation and water projects but targeted far more for road and airport construction and urban development. Of its aid to all countries between 1975 and 1978, the fund disbursed about 16 percent for agriculture. Similarly, the rich Kuwait Fund had in 1978–1979 set aside only 16 percent of its project aid for agriculture, while 30 percent was slated to go to developing energy resources, 29 percent to transportation, and 25 percent to industry.[41] Geographically, most of the attention of Arab creditors to agricultural development was focused on Sudan.

Financial aid to Sudan reveals how enlightened self-interest, far more than benevolence or a sense of responsibility, guides investment and support. If Sudan points up the importance of collaborative assistance efforts, it also shows the drawbacks of tying development policy to large-scale external financing. During the mid-1970s, a consortium of Arab governments and private investors committed themselves to ambitious agricultural development schemes in Sudan. With well-designed capital projects that could tap the country's water resources and greatly expand its cultivable area, improved methods would allow for crop diversification and large surpluses for export. Sudan seemed a sensible choice for several governments anxious to secure reliable food-supply sources for their expanding domestic consumption and seeking lucrative nearby investments for their surplus income. Significantly, it was unlikely that assistance would enable Sudan to become a political or military rival to donor countries in the Middle East.[42]

An agricultural survey of Sudan in 1974 by the Arab League's Fund for Social and Economic Development produced a comprehensive plan that offered the possibility of massive outside help. To administer the investment fund and program, Arab foreign ministers meeting in Rabat in 1976 created the Arab Authority for Agricultural Investment and Development (AAAID) and located it in Khartoum. It was projected that $6.5 billion from all sources would be invested in more than a hundred projects in Sudan over a ten-year period.[43] There was nothing to ensure, of course, that donors would continue high levels of financial assistance should world export markets and crop prices make investment in Sudan less attractive. These factors indeed contributed to the slowdown in governmental and private support during the late 1970s and to the lagging execution or suspension of many projects. The possibility of early surpluses and profits was also dimmed by the unanticipated technological and social problems encountered. The Sudanese government, which was expected to become a partner in most undertakings, felt the budgetary strains of development and was forced to retrench on its own agricultural plans.

By the early 1980s there was little talk of Sudan as the region's future breadbasket. The virtually dormant AAAID announced in 1979 its intention to spend $600 million over the next five years in thirteen projects. It had in the works in 1981, however, only four agribusiness companies in which the authority's share was limited to 25 percent.[44] Sudanese critics complained about the modest size of even these projects and the decisions to locate them all within 30 kilometers of the capital. The only sizable agricultural project remaining from the era of great optimism was the Kenana Sugar Scheme, financed by the Kuwait and Saudi governments, the Arab Authority, influential Arabs from the Gulf countries, Sudanese banks, and the Khartoum government, with the latter the largest shareholder. Slated to become the largest sugar factory in the world, the scheme was long under attack as too expensive and unsuited to Sudan's development requirements. Yet the project had survived and begun production, both because it offered a hope of handsome returns with climbing world sugar prices in 1980 and because President Numeiri had invested heavy political capital in the much-publicized company.[45]

The Middle East's other potential breadbasket, Pakistan, had also begun receiving the dole of the region's oil-rich during the 1970s. No Islamic state was more active after 1973 in trying to attract Arab aid to its economy. Between 1973 and mid-1976, five Arab countries—Abu Dhabi, Kuwait, Saudi Arabia, Libya, and Qatar—along with Iran, provided loans and credits worth $990 million. Aside from Iran's loans, which called for rapid amortization, intraregional aid was strongly concessional.

Although most of the financial assistance to Pakistan was of a general-purpose kind, any aid was bound to have an impact on the country's preeminent agricultural sector. In all, foreign assistance accounts for more than 50 percent of Pakistan's development budget.[46] By contrast to Sudan, however, the Arab countries have not rushed forward to invest in agriculture, specifically in the Indus River Basin, as a hedge against future food requirements. Most joint investment agreements, such as those with the United Arab Emirates (UAE), Libya, and Saudi Arabia, were designed to help finance turnkey projects intended for industrial and infrastructural development. In any event, very few of the companies and development projects planned in regional partnerships in the 1970s ever progressed beyond the planning stage.

Imports of agricultural commodities from Pakistan provided a firmer basis for assistance to the country's economy. A two-way trade that grew nearly 90 percent in the four years after 1973 naturally ran in favor of the oil-exporting Arab countries and Iran. Yet, as food demands increased in these countries, rice and other imports from Pakistan helped relieve the frequent food shortages. Saudi Arabia, with $80 million in purchases in 1976, became the region's single most important market for Pakistan's products; Iran and Kuwait also joined the ranks of valued customers. Cotton and rice exports alone accounted in the late 1970s for about two-thirds of Pakistan's foreign exchange earnings. The remittances of Pakistani workers in these same Middle East countries, totaling more than $1.1 billion in 1978, also contributed to the Islamabad government's ability to service its international loans.[47] The states employing these skilled and unskilled workers could normally go elsewhere for agricultural imports (with the notable exception of rice), but they could not so easily replace Pakistan's transfer of manpower and services.

Although they were mutually beneficial, aid and trade ties with Muslim countries in the region incurred political obligations for Pakistan. Prime Minister Bhutto had skillfully courted Arab and Iranian aid. In return he willingly played an active regional and Third World role on behalf of Arab causes—even while it was appreciated that Pakistan could not become a direct participant in the region's conflicts. For the shah, a strong, forward-looking government in Islamabad was considered critical to the defense and internal security of Iran. The postcoup government of General Zia ul-Haq was still more determined to retain its Islamic economic connections. The political considerations of aid were underlined for the new regime, however, by the early reluctance of major Arab donors and trading partners to provide financial assistance while it remained unclear whether the military regime would be more than transitory. Iran was least shy in linking its assistance to domestic politics in Pakistan. The Islamabad government's request in 1978 for additional economic aid and a moratorium on loan repayments was used in an unsuccessful attempt to restrain the Zia regime from taking the life of the then imprisoned former prime minister, Bhutto.[48]

Iran had begun to move, in the late 1970s, toward a food strategy that conceded the impossibility of producing enough for domestic consumption and that settled for using revenues from oil exports to invest in promising agricultural schemes in the region and long-term trade arrangements. The economic aid of Iran to neighboring countries was increasingly aimed at creating joint agricultural ventures as a means of lining up additional and convenient sources of scarce food commodities. An agreement with Turkey in 1975 was supposed to be a prototype. Iran committed $1.2 million in credits in order to finance, among other projects, food processing industries. The agreement also called for livestock raising in border areas and the importation of livestock, along with fruits and onions, by Iran. On the eastern frontier, Iran provided a $6-million grant that was combined with a World Bank loan to build a mutton-slaughtering facility in Herat, Afghanistan, for meat exports to Iran. Iran's assistance was in no small part motivated by the coup of July 1973 and concern about expanded Soviet influence in Kabul. To counter this, the shah offered President Daoud a lucrative alternative to Soviet aid. The government in Tehran proposed a lengthy list of development projects totaling $2.2 billion over a ten-year period to the Daoud regime. Had it been given—and Iran began to back away from its commitment even prior to the April 1978 Marxist coup—the assistance would have been equal to thirty years of development aid to Afghanistan from all sources.[49] An aid-cum-trade formula also marked Libyan assistance to Turkey. Libya extended a $100 million loan in 1978 and agreed to purchase surplus Turkish wheat. Hardly disguised in the deal was Colonel Qaddifi's intention to draw the Ankara government more closely into the Arab economic and political sphere.

Few policy leaders in the region now envision any quick schemes that would bring a cornucopia of food to consumers in the region. The oil-rich, food-poor states are not ready to disband all long-term regional investments in agriculture, but there appear more sober estimates of the enormous outlays required for developing highly productive new areas. Countries in which higher food consumption and security compete among national priorities show greater interest in projects with short-term payoffs and seek firm trade agreements with reliable sources of supply. Whatever the thrust of their policy, states of the Middle East continue to fashion assistance agreements and trade in ways closely coordinated with their foreign policy objectives.

### Assistance and Domestic Policies

For the Middle East's less affluent countries, concessional agreements and grants are a valued means of filling domestic food requirements and also freeing scarce resources for other budgetary purposes. Rising domestic demand, in the absence of increased agricultural output, must be met by increased purchases abroad and, in the case of low-income countries, the taking on of additional debts. In general, none of these countries possess the raw materials or trade potential needed for sufficient foreign exchange accumulation. To acquire the capital necessary to modernize their agricultural (and industrial) sectors, they depend on foreign investors and deficit financing rather than on domestic taxation and savings. The mounting debt has, in some cases, approached or exceeded the usually accepted limits of indebtedness. Aided countries also find themselves in the awkward position of having to plead regularly with their creditors for the rescheduling of debt payments.

Even successes in ensuring the flow of food imports and development aid cannot disguise building resentments in Middle East countries. Those on the receiving end of food aid include not only some of the region's most proud and populous states, but those that have been among its most politically prominent. Sustained food production deficits threaten their economic independence and, over time, sap their regional influence. To admit a chronic dependence on foreign economic assistance can be a domestic political handicap. And, by acceding to foreign-imposed monetary policies and loan agreements, governments expose themselves to charges of acquiescing in economic imperialism. Even though the Middle East's major creditors now include wealthy Arab regimes, the less well-off hardly relish having to go begging to states that only two or three decades ago made up the region's economic and political backwater.

Countries of the Middle East that are themselves able to finance their food imports, capital goods, and technological assistance retain greater control over their economic destiny. For all their economic muscle, however, these countries are also subject to price instability, in particular the steeply rising costs of foodstuffs and farm inputs on international markets. Throughout most of the 1970s, many of these costs grew at a more rapid rate than nations' oil-export incomes and were a significant drain on development budgets. Some nations have questioned the equity of the exchange between their own non-renewable natural resources and Western goods and services. The presence of a large foreign community participating in modernization programs is also a source of uneasiness, especially after the explosive events in Iran. The influx of skilled and unskilled employees creates resentments among native workers over the higher salaries of the former. The presence of an imported labor force in the cities and oil fields increases the possibility of economic and political agitation. These strains on social and economic institutions are felt mainly outside the agricultural sector. Yet the large foreign work force in some countries places a heavy burden on an already inadequate food production system and sharply raises import requirements.

It is an old saw that foreign assistance programs, especially food aid, contribute to problems they were supposed to help solve. Foreign food aid is often held responsible for distortions in national economies. Along with the financing for development planning, food aid is often accused of reinforcing questionable domestic priorities. Essentially, these results are thought to originate in the very success of foreign assistance programs—in making available relatively inexpensive and abundant food and supplying liberal international credits. There is little urgency to build more productive agricultural systems when, at least over the short run, it is less expensive to import most food commodities than to try to produce them domestically. Even where international prices are higher than local costs, the immediate attractions of concessional sales appear to encourage governments to subsidize imports to urban consumers rather than increase the incentives for domestic farmers to grow more. The accumulation of heavy foreign debts induces governments with an export crop to maximize foreign exchange income through depressed procurement prices for producers.

Foreign food and assistance programs have no doubt facilitated in some countries the observed sectoral transfers at the expense of rural areas. Project aid has permitted governments to divert a minimum of resources to the rural sector while maintaining the appearance of a commitment to agricultural expansion. It has also meant that public investment can be focused on a few highly visible rural projects, a strategy that is often pursued in the absence of foreign participation. Because project financing from outside sources has usually been available only for foreign exchange costs, aided countries are encouraged to seek agreements for capital-intensive projects. Smaller undertakings are necessarily overlooked even though their omission forfeits the benefits of generating demand for local production.[50] It is common practice to formulate projects calling for expensive farm equipment rather than to finance labor-intensive proposals. Requirements that procurements be funded only where foreign exchange is needed also ensures that a healthy domestic industry—for example, one that can produce farm machinery—will not emerge. Perhaps the most resented policies of foreign governments and banks are those that require assistance to be used for purchases in their countries. Recipient countries are often thereby constrained to buy commodities, equipment, and the services of specialists at prices higher than world-market levels.

Complaints are also raised that outright development grants by donor countries have diminished over the years in favor of loans and credits. The accompanying demands for economic belt-tightening by Western-dominated multilateral groups are often as politically difficult as they are economically distasteful. There is a widespread feeling that the United States and other advanced countries are able to dictate the path of development and that the world banking community is using Third World economies to test out theories of economic development. The trend among donors to substitute program assistance, which takes a broad view of the economy, for specific project aid is viewed as having the effect of allowing outsiders to manage the economy and impose their own development values. Critics of foreign aid can always cite how Western experts have fostered irrelevant technologies and then asserted that the region cannot adjust to a sophisticated agricultural technology. The United States and Western European countries are faulted at the same time for making it difficult for many Middle East countries to mature economically by earning hard currency through exports to more developed countries. Although most trade barriers against exports from the Middle East apply to manufactured and processed goods, tariff walls and quotas are also raised on some farm products. Concessional sales by developed countries can also reduce the market for those national producers in the region that in some years have exportable grain surpluses.

The willingness of many countries to accept foreign development and food aid is a risk-reducing political strategy. Whereas the job of increasing the flow of domestic savings to the public sector for local-cost financing will usually require increased taxes and be resisted by certain economic and political elites, foreign assistance financing can avoid these political and administrative difficulties.[51] Overall, foreign assistance in the form of food aid usually strengthens the politically powerful and economically advantaged in aid-receiving countries. By assisting ruling elements in coping with shortages and preventing urban unrest, donor countries unavoidably help to perpetuate a status quo. To the extent that assurances of adequate food stocks obviate the need for increased public resource transfers to the agricultural sector, foreign imports serve the interests of those groups favoring continued urban growth. High on this list are elites speculating in real estate, those with investments in industry and national bureaucracies fearful of a possible decentralization of administrative authority. Donor nations may find themselves caught between their desire to ensure the political and economic viability of aid-receiving countries through the financing of food purchases and the realization that continued aid can postpone necessary economic reforms.

A balanced view finds, of course, salutary influences on domestic policies from food and development aid. Large-scale food aid has probably not had in the Middle East the kind of retarding effects on agrarian reform that it is thought to have had in parts of Asia and Latin America. At least in recent years, foreign economic assistance programs have stimulated domestic interest in rural development and investment in agriculture. Project aid can serve to create a stronger consciousness of planning, organization, and evaluation among domestic officials, and agricultural research and training have probably received more attention than they would have received otherwise. Although food aid has not been used very creatively in rural development, as in crop insurance and work incentive programs, P.L. 480 shipments have ordinarily helped to stabilize domestic food prices and counter inflationary forces. By reducing the need for regular imports, they have provided a form of hard-currency assistance that eases governments over foreign exchange jams. Compared with the alternatives, concessionary imports may be inexpensive and politically attractive in the cities. While P.L. 480 sales have often succeeded in moving recipient countries further from foodgrain self-sufficiency, the shift to cash crops undoubtedly makes better economic sense for a number of countries in the region.[52]

### The Food-Oil Link

Self-interest has seldom been absent, as these discussions indicate, in U.S. or other donor-country aid to the Middle East. Indeed, it is difficult to imagine any country's agreeing to disavow self-interest entirely in its assistance programs or trade policies. Foreign policy and domestic economic goals by donors do not necessarily depreciate the value of commodity sales or technical aid in meeting real human developmental needs. During most of the history of U.S. food assistance, moreover, U.S. administrations found it possible to meet humane commitments to the Middle East while satisfying political and economic aims. Not until its involvement in Vietnam deepened and its wheat reserves dwindled was the United States forced to choose between political and nonpolitical objectives and to expose clearly the priority of its national interests.

A heavily politicized food and assistance policy shifted to the Middle East during the 1970s. The geopolitical aims of the United States and its allies became more imperative with the need to secure oil deliveries, especially after the decline in Iran's shipments after 1978. U.S. military assistance remains the prime means of strengthening the determination and capacity of those governments in the region prepared to act as bulwarks against the perceived threats to U.S. interests. But the cooperation and even survival of these regimes is greatly influenced by their domestic stability, on which any food trade and economic aid have a direct bearing. Dependence on the United States and other Western sources for agricultural commodities or development assistance creates a persuasive incentive. More problematic is the value to the United States of food as a coercive weapon.

The major test of food as a source of international power is whether it can act as an antidote to aggressive oil policies. The logic is uncomplicated: Both resources are critical to national survival, and the Middle East and the West, particularly the United States, have surpluses of the item in which the other is deficient. Specifically, food exports are expected to provide the West with a potent deterrent to oil-pricing pressures and politically motivated cutbacks in oil production. Exorbitant increases in the cost of crude oil would be matched by export controls and higher prices for grains, edible oils, and so on, while efforts to deny oil to U.S. or Western European markets would result in a halt in food commodity shipments. Proponents of this strategy see no reason for more selflessness in food policy than is shown in the sale of oil or raw materials.

In fact, food as an instrument of international power has dubious utility.[53] Food is an imprecise weapon, one that is potentially self-damaging. Although the food weapon is presumably capable of countering actions of the Middle East's major oil producers, its highest potential effectiveness is with those nations of the region that are relatively dependent on U.S. and Western European farm products—most of which are themselves oil importers. Ironically, the United States has been in the best position to threaten or punish countries with which it has maintained the closest ties and has least leverage against countries like Libya, Iraq, and Algeria, from which it is politically estranged. Any selective application of food as a weapon is also complicated by the common front the OPEC countries normally present, at least in matters of official pricing. As a class, the oil-producing countries are also least vulnerable to food price increases and direct boycotts. Their large foreign exchange reserves not only permit cash purchases at higher prices but also allow them to outbid other countries for available food stocks on world markets. One net effect of politicizing the market could be to drive up costs of commercial purchases to food-deficit, low-income countries that were not the intended targets of export sanctions. Any strategy that expects hard-pressed, less developed countries to pressure the OPEC producers to roll back oil prices is unrealistic.

If the United States has had at any time a strong agricultural export lever over an oil-exporting country, it would seem to have been Iran between 1974 and 1978. Over this period, the United States supplied between 70 and 80 percent of the wheat and nearly all of the rice the country purchased abroad. The logic of using agricultural exports along with arms sales to induce the shah to moderate his support for (some would say, stop his instigation of) OPEC price hikes was impelling for high officials in the Ford administration. The shah was already on record, however, as insisting that any attempt to link U.S. exports and oil would fail, as his country had many other markets for purchases. Allegedly because Secretary Kissinger had no desire to call the shah's bluff, he vetoed the proposed food-power strategy.[54] That the shah was not in fact all bluff was demonstrated following the monarch's fall, when Iran succeeded in reducing its total imports from the United States from $3.7 billion to $1.0 billion in a single year.[55] Although food imports from the United States in calendar years 1978 and 1979 declined more slowly, from $493 million to $415 million, after years of growth Iran proved itself able to find substitutes and do without agricultural products it once bought from the United States.

The diversification of food imports was well under way when the hostages were taken at the U.S. Embassy in November 1979. There were calls in the

American press and the Congress for the United States to unleash its food weapon on Iran either as a tough bargaining device or as a way to stimulate political opposition to the regime. Although the Carter administration declined to add a food cutoff to its list of commercial and diplomatic pressures on the Iranian government, a de facto end to direct U.S. food exports and other items was already in force with an embargo on all shipments to Iran initiated by longshoremen in U.S. ports. Throughout 1979, Iran was able to compensate for many U.S. goods with imports from Australia, Western Europe, Thailand, Turkey, and India, among others.[56] Also, good growing seasons in 1979 and 1980 and official exhortations helped to raise domestic grain production and lessened somewhat the pressures for imports. But the freeze of Iranian assets by the United States until January 1981, a sharp reduction in Western European trade, and the Iran-Iraq war forced an unplanned drop in agricultural imports. Iranian consumers were forced to endure higher food prices and reduced meat consumption. Even so, Iran exhibited many domestic defenses against the use of food as an instrument of coercion.

The United States holds a commanding position in the world's grain export trade, in recent years increasing its share to 63 percent of the total. But U.S. sales of agricultural products to the Middle East's five major oil-exporting countries, totaling $1.1 billion in 1979, still accounted for a minor, if also expanding, share of their food needs. A more effective political allocation of food would require the collaboration of other major food-exporting countries. However, the world's food production and marketing systems can be highly pluralistic and adaptable. Both the mechanisms and the will for united action to control food prices and supplies are absent, at least in part because many Western food-surplus states—together controlling as much as 85 percent of all wheat exports—expect to be treated preferentially in the event of an oil boycott. International market prices for food commodities are far more at the mercy of supply and demand factors than are oil prices; and there are no easy ways to prevent the resale of food imports to third countries. The influence of food-export allocations is potentially greatest when there is a world scarcity—but this is also a time when they would be least available to offer or withhold. Experience with export restrictions has shown that production may be stimulated in countries that were previous nonexports and substitute crops developed that then become highly competitive exports. Good customers may be forced to diversify their sources of supply. The oil-importing countries have also to contend with the domestic fallout of a decision to block agricultural export sales. A loss to the United States of markets in Middle East oil-rich countries would not at present have a heavy balance of payments impact. But after the largely ineffective and resented boycott of sales to the Soviet Union in 1980, U.S. farmers and agribusinesses and the transportation industry, all politically articulate groups, are unlikely to be as tolerant of so debatable a foreign policy strategy.

Middle East oil-exporting nations are not constrained in the same fashion by domestic interests. Food boycotts are potentially able to bring about mass discontent through spot shortages and higher prices that erode confidence in ruling authorities and prepare fertile ground for opposition elements. But a determination to stand up to Western pressures may, at least over the short run, rally citizens behind those in power. People are more likely to make adjustments and to tolerate considerable deprivation when the cause is identified as an external enemy. The food weapon is obviously most opportune at a time of famine, war, or severe economic crisis. Yet on these occasions disruption in the movement of food would seem especially callous and inhumane and would draw the certain censure of the international community. Sustained crises could also lead to public disorder that would force Middle East governments to use repressive measures to keep their citizens in check. Still more, hardships due to higher-priced or denied foodstuffs would be felt most immediately by those elements of the populations least able to cope with shortages.

Oil and food are, then, asymmetrical in the political and economic power they bestow. There seems little chance that a U.S. administration will pretend, as it did after 1973, that a quid pro quo can hold down oil price rises. Even so, food exports remain a not inconsiderable bargaining chip.[57] The economic interdependence of oil- and food-surplus countries is an increasing reality. Economic policy makers in the oil-exporting states are keenly aware that their agricultural as well as industrial purchases from the United States, Western Europe, and Japan are critical not only to their own economic development but also to the maintenance of a viable international trade. Officials on both sides understand the interconnections between rising prices for petroleum and food costs. Food exports are typically part of a broader trade that is mutually beneficial, even with politically unfriendly countries. A reciprocity of sorts will continue so long as food requirements in the Middle East outstrip production and Western stocks are reasonably plentiful.

No necessary contradiction exists between the desire of the United States to retain the Middle East as an attractive market for food exports and aid policies that aim to increase agricultural self-sufficiency across the region. The United States and other food-surplus countries cannot expect to cover indefinitely the region's deficiencies. To perpetuate a heavy dependence will no doubt increase resentments over the short run and assure even more bitter reactions later. Greater agricultural productivity in both high- and low-income countries can be profitable to the West, however, in stimulating imports from the West of farm inputs, equipment, and technology. At least in the case of poorer countries, a failure to strengthen their export-crop capabilities increases the likelihood of loan defaults and shocks to the international banking system. The yardstick for successful U.S. policies in the Middle East during the 1980s will be their contribution to stabilizing and pacifying the region. Food aid, trade, and development are active policy instruments in this security-oriented foreign policy.

## Notes

1. William D. Anderson, "The Intersection of Foreign and Domestic Policy: The Example of Public Law 480," Ph.D. dissertation, University of Illinois, 1970, p. 14.

2. Daniel E. Shaughnessy, "The Political Uses of Food Aid: Are Criteria Necessary," in Peter E. Brown and Henry Shue, eds., *Food Policy* (New York: Free Press, 1977), pp. 94–97.

3. *Foreign Agriculture,* September 1980, p. 14.

4. Ibid., June 1980, p. 38.

5. Ibid., November 1979, p. 34.

6. U.S. Department of State, "Assistance Proposals for FY 1981," *Current Policy,* no. 148 (March 20, 1980), p. 3; U.S. Department of State, "Achievement and Future Challenge," *Current Policy,* no. 63 (April 1979), p. 2; "U.S. Controversy Over AID Size, Scope," *Middle East,* January 1979, pp. 118–119. By FY 1980 the SSA program had been redesignated as the Economic Support Fund (ESF). In all, funding from ESF and SSA provided $4.2 billion for Egypt between 1975 and 1980. Food aid under P.L. 480 allotted an additional $1.2 billion during the same period. U.S., General Accounting Office, *U.S. Assistance to Egypt: Slow Progress After Five Years,* Report to the U.S. Congress (Washington, D.C.: General Accounting Office, March 1981), p. 1.

7. An exception of sorts occurred in a proposed commercial transaction between the Libyan government and Iowa farmers during late 1978. The Libyans held up the sale because U.S. officials would not guarantee that the shipments would be exempt from a U.S. embargo on strategic goods to Libya. The embargo had already been extended to cover American heavy-duty trucks and commercial aircraft purchases.

8. For a careful examination of this period, see John G. Merriam, "U.S. Wheat to Egypt: The Use of an Agricultural Commodity as a Foreign Policy Tool," in Richard M. Fraenkel, Don F. Hadwiger, and William P. Browne, eds., *The Role of U.S. Agriculture in Foreign Policy* (New York: Praeger Publishers, 1979), pp. 90–106. Also see Mitchell B. Wallerstein, *Food for War – Food for Peace* (Cambridge, Mass.: M.I.T. Press, 1980), pp. 125–129; and Anderson, "The Intersection of Foreign and Domestic Policy," pp. 422ff.

9. Merriam, "U.S. Wheat to Egypt," p. 98.

10. Wallerstein, *Food for Peace – Food for War,* p. 129.

11. Richard Fraenkel, "Introduction," in Fraenkel et al., *The Role of U.S. Agriculture in Foreign Policy,* p. 5.

12. Norman K. Nicholson and John D. Esseks, "The Politics of Food Scarcities in Developing Countries," *International Organization* 32, no. 3 (Summer 1978):679–719.

13. M. G. Weinbaum and Gautam Sen, "Pakistan Enters the Middle East," *Orbis* 22, no. 3 (Fall 1978):599–602.

14. For an extensive discussion on the topic, see John Waterbury, "The Opening, Part I: Egypt's Economic New Look," *American Universities Field Staff Reports,* Northeast Africa Series 22, no. 2 (June 1975), especially pp. 6 and 7.

15. U.S. Agency for International Development, "U.S. Economic Assistance to Egypt," report of a special interagency task force, February 15, 1978, p. 46.

16. Ibid., pp. 55–56.

17. The evidence, in fact, appears to suggest that where U.S. food policy was intended to help a friendly regime deal with internal opposition, the outcome has frequently been disappointing. Leon Bagramov ("Food and Politics," *International Affairs* [Moscow] 3 [June 1977]:3), cited a study by a Swedish economist that reportedly found that of fourteen countries allied to the United States in 1973 and receiving food aid, only seven had been able to maintain "social stability" by 1976.

18. See Wallerstein, *Food for War—Food for Peace,* pp. 67–89, for a description of the European role in food aid.

19. *Middle East,* December 1979, p. 74.

20. Alan R. Taylor, "The Euro-Arab Dialogue: Quest for an Interregional Partnership," *Middle East Journal* 32, no. 4 (Autumn 1978):429.

21. John B. Parker, Jr., "Subsidies Help Boost EC Farm Exports to OPEC," *Foreign Agriculture,* February 1980, pp. 13–14. See also Hilton C. Settle, "EC Poultry Meat Subsidies," *Foreign Agriculture,* October 1979, pp. 7–8.

22. Parker, "Subsidies Help Boost EC Farm Exports to OPEC," p. 14.

23. U.S., Congress, Joint Economic Committee, *Economic Consequences of the Revolution in Iran* (Washington, D.C.: Government Printing Office, 1980), p. 12.

24. U.S., Central Intelligence Agency, National Foreign Assessment Center, "Communist Aid Activities in Non-Communist Less Developed Countries, 1979 and 1954-79," research paper ER 80-10318U, October 1980, pp. 18–20. Also see idem, "Communist Aid Activities in Non-Communist Less Developed Countries, 1978," research paper ER 79-10412U, September 1979, pp. 7–10.

25. U.S., Central Intelligence Agency, National Foreign Assessment Center, "Communist Aid to Less Developed Countries of the Free World, 1977," research paper ER 78-10478U, November 1978, pp. 28–35.

26. *New York Times,* May 26, 1979.

27. Louis Dupree, "Afghanistan: 1977: Does Trade Plus Aid Guarantee Development?" *American Universities Field Staff Reports,* South Asia Series, 21, no. 3 (August 1977), p. 2.

28. David Chaffetz, "Afghanistan in Turmoil," *International Affairs* (London) 56, no. 1, (January 1980):18.

29. World Bank, *Annual Report 1980* (Washington, D.C.: World Bank, 1980), pp. 119–122. Also idem, *Annual Report 1979,* pp. 95–98.

30. "How the World Bank Works in the Middle East," *Middle East,* November 1979, p. 120.

31. World Bank, *Annual Report 1979,* pp. 73–80; idem, *Annual Report 1980,* pp. 97–104.

32. See *Finance and Development,* December 1978, pp. 2–4.

33. *Middle East,* February 1980, p. 58.

34. O. H. Goolsby, "LDC's May Need More Aid to Maintain Food Imports," *Foreign Agriculture,* October 1980, p. 19.

35. *New York Times,* February 5, 1980.

36. "IMF Policy: Medicine Now Rather than Surgery Later," *Middle East,* July 1978, p. 71; "IMF Keeps Watchful Eye on Belt-Tightening in Sudan," *Middle East,* December 1978, p. 111.

37. Ibid., December 1978, p. 108.

38. World Bank, *Annual Report 1980,* pp. 99–104.

39. "Arab Institutions for Development Aid," *Pakistan Economist,* February 24, 1979, p. 23.

40. U.S. Agency for International Development, "U.S. Economic Assistance to Egypt," a report of a special interagency task force, February 15, 1978, p. 52. Aid from Kuwait, Saudi Arabia, the United Arab Emirates, and Qatar in grants, bank deposits, loans, and loan guarantees accounted for 60 percent of total aid over this period. Egypt additionally receives $2 billion yearly in remittances from nationals working abroad.

41. *Middle East,* May 1978, p. 75; and *Arab Economist,* June 1981, p. 12.

42. John Waterbury, "The Sudan, In Quest of a Surplus, Part III: Capital Packages and Regional Prospects," *American Universities Field Staff Reports,* Northeast Africa Series 21, no. 10 (August 1976), p. 2.

43. "AAAID Slowly Silences Critics," *Middle East,* March 1981, p. 56. Also see *Arab Economist,* June 1981, p. 14.

44. "Agriculture Gets Arab Finance," *Middle East Economic Digest,* August 10, 1979. Also see *Middle East,* March 1981, p. 56.

45. *Middle East,* May 1980, p. 60.

46. *Pakistan Economist,* March 19–25, 1977, p. 22.

47. Weinbaum and Sen, "Pakistan Enters the Middle East," p. 603.

48. Ibid., pp. 610–611.

49. Dupree, "Afghanistan: 1977," pp. 3–5.

50. See discussion by Judith Tendler, *Inside Foreign Aid* (Baltimore: Johns Hopkins University Press, 1975), pp. 73–84.

51. Ibid.

52. Recognition of the need to improve recipient countries' capacity to produce basic food crops was reflected in the 1977 passage of a new Title III under P.L. 480 legislation. For the first time, the United States committed itself to a multi-year commodities agreement and loan repayment forgiveness in exchange for a commitment by aid-recipient countries to undertake specific, comprehensive development efforts over and above existing programs. The long-term assurances of commodities aid were expected to provide incentives previously lacking for governments to use P.L. 480–generated income as an effective resource for agricultural development. A percentage of the revenues accruing from local sales of P.L. 480 commodities and invested in these new projects could be applied against repayment obligations to the United States.

53. See Emma Rothschild, "Food Politics," *Foreign Affairs* 54, no. 2 (January

1976):285–307. Also, Nasir Islam, *World Food Shortages: Ethics, Politics and Policies* (Lahore, Pakistan: Progressive Publishers, 1976), pp. 16–21. For more recent examinations of the subject of the limitations of food as a political weapon, see Robert L. Paarlberg, "The Failure of Food Power," in Fraenkel et al., *The Role of U.S. Agriculture in Foreign Policy,* pp. 38–55; and Thomas J. Sloan, "The Political Role of U.S. Grain Exports in a Hungry World," ibid., pp. 19–37.

54. See Paarlberg, "The Failure of Food Power," p. 47.

55. U.S. Department of Agriculture, *Foreign Agricultural Trade Statistical Report, Calendar Year 1979* (Washington, D.C.: U.S. Department of Agriculture, 1980), p. 32.

56. In its urgent need for food, Iran had expanded its agricultural trade with India tenfold between 1979 and 1980, buying from the Indians large amounts of rice and onions. Further agreements called for the export to Iran of wheat, barley, animal feed, and potatoes. During 1975–1978, India had shifted its imports of petroleum away from Iran to Iraq, and total two-way trade had dwindled before 1979. *Foreign Agriculture,* October 1980, p. 32.

57. A linkage of another sort probably occurred during this same period and involved the Soviets' acceptance of Secretary of State Henry Kissinger's Middle East peacekeeping efforts. Officials in the U.S. State and Agriculture Departments believed that the massive sales of wheat to the Soviet Union help to explain Moscow's restraint during the Egyptian-Israeli negotiations. "U.S. Food Power: Ultimate Weapon in World Power?" *Business Week,* December 15, 1975, p. 56. At the same time, renewed U.S. shipments of wheat to Egypt in 1974 helped to ensure minimal domestic opposition to President Sadat's acceptance of Kissinger's step-by-step approach.

# 6
# Food and Political Stability

Domestic instability and regional political tensions have an obvious bearing on the pace of agricultural development and on consumer access to food. By the same token, government decisions on issues like land reform, farm subsidies, and food pricing are frequently contentious, inciting elite resistance and popular discontent. As this book has stressed, agrarian policies are caught up in class-related conflicts, in competing sectoral demands, and generally, in differences over how a country's productive assets should be allocated. Food deficits and failures in agriculture in the Middle East cannot be understood apart from the way governments have fashioned policies to placate dominant national interests and have chosen among alternative development norms. In turn, the fate of regimes hangs increasingly on how well they manage crises of food supply and distribution. Although it is probably an overstatement to assert that as long as people have food in their stomachs political leaders need not fear popular uprisings, it has become apparent that in the absence of food security no regime in the Middle East can have a firm grip on power.

Cases in recent years in which food and agricultural development policies have been closely linked to civil unrest and intraregional discord are readily cited. Disarray in Iran's agricultural sector and a consequent mass urban migration helped to point up the disparities in national income and life styles and multiplied the ranks of the disaffected, who in 1978 openly challenged the shah's political order. The bungled food relief during the 1971–1972 rural famine in Afghanistan is conceded to have encouraged radical dissidents in the military to mount a coup against the monarchy in July 1973. Later, the heavy-handed efforts at land reform activated conservative Afghan elements against the Marxist Khalq regime. Serious challenges to reigning political authority were posed by the violent demonstrations over government food and fuel increases that occurred in Egyptian and Sudanese cities in January 1977 and August 1979 respectively. During the 1970s sorely strained relations between Syria and Iraq and between Iran and Afghanistan were raised to near flash point over competing claims to water resources. No doubt the most intriguing case, Egypt's

desperate need to find hard currency to pay for wheat purchases, may have
served as a proximate cause of the October 1973 war. President Anwar Sadat
reportedly concluded that only through an early crossing of the Suez Canal
could the government hope to rally financial backing from wealthy Arab
states and thus spare Egypt a major grain crisis.[1] That food and agricultural
problems have not to date loomed even larger in government change and in-
terstate conflict in the Middle East probably reflects the normally acute sen-
sitivity of policymakers, whatever their ideological persuasion, to the likely
political consequences of soaring food prices and painful shortages. For
several reasons, however, food and agricultural issues are almost certain to
become more conspicuous and politically explosive during the 1980s.[2]

### Food and Urban Violence

Few areas of public policy compare with food decisions in immediacy,
universality, and tangible meaning. A consciousness of government actions
affecting basic foodstuffs requires little or no political sophistication—the
impact of slight changes in cost and temporary disappearance of staples
registers quickly on consumers. Food is an inescapable issue in the larger
cities of the Middle East, where consumption patterns serve as a common
measure of economic status. A high proportion of urban family income goes
toward purchasing food; and regular enjoyment of items like meat, rice, and
fruit is a conspicuous mark of well-being. Food consumption is closely tied
to a sense of overall security. This is especially true for factory and construction workers, often recent arrivals from the countryside. Those who once
provided for their own sustenance on the land feel a particular vulnerability
in their dependence on remote and impersonal food distribution systems.
Cut off from the land and from traditional sources of authority, former rural
dwellers are more readily mobilized by the government as well as by its
enemies. In protesting official policies that threaten access to plentiful, inexpensive food, the urban lower classes find common cause with public
employees and students.

The potentially disruptive effects of food costs and supply problems are
most directly managed through official intervention to keep consumer prices
lower artificially. As described in previous chapters, heavy public subsidies
of domestically procured crops are meant to hold down the costs of commodities essential to basic nutritional needs. By also depressing the prices
paid to farmers for their crops, policymakers are able to ease the financial
burdens on the public exchequer. In effect, the tax exacted on the
agricultural sector is calculated to improve chances of peace in the urban
centers. Most governments accept the need to divert foreign exchange to pay
for food imports and to absorb the higher costs rather than pass them on to

the consumer. Despite questions raised about the wisdom of sectoral resource transfers and the financial drain of food imports, when the alternative has been to ask urban dwellers to assume added costs or to reduce their consumption and thereby alter their accustomed life style, governments have typically followed the politically expedient course.

Regimes anxious to divert attention from other sacrifices asked of citizens have gone to great lengths to try to normalize food supplies and moderate prices. The Babraq government in Afghanistan ensured ample supplies with the help of an airlift and the trucking of wheat and rice from the Soviet Union. Unpopular government officials and party members in Kabul could frequently buy rice at a fraction of the going price in the local bazaars. City consumers in Iraq during the war with Iran found available fresh produce in unaccustomed quantities and were treated to suddenly efficient government-organized distribution. Iran's ruling authorities were helpless to stem the wartime inflation, but they strained the country's poor transport system and dug deep into the foreign exchange reserves to keep up a reasonable flow of grains, oils, and vegetables to population centers during the conflict.

Ever mindful that food shortages could serve as a catalyst to urban unrest, the authorities in prerevolutionary Iran also did not chance a long absence from the shelves of staples in the country's diet. When onions and potatoes disappeared from Tehran's shops during the winter of 1976 and sporadic street disturbances occurred, the government rushed to buy up all available surpluses from neighboring countries. Policies attempting to stabilize and hold down food prices were meant to compensate for the government's limited success (some would say limited efforts) in curbing runaway inflation in urban housing costs and other areas.[3] But in spring 1978, Iranian officials relaxed their accustomed vigilance in protecting the urban consumer. Faced with a drop in oil revenues and rapidly growing food imports, the regime sought to trim its $1-billion food-subsidy bill while it offered high prices for crops and more generous credits to farmers in hopes of stimulating domestic agricultural production. Subsidies came down in particular on milk, chickens, and imported eggs. Any increase in salaries to cover these rising food costs was linked by the government to evidence of greater worker productivity. The subsequent wave of strikes by workers and civil servants for higher wages rapidly undermined the shaky Iranian economy and, by forcing the shah into a series of economic concessions, raised doubts about his previously unquestioned political sagacity.

Ill-timed policies and errors in judgment took place in Sudan in 1979, when President Numeiri ordered price increases in several basic commodities. Pressed by Sudan's international creditors to cut a massive budget deficit, officials allowed the price of sugar to rise by 33 percent. Because sugar, in short supply, was already selling for a higher price on the black market, the initial public reaction was muted.⁴ But a second round of increases in the prices of food, fuel, and transport weeks later brought mobs into the streets of Khartoum and other cities. The police finally gained control after ten days of disturbances, but not before the government cancelled the price increases. One-third of all meat earmarked for export was quickly diverted to local markets, and authorities ordered that bread supplies be kept adequate.⁵

The removal or reduction of food subsidies did not bring down Israel's governing coalition in early 1980, but this action did further reduce popular support for the fragile government of Prime Minister Menachem Begin and created doubts for a time that it could survive the June 1981 parliamentary election. Dissatisfaction with higher food prices far overshadowed misgivings in some sectors of the population over Israel's settlement policy for the West Bank or negotiations with Egypt over Palestinian autonomy. The 135 percent inflation in food prices during 1980 was buffered for many Israelis, however, by an indexing system inherited from the previous Labor government that adjusted salaries to the rising consumer prices.

The food issue as a convenient vehicle for articulating popular urban discontent is dramatically illustrated by the Egyptian food riots of 1977. Advised by the International Monetary Fund and other financial backers in the West and the Arab Middle East to reduce a budget deficit of $3.2 billion, President Sadat cut or eliminated subsidies on a wide range of basic consumer items that totaled some $700 million annually. The resulting increases on such foodstuffs as rice, sugar, and bread were modest, although on other items, including an extensively used bottled cooking gas, the prices were hiked by 50 to 100 percent. The net effect on Egyptian workers, whose average monthly wage was $80, was the loss of a sizable portion of their purchasing power. The government hoped to cushion the impact of the increases by promising pay raises to public service employees; instead the new policy heightened general resentment, and the clumsy way it was announced by official spokesmen did little to help the regime to make its case.⁶

The street demonstrations, some spontaneous, others well organized, quickly assumed a violent, strongly antiregime tone. President Sadat and his close advisers were criticized for Egypt's deteriorating economic condition and for a de-emphasis of the socialist policies identified with the late President Nasser as well as for lifting the subsidies. The wartime image of Sadat as the leader of a nation that had reclaimed its honor by crossing the Suez Canal was forgotten in bitter denunciations of the president and his luxurious life style. When the police were unable to halt the rioting of tens of thousands of young workers and students in Cairo, Alexandria, and several other cities, the army was brought in to contain the troubles. Over a two-day period, seventy-nine people were killed, hundreds injured, and nine-hundred arrested. Damage to the economy was estimated at more than $1 billion. Only Sadat's early decision to wholly rescind the price increases averted a more serious test of his ability to hold power.

The effectiveness of the food issue in mobilizing the disaffected masses was plainly apparent in the January 1977 events. The sudden imposition of price increases was perceived by many as a token of the underlying insensitivity of authorities toward the public. Yet the riots also had some value for the regime. In subsequent months they provided President Sadat with added leverage in dealing with his foreign creditors. He was able to argue more convincingly with his financial backers that the Egyptian public would not tolerate most of the fiscal reforms they demanded. Still more, the aggressiveness of the Egyptian left, which according to government accounts had instigated the riots, strengthened Sadat's appeals to the West and to conservative Arab states for additional aid. Without help, it was intimated, the government might succumb to domestic communists.

Over the next few years, Egyptian authorities were determined not to repeat the errors of January 1977. President Sadat personally earned much of the credit for averting civil unrest. In the aftermath of January 1977, he campaigned hard to convince citizens of his determination to see food production expanded. The president traveled widely to promote the development of reclaimed lands and received generous publicity as he inaugurated food processing plants and distributed land titles to poor farmers. Sadat reiterated his commitment to spend hard currency to maintain the level of foreign food imports. By late 1977, he was also buoyed by peace talks with the Israelis that convinced educated and uneducated Egyptians alike that the country's economy was headed for better times. Peace, people were anxious to believe, would attract foreign private investment and create new jobs in industry.

In April 1978, unusually severe seasonal shortages drove up food prices at a rate sharper than that experienced prior to the 1977 riots. Yet the public's indignation failed to erupt into demonstrations; few Egyptians seemed to hold the government directly responsible.[7] Urban consumers had no doubt become accustomed to steadily rising prices in a period of general inflation. More important, officials, rushing delivery of tomatoes from the countryside and importing butter for the Cairo market, repeatedly assured the public of ample supplies. Authorities also promised to deal harshly with speculators.

Again, early in 1980, the government weathered a consumer crisis, this time brought on by shortages of balady bread, a flat brown bread favored by Egypt's masses. With the bread selling at a subsidized price one-fifth below its real market value, bakers had diverted flour to make uncontrolled, higher-priced breads and cakes. But government warnings to bakers and a shifting of supplies headed off street demonstrations.[8] Despite a deficit believed to be as high as $4.3 billion out of a total budget of $10 billion, authorities continued to subsidize, along with bread, the costs of such food staples as rice, beans, sugar, tea, and edible oils. Imported tractors, fertilizers, and insecticides were also insulated from rising international prices. The unmanageable deficit notwithstanding, President Sadat refused to try to curb domestic consumption or public expenditures.

Carrying the deference to consumerism further, Sadat's policies in mid-1980 ensured still larger budget deficits. He ordered increased wages for workers and public employees, stricter enforcement of laws against black market activities, better prices to farmers for their crops, and even higher subsidies on a number of food items. The total cost of subsidies, direct and indirect, rose during 1980 to somewhere between $2.2 and $3 billion, with food taking more than 70 percent of the outlays.[9] Defying domestic and foreign economists who had counseled more financial rigor, the Egyptian president sensed in Egypt's mounting economic discontent an imperative to deliver soon on outstanding promises for improved material well-being for all Egyptians, not just the middle class. By trying to reduce repeated shortages and increase mass buying power in a situation of 30 percent annual inflation, Sadat underscored his determination to deny political opponents the potent food weapon.

### Rural Discontent

Rural populations in the Middle East do not, as a rule, instigate revolutions and are rarely active in making or unmaking governments. By comparison with their urban counterparts, the rural masses seldom react strongly or spontaneously to official food or agricultural policy decisions. At least three reasons seem to account for this: the economic and psychological detachment of the rural poor, coercive regime policies, and the co-optation of the more successful farmers. For the great majority of small farmers who consume most of what they grow and trade their few surpluses locally, government agricultural policies have a marginal impact at best on their economic condition. Landless laborers, sharecroppers, and small owner-cultivators, those normally preoccupied with subsistence activities, traditionally neither envision political solutions to their hardship nor believe in their ability to improve their circumstances. Even for the increasing number of farmers organized cooperatively by government and to a great extent dependent on public subsidies, credits, and marketing facilities, official decisions may be poorly understood and associated with distant and immovable authority. With few exceptions, these farmers show little inclination toward collective action. Given the obstacles, mobilization of the agrarian underclass is difficult, even with rising class consciousness.[10]

The frequently observed quiescence of the rural poor in the face of exploitative relations and the denial of supposed benefits or rights may also be explained by various forms of coercion. Economic independence and political leverage are hardly possible for those who are liable to be severely penalized by the denial of farm credits, either by government or private sources. With local administrative and judicial institutions typically penetrated by rural elites, the poor have little opportunity to press their grievances or to assert their rights. In most countries the physical isolation of village populations, together with limited resources, virtually precludes organized activities by small producers and denies these farmers effective leadership. Authorities have reason to fear the countryside only when regional, ethnic, and other broad communal demands serve as a basis on which to unite the rural poor with the middle classes. More often, factional struggles divide those with common economic cause. Where they are held, elections offer little outlet for political expression, as peasants are regularly intimidated or manipulated in voting by landlords or government party agents. There is perhaps no example, outside of Turkey's Democratic party in the late 1940s, of an urban-led opposition party that was allowed to stimulate and then channel rural discontent. If electoral or other forms of mobilization occur, authorities are normally able to ensure that these are carefully orchestrated by themselves.

Just the same, rural discontent has increased throughout the region since the mid-1960s. The introduction of new agricultural technologies and revised development strategies is believed to be in large measure responsible. As has been pointed out, farmers have not benefited evenly from the gains registered in agricultural production. Modern farming practices have instead widened economic disparities in most countries, as only the larger, already more progressive farmers are able to absorb capital-intensive approaches or afford the expensive inputs required. Modernization and commercialism have also altered the management of many larger units in a way that makes tenant farming less secure and expands a wage-labor market. Land reform intended to reduce restlessness has made cynics of the great majority of the landless, who are bypassed in redistributions, and new smallholders, who are left without adequate government assistance and services. Often, highly publicized rural schemes have foundered as a result of inadequate planning, weak institutional supports, and urban elite resistance to the transfer of resources. Ambitious designs for public works and large-scale nonfarm employment, aimed at raising rural incomes, remain largely unfulfilled. For the present at least, much of the mass rural discontent is siphoned off through the continued exodus of peasants to the larger cities and to oil-rich, labor-short countries of the region.

Middle-level farmers form a more politically conscious and potentially dynamic element in the rural population. Because they are integrated into a nonlocal, commercial market, they differ from smaller farmers in their measure of economic and political independence of the large landlords. Most middle-level farmers have exchanged this dependency, however, for a new one with the state. Few can prosper without government support programs. As a result, they are an economically insecure group, vulnerable to unstable market conditions and frequently contradictory government policies. They complain of low official prices for crops, shortages of credits, and delays in the delivery of fertilizers, seeds, and other inputs. The widening gap between rural and urban income—in some countries better than a 3 : 1 ratio—is bitterly resented. And yet middle-level farmers do not constitute a destabilizing force over most of the contemporary Middle East. In some systems they may be too few in number to lead a rural opposition.[12] More commonly, these farmers have acquired enough of a stake in the economic and social order to be fearful of radical agrarian reforms.[13] Middle-level farmers are, then, given a place in national agricultural policy, not only for their ability and inclination to make demands on bureaucracies but also for the role they fill in feeding urban dwellers. Governments may squeeze the more progressive farmers economically, but no rational policymaker seeks to cripple them as producers.

### Conflict and Production

It is in the interest of every government of the region to maintain rural stability, if only to ensure that agricultural production is not disrupted. Unrest influences planting decisions, and if the political uncertainty also carries the threat of land confiscation, farmers may choose to reduce the area under cultivation. Armed conflict creates labor shortages and preempts transport. Farm equipment is often allowed to lie idle for lack of fuel and parts. Yields are likely to be lowered by a breakdown in the importation and distribution of fertilizers and seeds and an exhaustion of credits. Rich areas of cultivation may be devastated by fighting, and failure to keep irrigation systems in repair can have long-term effects. Wealthier farmers typically withhold crops in hopes of gaining higher prices, and in the absence of contingency reserves, food stocks are rapidly depleted by consumer hoarding or may be removed by combatants. Fortunately, the major wars engaging states of the region have largely been fought over sparsely populated, arid terrain. Even where food stocks were low, hostilities were usually brief, if intense.

Minimally adequate food consumption is most threatened in circumstances of prolonged domestic communal strife and ideological struggle, as in Lebanon, North Yemen, Iran, and Afghanistan. In each of these cases, the problem has been as much one of food price as food availability, especially for the urban lower class. When scarcity results largely from natural conditions, the rural poor, notably the landless, suffer most; what food is accessible on local markets is beyond their purchasing power. Even small farmers are rarely self-sufficient in all their food requirements. The rural masses are, importantly, beyond the reach of most food relief efforts or are the easy victims of diverted supplies and price gouging. But where political events play a central role in shortages, the breakdown of food delivery systems frequently leaves sufficient supplies available in rural areas as farmers are forced to sell off their produce locally at a sacrifice. City dwellers are most adversely affected. Not only are supplies from the countryside disrupted, but food imports, which often account for a major fraction of urban consumption, are normally curtailed. Of those stocks on hand, more affluent city dwellers command a disproportionate share through their ability to pay the higher prices. Urban food shortages may linger, moreover, long after the conflict has passed.

The once valuable crops of Lebanon were significant casualties of the civil war of 1975–1976. Prior to the Syrian intervention, losses in agricultural production ran to hundreds of millions of dollars, and for the first time in its history, Lebanon was forced to import olives and olive oil. The important poultry industry was nearly destroyed in the heavy fighting in 1976. Sudan's efforts to develop its agricultural export potential could not get under way until a political settlement had been reached with rebels fighting in the south. The Algerian civil war, however, offers the best example of the long-term impact of internal conflict. After several years in which the French deliberately denuded the countryside in order to deny refuge to the insurgents, the fighting left enduring scars on the traditional agricultural sector.[14]

Ironically, the very marginality of much agriculture in the Middle East can sometimes militate against a sustained high level of hostilities. The need to get crops into the ground as well as harvest them may require combatants to break off fighting and return to their villages. This occurred in Afghanistan during the late spring of 1979, when clashes between provincial Islamic and nationalist insurgents and the army of the Marxist government in Kabul fell off sharply for a time. Prior to armed Soviet intervention, the opposition banked, however, on food shortages' becoming the undoing of the central government. The combination of light winter snows that reduced the season's wheat output and farmer reluctance to cultivate land threatened by government confiscation had been expected to create bread shortages that would carry the unrest to the capital. With the intensification of fighting, much of it in areas close to the cities and major towns, both sides deliberately burned food crops and stockpiles in order to disable the other's efforts. Fleeing refugees herded off when possible their goats and sheep, the principal sources of meat for the urban bazaars. Thousands of animals also perished during armed attacks. After depositing their families in Pakistan, many farmer-rebels from Eastern Afghanistan returned to their villages to cultivate fields of wheat, rice, and spinach and valuable opium poppy crops. The highly decentralized, frequently primitive agricultural system of Afghanistan in some ways worked to the advantage of rural populations cut off from markets and modern farm inputs. Still, supplies were uncertain across much of the countryside and the insurgents' operational range was limited to areas close to their sources of food. When they were near larger cities, raids on granaries were not uncommon.[15]

Armed conflict that reduces agricultural output ordinarily cuts heavily into export crops, unbalancing national budgets and, in some cases, further destabilizing political authority. The sabotage of transport in a countryside under the control of antigovernment forces crippled Afghanistan's agricultural export trade. In Jordan, more than 60 percent of the agricultural lands and a principal source of foreign exchange were removed with Israel's capture of the West Bank in 1967. Hostilities caused physical damage to irrigation works in the Jordan Valley, and plans for the Yarmouk water development project were upset. Many farmers who fled the valley's East Bank remained away for several years. Sporadic border raids between 1967 and 1970 and the kingdom's attack on armed Palestinian forces during 1970 delayed the area's recovery. Farmers also had little incentive to resume cultivation while the delivery of technical, credit, and marketing services was curtailed.[16]

The effects of the 1967 war on agricultural production continue to be felt in the military administration and Jewish settlement policies in the West Bank. Crop yields on some Arab farms have improved with more modern cultivation practices copied from the Israelis. A cooperative system, dormant after 1967, was revived in 1975, and loans to Palestinian farmers became more available in the late 1970s.[17] But the agricultural sector on the West Bank is hardly robust. Local Arab investment in agriculture is meager, and overall agricultural output from the West Bank has not increased. The sector's contribution to the local economy fell steadily under Israeli occupation, along with a drop of more than 10 percent in agricultural employment. The day labor available in Israel for 100,000 Arabs from the West Bank and Gaza has escalated the costs of agricultural labor on Arab farms. And although most Israeli exports move freely to the West Bank, the sale of agricultural and other goods to Israel from the occupied territories is restricted.[18]

The amount of good agricultural land appropriated in one way or another by Israeli settlements is not extensive. But the government—for security reasons, it has stated—controls an estimated 150,000 hectares, or 27 percent, of the West Bank and has placed off limits land once regularly used by Arabs for cultivation or grazing animals.[19] Some reports allege that the Israeli military have used defoliants to destroy food crops in areas where Arab farmers have continued to work confiscated lands.[20] Curfews and other security measures frequently interfere with farm schedules and the export of perishable crops. Some Israeli policymakers make no effort to hide their desire to block Palestinian agricultural development.[21] But whatever its motives, the government has contributed very little toward stimulating the sector. At most, West Bank authorities allow external development assistance from USAID-supported American voluntary organizations for some projects in politically favored locales and credits and grants from Jordan and oil-producing Arab countries. In 1979, for the first time, aid projects in the West Bank and Gaza were planned by the U.N. Development Programme.

Conceivably more serious for agriculture than Israel's land policies in the occupied territories is the competition between Arabs and Jews for desperately scarce water resources. Although extensive and sophisticated water systems have been constructed for West Bank settlements, including more than twenty deep wells by 1980, no permits for irrigation wells have been issued to Arab farmers since 1967, and drilling was authorized to only a handful of West Bank municipalities. Arabs claim they have difficulty, moreover, in expanding the capacity of existing wells and buying spare parts.[22] More important for the long run, pumps on the other side of the Green Line, that is, in Israel proper, draw heavily on the aquifers that lie under the West Bank, increasing salinity and drying up the older Arab wells and springs vital for town and agricultural use. Israel's exploitation of West Bank water resources, currently meeting a sizable share of national requirements, poses one of the thorniest problems in trying to establish Palestinian claims under a plan for West Bank autonomy.

In the region's armed conflicts, the fragility of an agricultural system may be more significant then the fact of direct involvement in determining the impact on production. This conclusion is suggested by Table 6.1, which presents food production indices for belligerents and selected nonbelligerents in the 1973 Middle East War. With 1969–1971 as a base, overall food production was down sharply in 1973 for both Syria and Jordan, in both cases declining from impressive 1972 growth figures and in each instance rebounding impressively in 1974. Production also dropped precipitously in Iraq, although it failed to recover in 1974 and remained low throughout the following year, during which Iraq's Kurdish rebellion came to a climax. By contrast, food production in Egypt and Israel, with their better-developed agricultural institutions and infrastructures, remained

TABLE 6.1
Food Production Indices among Belligerent Countries and
Selected Non-Belligerents in the 1973 Middle East War

|  | Total Food Production (1969-71=100) | | |
| Country | 1972 | 1973 | 1974 |
| --- | --- | --- | --- |
| Egypt | 104 | 104 | 103 |
| Iraq | 128 | 94 | 93 |
| Israel | 120 | 119 | 128 |
| Jordan | 123 | 81 | 141 |
| Syria | 136 | 90 | 144 |
| Iran | 112 | 115 | 120 |
| Lebanon | 119 | 111 | 124 |
| Libya | 138 | 140 | 144 |
| Sudan | 105 | 103 | 122 |
| Turkey | 109 | 101 | 112 |

Source:  Food and Agriculture Organization, Production
Yearbook, 1978.

reasonably level over the period examined, neither declining in the 1973
conflict nor showing the pattern of growth, modest in the case of Egypt, that
had been registered since 1969–1971. The nonbelligerent countries in Table
6.1 exhibited either continued food production growth between 1972 and
1974 or slight declines in 1973, as in Lebanon, Sudan, and Turkey. Drought
conditions in portions of the region during 1973 no doubt contributed to
the generally lower output levels, especially in those countries without extensive irrigation systems. But the production figures shown here
nonetheless make a case for the impact, however uneven, of domestic
dislocations and diverted energies during the fall of 1973.

Regime instability, which so often appears to deprive industrial sectors of
discipline and direction, can take a similar toll on agricultural and food
planning. Repeated political elite turnover results in a discontinuity of
development ideas and personnel and a failure to accomplish many
realizable objectives. Worthy projects are likely to be abandoned simply
because of their identification with the discredited officials and deposed
cliques. As noted in Chapter 2, the turmoil in Iran during 1978 froze new
initiatives, including a development plan. Subsequent shuffling of ministry
personnel in post revolutionary Iran left few administrators sufficiently
secure or certain of the direction of the government to commit themselves to
any policies. Agricultural planners were especially apprehensive after the
government's execution of a former minister who was alleged to have
"destroyed the country's agriculture."[23]

Newly installed regimes in the Middle East regularly pay homage to their agrarian toilers. Meaningful reforms are high on the list of promises in recent years, as are assurances of raising domestic agricultural production and farm income. Once faced with shaping policy, however, leaders are ordinarily too preoccupied with the need to consolidate power and too constrained by the necessity of winning over key urban constituencies to commit substantial transfers of resources to the rural sector. Rural masses, trucked in from the countryside to demonstrate, may be convenient for providing the appearance of popular backing for a regime, but they are seldom considered a reliable force in defending power. New governments prefer policies with short-term economic impact rather than the longer-term payoffs associated with agricultural investments. Small farmers are widely thought to have an almost infinite ability to absorb assistance without any demonstrable returns to the national economy. Development programs already in effect in the countryside become paralyzed with regime change. Government employees sharply curtail their activities to wait out power struggles, in hopes that a low profile may allow their jobs and programs to survive.

When nations of the region have experienced high (or low) levels of turnover of political leadership, it is reasonable to anticipate finding some impact on their agricultural effort. Table 6.2 takes as a measure of national attention crop yields (in kilograms per hectare) recorded over the periods 1952–1956 and 1961–1965. These years are selected because they fall within the period of 1948–1967, for which we also have a reliable record of regular and irregular national executive transfers.[24] In the table sixteen Middle East countries are ordered by the number of transfers and compared by wheat yields in 1952–1956 and total cereal yields in 1961–1965.

It is of course improbable that a direct relationship exists between political turnover and agricultural effort. Obviously, many factors contribute to agricultural productivity besides political change. Moreover, the impact of instability on planning and investment may take various forms in addition to crop yields. Table 6.2 finds, predictably, no simple connection between instability and yields such as would be indicated by a significant rank order correlation of the two factors. If nations with high political turnover should tend toward lower yields, then Lebanon in 1961–1965, for example, is clearly out of order among countries with the highest number of transfers, and yields in Sudan in 1961–1965 and Pakistan in both periods are far lower than would be expected for countries with relatively few political changes. Intensively cropped Egypt is of course a special case. Still, some linkage between political change and national agricultural effort is suggested by the figures. The average wheat yields for the five most unstable countries was 668 kg/ha in 1952–1956, as contrasted with 1,116 kg/ha in the same period for the five with the lowest political executive turnover. The former was 225

TABLE 6.2
Political Instability and Crop Yields in Sixteen Middle East Countries

| Country | Regular and Irregular Executive Transfers 1948-67 | Wheat Yields (kg/ha) 1952-56 | Total Cereal Yields (kg/ha) 1961-65 |
|---|---|---|---|
| Syria | 54 | 620 | 816 |
| Iraq | 31 | 580 | 652 |
| Jordan | 30 | 640 | 681 |
| Lebanon | 26 | 810 | 1027 |
| Morocco | 23 | 690 | 820 |
| Egypt | 23 | 2170 | 3310 |
| Israel | 20 | 1010 | 1471 |
| Iran | 19 | 930 | 927 |
| Algeria | 16 | 680 | 624 |
| Libya | 15 | 90 | 251 |
| Tunisia | 14 | 500 | 427 |
| Pakistan | 13 | 750 | 874 |
| Sudan | 12 | 1430 | 815 |
| Turkey | 11 | 1000 | 1146 |
| Afghanistan | 6 | 1020 | 1076 |
| Saudi Arabia | 4 | 1380 | 1283 |

SOURCES:  Charles L. Taylor and Michael Hudson, World Handbook of Political and Social Indicators, Second Edition (New Haven; Yale University Press, 1972), pp. 128-135, 150-153.  Food and Agriculture Organization, FAO Production Yearbook 1967 and Yearbook 1974.

kg/ha below the sixteen-country average and the latter 223 above. The comparable figures for 1961–1965, for which total cereal yield statistics are available, are 799 and 1038 for high- and low-turnover countries, with the more unstable 213 kg/ha below the regional average and the more stable 26 kg/ha above. Probably the case that two decades of continuous political change had a hand in retarding agricultural sector investment and energies can best be made for Syria, Iraq, Jordan, Morocco, and perhaps Lebanon.

## Islamic Resurgence and Agrarian Policy

A revival of Islamic orthodoxy in political movements across much of the Middle East brought a new source of instability in the late 1970s. The heightened salience of religion in national politics found expression in elections and the drift of public policies, as well as in opposition to incumbent regimes and leadership turnovers. The ascendance in Iran of a government dominated by Ayatollah Khomeini was only the most newsworthy example. Although the unique doctrinal features of Shiite Islam strengthened claims of Iran's *ulema* (clergy) to a central political role, the popular enthusiasm for religious authority and the political vigor of traditionalist forces in Iran were by no means isolated phenomena. Ayatollah Khomeini indeed sought to export his revolution to Shiite populations in neighboring Iraq and the Gulf countries. Pakistan's military government assumed power in 1977 following on the heels of clergy-backed civil disorders that aimed at reviving an Islamic way of life. In Afghanistan, religion rallied insurgent groups battling Marxist governments and their Soviet partners who were characterized as anti-Islamic and godless. Social and economic cleavages reinforced and politicized religious ones in Lebanon's civil war, and militant Muslim brotherhoods made life difficult for Syria's largely Alawite political elite and Sudan's military leadership. Egypt's President Sadat has given wide berth to the country's religious leaders in return for support for his political initiatives. A common element throughout much of the region is the increasing need of political leaders to accommodate popular religious forces and employ religious piety to legitimize political authority. There is growing currency in the idea that Islam offers a realistic alternative to the frustrations and inequalities left by Western-induced economic change and social values. Because a strengthened Islamic consciousness influences policymaking in the broadest sense, it cannot but affect national choices in agricultural modernization and food policy. The political divisions that this resurgence has cast up also find expression in competing attitudes toward agrarian reform and income redistribution.

The Koran prescribes that a man is entitled to use only so much land as he can work himself; he is denied the right to exploit the labor of others. Strictly interpreted, these principles could justify ending many tenancy arrangements and prohibiting larger private agricultural enterprises. Similarly, the imposition of *ushr* (a Koranic tithe on agricultural land) could, when joined with *zakat* (a tax on wealth for purposes of charity), provide an alternative to prevailing private and public credit arrangements, as well as a basis for redistributive economic policies. *Zakat* could be used to compensate farmers whose expenses for production outweigh the profits they can realize, thus spreading the risks in tenancy and sharecropping. Ideally, it would end the usurious practices that scriptures preach against and that economically enslave poor farmers.

But tenancy and sharecropping are deep-rooted in traditional Middle East society. And in those states where religious taxes have long been in force, most notably Saudi Arabia, there is little evidence of a narrowing of incomes, particularly the disparities between the urban and rural dwellers. In practice, Islam has been permissive on the central issue of landownership. Religious authority has sanctioned through time a wide variety of ownership forms. State lands and religious endowments have existed side by side with private ownership, under clear deed of title and in its absence. If no claims are in fact made for the higher legitimacy of a single form, neither has religious authority been used to deny the acceptability of any ways of organizing agricultural production, collective or individual.

By itself, Islamic doctrine, not to mention an Islamic past and the example of contemporary states, offers a contradictory basis for challenging secular authority. Muslims are enjoined by the Koran to oppose social injustice, political oppression, and economic exploitation. Taken literally, the masses may be justified in actively resisting those in authority. But an Islamic society is more often viewed as encouraging passive obedience. The warrant to rise against abusive social, economic, or political power can be very narrowly defined, limited to only those offenses specifically proscribed by law. Fatalism that issues from the acknowledgment of God's omnipotence and a tradition that draws no fast lines between religious and secular authority normally result in submission.[25]

The *ulema* is understandably supportive of a social and economic order that furnishes it prestige and sometimes considerable wealth. Islam has in fact not provided much of a barrier against the transfer of political power, but it often stands in the way of radical transformations of prevailing economic and social structures. Much of the clergy's influence during the twentieth century has come from its alliance with the commercial middle classes and traditional rural leadership. Events in post-Bhutto Pakistan bear out this conservative bias. The pious military leadership in Islamabad permitted rural elites to reassert their influence over the countryside while promises to implement lower limits on land ownership were all but forgotten. Religious authority was poised against Afghanistan's agrarian campaigns, forcing the Taraki and then the Amin and Babraq governments to soft-pedal land reforms. In Iran, revolutionary guards under the direction of the country's top religious leaders clamped down hard on peasant farmers who had seized land from large landowners in the Turkoman tribal regions. Around the country landlords, aided by armed Iranian government cadres, were often able in the postrevolutionary period to retrieve land occupied by agricultural laborers. Many peasants had anticipated an immediate land redistribution and found justification of their seizures in the Koranic injunction that the land belongs to those who till it.

What was heralded as an Islamic approach to land reform was proclaimed by Iran's Revolutionary Council early in 1980. The plan delegated authority for dividing the larger estates to seven-member regional committees that acted independently of regular government departments. These committees were, however, slow in getting started and were not always sensitive to the economic impact of changes or the physical constraints on successful farming.[26] They managed during 1980 to allocate only a small fraction of the potentially affected holdings. Indecision and delay in implementing policy in agricultural reform and the sector as a whole was in part at least a reflection of the struggle among Iran's ruling groups. Although a few ministry officials, members of the ruling Islamic Republican Party, hoped to use the reform to identify the regime with a popular radical agrarian cause, more pragmatic officials, especially those close to then President Bani-Sadr, cautioned against land fragmentation and its adverse impact on short-run food supplies.[27] Definition of the plan's ideological thrust was, in any case, blurred by the refusal of religious authorities to designate a preferred Islamic form of land ownership. In operation, an Islamic agricultural policy for Iran, although insisting on economic independence that would contrast with policies of the shah, merely found new sources of supply and adopted many latter-day priorities of the former regime, namely the aims of expanding agricultural output and promoting nonagricultural development in the countryside.

Aside from prohibitions on certain food items, alcohol, slaughter of animals by non-Muslims, Islam dictates no particular food policies. Yet the nationalism that almost everywhere—notwithstanding the doctrinal denial of political loyalties separate from the Islamic community—accompanies a resurgent religious consciousness emphasizes the need for greater national self-reliance in agriculture. The prevailing ideology holds that the region's agricultural systems have been deliberately destroyed by Western economic imperialism, with resulting social problems and moral decadence. Preferably, an Islamic country will shed much of its dependence on trade and aid from outside the Muslim world. The import of luxury food items should be sharply curtailed, and such alien concepts as agribusiness joint ventures and Soviet-style state farms may be unacceptable. Transplanted rural populations will be encouraged to return to the countryside where generous government investment in agricultural development will again make farming a viable occupation and restore the virtues of village life.

An Islamic approach, so conceived, is likely to be pursued only so long as it remains compatible with larger economic goals and the practicalities of regime political survival. It seems doubtful that even those regimes claiming the strongest dedication to Islamic principles will ask their citizens to endure for very long in the name of religion or economic independence soaring food prices or shortages. No government seems likely to dismantle an industrial base in favor of its agricultural sector or to pose serious obstacles to continued urban settlement. In Iran, the call by Khomeini for peasants to return to their villages and grow wheat was less idealistic than pragmatic; the country's stagnant economy had left thousands of former peasants, especially those employed in urban construction, without any income. For Saudi Arabia and other wealthy desert nations, food imports are too important to be left to symbolic politics. Their *ulema* raise no objections to increased imports of processed food from the West. Nor does Egypt's religious establishment criticize new economic policies requiring foreign cooperation that are designed to lift the country out of its economic doldrums. Islam may be cited as a source of innovative ideas in food and agricultural policy. But it is far more likely to serve as a powerful rationale for policies for which there are already political constituencies and good economic imperatives.

### Prospects for the 1980s

It is reasonable to assume that the net food deficits that exist in nearly every country in the Middle East will continue to mount during the 1980s. Individual states may boost domestic production in some food crops in some years, particularly if public policy favors certain agricultural exports. Over longer periods, the opening of new lands, improvement of irrigation systems, and more extensive and effective use of chemical fertilizer can more than compensate for spreading desertification or losses to waterlogging and salinity. Still, the major forces behind higher food requirements in the region—rapid urbanization, population growth, and rising disposable income—show no signs of reversal and are expected to push overall consumption well beyond supplies from domestic sources. Nor is there much cause for optimism while the vast majority of those still attached to the land fail to receive the resources or the incentives needed to produce surpluses for an expanding urban market.

The countries of the Middle East are obviously not similarly equipped to deal with future food and agricultural development problems. Without exception, the region's oil-exporting nations have the capacity to set aside a large portion of their national wealth for agricultural activities and to afford the prevailing international prices of food commodities, farm machinery, and other modern farm inputs. Most can easily accept the burden of defraying the costs of food to their citizens through generous subsidies. For the oil-rich, the management of food scarcities and efforts to cope with low agricultural output come down largely to a matter of national priorities, administrative capability, and political will. Moreover, with the exception of Iran and Algeria, the oil-wealthy nations have small populations and relatively few mouths to feed.

The larger number of states in the Middle East resemble capital-deficit countries elsewhere. Their policy options ordinarily involve trade-offs, none very palatable, and no dramatic breakthroughs in agricultural production are likely. The less well-off countries are denied the luxury of parallel programs that could aid experimentation and help to identify optimal sets of policies. Many are locked into an international food system that eliminates the possibility of more self-reliant, autonomous forms of development. And few are able to alter investment strategies that aim for immediate production gains in favor of slower structural changes intended to ensure long-term productivity. On world food markets, these states are at a decided disadvantage with respect to wealthier countries, forced to spend scarce foreign exchange and dependent on international credits. Energy costs, always high for the low-income countries of the region, are increasingly competitive with food imports for foreign exchange. Outlays for cereal and other food imports must be subtracted from what little is available for development, agricultural or industrial. High fossil fuel prices pose special hardship for countries reliant on agricultural exports when the increase shows up in the cost of imported farm inputs and the transport of food and fibers. Rising costs of oil and petrochemicals leave many states hard-pressed to sustain their expensive food subsidy programs.

The region's rich and poor nations alike have a common, overriding concern that food prices paid by their citizens be kept from soaring and that food stocks be adequate. In both, any acute shortages of food are likely to increase national tensions by underscoring the economic advantages of particular societal groups in their access to food. The economically weak and strong countries face, moreover, the possibility that during the 1980s, global food-exporting countries may be increasingly unable — perhaps unwilling — to cover the region's food deficits at any price.

Prospects for reducing extraregional dependencies rest in large measure on increasing economic integration and cooperation among Middle East states. If identity and ample resources mean anything, the Islamic Middle East forms a regional whole that is unmatched in the developing world. Cultural homogeneity and political awareness give it what appears to be a decisive advantage in building a basis for food trade. The region's oil-exporting countries have the accumulated capital to assume a larger share of the financial assistance and development aid required by their less affluent neighbors. Intraregional transfers of skilled and unskilled labor, as well as valued remittances to home countries, are already dominant features of the Middle East and will continue to underpin development plans and relieve budget problems. But the centerpiece in a complementary agricultural policy for the region would be a system of free trade in which countries of the region specialized in cultivating those crops that they produced most efficiently and with their export earnings imported what others in the region have grown. Accordingly, Egypt might be expected to specialize in sugar and cotton, the Sudan in corn, edible oils, and animal raising, Pakistan in rice and cotton, Turkey and Syria in wheat, and Lebanon in fruits and vegetables. Collaboration would also extend to the manufacture of farm machinery, fertilizers, and other imports, as well as a sharing of agricultural research. Aside from minimizing the hazards to their economies of a dependence on a single major export crop subject to wide international price fluctuations, economic cooperation allows the region's less well-off states to gain some of the protection that is enjoyed by their oil-rich neighbors in their bargaining with the industrial West.[28]

If the recent past is any guide, regional integration of economies is a distant goal at best. At present all trade among countries of the Middle East is modest. Among Arab states, only Jordan found a major export market in 1977, about 60 percent of the country's total world trade, in the region's Arab countries. Oil trade aside, Iraq was second to Jordan, with merely 19 percent of total exports to countries in the Arab world.[29] Saudi Arabia had the highest share of imports from fellow Arab states, some 24 percent of all it bought abroad. Otherwise, inter-Arab trade in the late 1970s, whether imports or exports, accounted for less than 15 percent of their commerce with all countries. Egypt's trade with Arab states, for example, which had been reduced but not entirely stopped by the 1979 embargo by other Arab countries, had amounted to only 12 percent of its total exports and 3 percent of all its imports. Overall, intraregional trade has grown relative to world trade, but only slowly from its average of less than 10 percent in 1974.[30] Intraregional increases in recent years have been discontinuous and between some regional subgroups trade has actually declined from peaks reached during the 1970s.[31] Meanwhile, the trade flow, including food, with industrialized countries has continuously expanded. There is, after all, much that is uncomplementary about the agricultural systems of the region, and the job of reorienting trade would be formidable. Not only do they presently compete in many food crops, but countries of the region often advocate highly contrasting public policies, ranging from largely unfettered private enterprise to state-domination of the rural economy.

Prospects for integration of the agricultural systems in the Middle East would seem to be predicated on a level of political cooperation that has rarely been witnessed in the region. A good case can be made that so long as national rivalries and suspicions remain strong, collaborative efforts to solve the region's food and agricultural problems are probably precluded. If cooperation throughout the region is contingent on first compromising major differences over ideologies, over national goals, or between leaders, the outlook cannot be promising. The periodic efforts of Arab countries to unite for essentially political and strategic reasons have regularly failed, carrying down with them plans to integrate economic institutions. Yet agreements between Middle East countries that rest in the first instance on economic convenience, even if system or ideological differences are not resolved, stand a better chance of success. Practical economic understandings, initially of limited scope, may provide the firmest basis for eventual political agreements. This kind of thinking appears to have guided the joint projects that have taken shape in recent years between Egypt and Sudan. By contrast, the overshadowing of economic talks by political exigencies, as between Iraq and Syria and between the two Yemens during the late 1970s, helps to explain their breakdown or failure to make progress. Similarly, the convergence of interests among both conservative and radical Arab states in the wake of the Egyptian-Israeli agreements offered a weak foundation for economic cooperation, as it was based primarily on the politics of revenge.

Common visions of massive food shortages in the region could provide a powerful stimulus for economic cooperation, and with it an easing of political antagonisms. One perennial source of political tensions, disputes between countries over the diversion of river headwaters, would be likely to fade as an issue in the context of integrated agricultural policies. Governments in the Middle East would also be less compelled to compete with one another in any future fall-off in foreign food exports. The current preoccupation of regimes with national defense absorbs resources that might otherwise be allocated for agricultural development. A competition that favors huge military budgets has been particularly evident in such capital-deficit countries as Egypt and Pakistan but has also been a feature of oil-rich Iran and Iraq. To be sure, the cooperation of Arab states might heighten Israel's fears over its continued exploitation of the water of the Jordan River and end its hopes of siphoning other rivers of South Lebanon. A carefully coordinated regional food system may intensify Israel's feelings of isolation, while emboldening the Arab countries for confrontation with the Jewish state. Alternatively, a broadly beneficial regional food policy can create greater stakes for everyone in political stability throughout the Middle East. A sense of urgency over agricultural development and production could also focus on Israel's potential technological transfers to the region, thereby strengthening incentives for joining in a comprehensive peace.[32]

Any progress toward a regional perspective is unlikely to alter the strongly national character of policy implementation in the Middle East. Just as nothing in the foreseeable future suggests the emergence of an overarching organizational framework for the aggregation of regional interests, external influences able to penetrate countries to enforce collective decisions are presently weak. Governments are willing to accept ideas, technologies, and financial assistance from the outside and may be resigned to having these on terms other than their own. But political leaders are likely to guard carefully the job of mobilizing and motivating people and to ensure that policies are implemented according to their values and priorities. It is quite another matter that governing elites may be unable to muster the strength or will to overcome domestic resistance and apply policies they accept in principle. The political instability that reemerged in the region in the late 1970s has no doubt restrained many leaders from taking undue risks in pressing for rapid change and modernization.

Reliable sources of supply, secured by a greater reliance on domestic production, should be the cornerstone of national food planning in the Middle East for the 1980s and beyond. There is a sense of urgency, if not yet crisis, in most countries over their ability to meet both the demands of the masses for basic nutritional needs and also those of strategic segments of the society for higher consumption. In the more populous, low-income countries, deficits have already brought heavy economic burdens and laid down conditions for civil unrest. These countries have for some time recognized the high stakes in providing ample affordable food for their citizens. Yet even the more economically advantaged, oil-producing states of the region have come around to the view that there is no certainty, even should they succeed in expanding urban industrial sectors, that international markets for manufactured goods will exist to replace the diminishing income from oil. The recent slogan in one oil-rich country, that "agriculture is permanent oil," needs little explanation in a region where land has historically been considered as the only sure basis of wealth and security.

Countries with a surfeit of food and the means to sustain high levels of production have potent, if flawed, instruments of regional and international power. Although it is unlikely that food as a commodity will acquire the value of oil as a political and economic weapon, for a number of countries in the Middle East there is a deepening concern that imports can become the basis for checking their present economic leverage and undermining their political integrity. As this volume has pointed out, despite a rude awakening among policymakers about agriculture, governments across the region have repeatedly stumbled in husbanding their resources and developing the administrative capacity needed for constructive, attainable policies. Most regimes in the region have never discovered and sustained a satisfactory balance of national goals aimed at extending productivity, equity, and political order. Still, the region as a whole, given its enormous aggregate wealth, has an unparalleled opportunity to modernize agricultural production and realize the aspirations of most of its people.

## Notes

1. John Waterbury, "Aish: Egypt's Growing Food Crisis," *American Universities Field Staff Reports* Northeast Africa Series 19, no. 3 (December 1974), p. 11. Waterbury wrote that Sadat shared this reasoning with his National Security Council in explaining the decision to fight.

2. Some materials in the chapter appear in an earlier form in Marvin G. Weinbaum, "Food and Political Stability in the Middle East," *Studies in Comparative International Development* 15, no. 2 (Summer 1980):1–26.

3. M. G. Weinbaum, "Agricultural Policy and Development Politics in Iran," *Middle East Journal* 31, no. 4 (Autumn 1977):437.

4. *New York Times*, August 12, 1979.

5. *Middle East*, September 1979, p. 13.

6. *Middle East Economic Digest*, January 21, 1977, p 57.

7. *New York Times*, April 23, 1978.

8. Ibid., February 8, 1980.

9. Ibid., June 16 and 23, 1980, and April 5, 1981.

10. Ronald J. Herring and Charles R. Kennedy, Jr., "The Political Economy of Farm Mechanization Policy: Tractors in Pakistan," in Raymond F. Hopkins, Donald J. Puchala, and Ross B. Talbot, eds., *Food, Politics, and Agricultural Development: Case Studies in the Public Policy of Rural Modernization* (Boulder, Colo.: Westview Press, 1979), p. 217. Although the authors make this observation for Pakistan, it has validity for the greater region.

11. A case in point is the dismantling of the militant Gezira Tenants Union in 1974 after it had led a protest burning of crops. The Numeiri regime formed a new tenants' organization under the direct tutelage of its Sudan Socialist Union. Carole Collins, "Sudan: Colonialism and Class Struggle," *MERIP Reports*, no. 46 (April 1976), p. 13.

12. See Fahad Kazami and Ervand Abrahamian, "The Unrevolutionary Peasants of Modern Iran," *Iranian Studies* 11 (1978):259–304.

13. This conclusion is at some variance with that reached by Eric Wolf, *Peasant Wars of the Twentieth Century* (London: Faber, 1971), p. 291. Wolf found that the middle peasantry, in general, enjoys enough economic security to be in a position to challenge large landlords and government officials. Although the better-off peasants in the Middle East have typically abetted the breaking up of large estates, they have been as conservative as the landlords they replaced when it came to the extension of reforms to others.

14. John Waterbury, "Land, Man, and Development in Algeria, Part I: Problems of Trained Manpower, Industry and Agriculture," *American Universities Field Staff Reports*, North Africa Series 17, no. 1 (March 1973), p. 11.

15. Francis Fukuyama, "The Future of the Soviet Role in Afghanistan," Rand Report no. 1579, September 1980, pp. 27–28. Also see *Omaha World-Herald*, May 6, 1981.

16. Jared E. Hazelton, "Land Reform in Jordan: The East Ghor Canal Project," *Middle Eastern Studies* 15, no. 2 (May 1979):267.

17. Peter Gubser, *West Bank and Gaza Economic Development: Now and the Future*, Middle East Problem Paper no. 20 (Washington: Middle East Institute, 1979), p. 607.

18. Ibid.

19. Rami G. Khouri, "Israel's Imperial Economics," *Journal of Palestine Studies* 9, no. 2 (Winter 1980):75. Khouri drew his statistics from a Royal Society of Jordan report and a task force report by the U.N. Development Programme submitted in April 1979.

20. *Middle East*, August 1980, p. 53.

21. Michael Hudson, "The Scars of Occupation," *Journal of Palestine Studies* 9, no. 2 (Winter 1980):36.

22. "Israel Drains West Bank Waters," *Middle East,* September 1979, p. 38.

23. *New York Times,* April 12, 1979.

24. Executive transfers refer (in Charles Taylor and Michael Hudson, *World Handbook of Political and Social Indicators,* 2nd ed. [New Haven: Yale University Press, 1972]) to changes in the office of national executive from one leader or ruling group to another. The combined figures used in Table 6.2 include both transfers accomplished through conventional legal or customary means and those that are procedurally irregular. The findings suggested by using the Taylor and Hudson data are largely supported in a study by M. G. Weinbaum, "Dimensions of Elite Change in the Middle East," *Comparative Political Studies* 12, no. 2 (July 1979):123–150.

25. Michael Hudson, *Arab Politics* (New Haven: Yale University Press, 1977), p. 48.

26. *New York Times,* January 1, 1980; also "Which Land Is My Land," *Middle East,* September 1980, p. 75.

27. *Middle East,* September 1980, p. 75.

28. Mehmet Ali Cicekdag, "The Dependence of Middle Eastern Countries on Foreign Food," a paper delivered at the annual convention of the Western Political Science Association, Portland, Oreg., March 22, 1979, p. 15.

29. Central Bank figures for a number of countries are found in "Arab Common Market Still At Square One," *Middle East,* July 1979, p. 90. Also see "More People, Produce in Jordan Valley Project," *Middle East,* December 1979, p. 79.

30. U.N. Economic Commission for Western Asia, *Studies on Development Problems in Western Asia* (New York: United Nations, 1975), p. 38.

31. Barry W. Paulson and Myles Wallace, "Regional Integration in the Middle East: The Evidence for Trade and Capital Flows," *Middle East Journal* 33, no. 4 (Autumn 1979):466, 470–472.

32. Agriculture is one of the main fields of potential cooperation between Israel and Egypt, involving possible joint ventures in irrigation and vegetable production and paving the way for Egyptian purchase of Israeli-made insecticides and other inputs. Through private sales, a modest flow of agricultural exports was under way in 1980 (*Jerusalem Post,* December 22, 1980). Israel's agricultural assistance, once broadly dispensed on the African continent, had an earlier Middle East counterpart. Teams of agronomists, food specialists, economists, and engineers were sent to Iran to plan the restoration of the Ghazvin area, devastated by a 1962 earthquake. Another development assistance project was started up in Iran's Khuzistan Province. The Ghazvin mission introduced modern agricultural methods to an area of once traditional subsistence farming by recommending improved crop rotations and new crops, more effective irrigation and land utilization, marketing, and agricultural industry, as well as agrarian reform. Although the comprehensive plan fell far short of its objectives, the low-profile Israelis worked easily with peasant farmers and Iranian extension workers, who viewed them as just another "European" team.

# Selected Bibliography

Abrahamian, Ervand. "Structural Causes of the Iranian Revolution." *MERIP Reports,* no. 87 (May 1980), pp. 21–29.

Alavi, Hamza. "The Rural Elite and Agricultural Development in Pakistan." In *Rural Development in Bangladesh and Pakistan,* edited by Robert D. Stevens, Hamza Alavi, and Peter J. Bertocci, pp. 317–353. Honolulu: University Press of Hawaii, 1976.

Anderson, William D. "The Intersection of Foreign and Domestic Policy: The Example of Public Law 480." Ph.D. dissertation, University of Illinois, 1970.

Aresvik, Oddvar. *Agricultural Development of Iran.* New York: Praeger Publishers, 1976.

———. *The Agricultural Development of Jordan.* New York: Praeger Publishers, 1976.

Askari, Hossein, and Cummings, John T. *Middle East Economies in the 1970s.* New York: Praeger Publishers, 1976.

Askari, Hossein, Cummings, John Thomas, and Toth, James. "Land Reform in the Middle East: A Note on Its Redistributive Effects." *Iranian Studies* 10, no. 4 (Autumn 1977):267–279.

Aziz, Sartaj, ed. *Hunger, Politics and Markets: The Real Issues in the Food Crisis.* New York University Press, 1975.

Baber, Sattar. *United States Aid to Pakistan.* Karachi: Pakistan Institute of International Affairs, 1974.

Bagramov, Leon. "Food and Politics." *International Affairs* (Moscow) 3 (June 1977): 45–53.

Balaam, David N. and Carey, Michael, eds. *Food Politics: The Regional Conflict.* Montclair, N.J.: Allanheld, Osmun & Co., 1981.

Barkai, Haim. *Growth Patterns in the Kibbutz Economy.* Amsterdam: North-Holland Publishing, 1977.

Berger, Morroe. *The Arab World Today.* Garden City, N.Y.: Doubleday and Company, Anchor Edition, 1964.

Bill, James A., and Leiden, Carl. *The Middle East: Politics and Power.* Boston: Little, Brown and Company, 1979.

Binder, Leonard. *In a Moment of Enthusiasm.* Chicago: University of Chicago Press, 1978.

Brown, Lester R. *Redefining National Security.* Worldwatch Paper 14. Washington,

D.C.: Worldwatch Institute, October 1977.

Brown, Peter E., and Shue, Henry, eds. *Food Policy.* New York: Free Press, 1977.

Brunner, Christopher J. "Afghanistan's Agrarian Policy." An unpublished paper read at a conference, "Rural Life in Afghanistan: The Prospects for Development." Center for Afghanistan Studies, University of Nebraska at Omaha, September 23-26, 1976.

_____. *New Afghan Laws Respecting Agriculture.* Occasional Paper no. 12. New York: Asia Society, Afghanistan Council, October 1977, pp. 3-9.

Burki, Shahid Javed. "The Development of Pakistan's Agriculture: An Interdisciplinary Explanation." In *Rural Development in Bangladesh and Pakistan,* edited by Robert D. Stevens, Hamza Alavi, and Peter J. Bertocci, pp. 290-316. Honolulu: University Press of Hawaii, 1976.

Chaffetz, David. "Afghanistan in Turmoil." *International Affairs* 56, no. 1 (January 1980):14-36.

Christensen, Asger. "The Pashtuns of Kunar." *Afghanistan Journal* 7 (1980): 80-91.

Cicekdag, Mehmet Ali. "The Dependence of Middle Eastern Countries on Foreign Food." An unpublished paper read at meetings of the Western Political Science Association, Portland, Oreg., March 22, 1979.

Collins, Carole. "Sudan: Colonialism and Class Struggle." *MERIP Reports* 46, (April 1976):3-20.

Cool, John. "The Great Indus Food Machine." *Pakistan Economist,* March 18, 1978), pp. 13-17.

Cooper, Mark. "Egyptian State Capitalism in Crisis: Economic Policies and Political Interests, 1967-1971." *International Journal of Middle East Studies* 10 (November 1979):481-516.

Craig, Daniel. "The Impact of Land Reform on an Iranian Village." *Middle East Journal* 32, no. 2 (Spring 1978):141-154.

Critchfield, Richard. "The Changing Peasant: Part I: The Magician." *American Universities Field Staff Reports,* Africa Series no. 28, March 1979.

Curtis, Michael. "Utopia and the Kibbutz." In *Israel: Social Structure and Change,* edited by M. Curtis and Mordecai Chertoff, pp. 101-113. New Brunswick, N.J.: Transaction Books, 1973.

Daftary, Fahad. "Development Planning in Iran: An Historical Survey." *Iranian Studies* 6, no. 4 (Autumn 1973):176-228.

Davis, Uri, Maks, Antonia E. L., and Richardson, John. "Israel's Water Policies." *Palestine Studies* 34 (Winter 1980):3-31.

Dupree, Louis. "The Democratic Republic of Afghanistan, 1979." *American Universities Field Staff Reports,* South Asia Series, no. 32, (September 1979).

_____. "Afghanistan: 1977: Does Trade Plus Aid Guarantee Development?" *American Universities Field Staff Reports,* South Asia Series, no. 21, August 1977.

Eckholm, Eric. *Losing Ground.* New York: W. W. Norton, 1976.

El-Tobgy, H. A. *Contemporary Egyptian Agriculture.* 2nd ed. Cairo: Ford Foundation, 1976.

"Farming in the Arab East," *ARAMCO World Magazine,* May-June 1978.

Fitch, James B., Khedr, Hassan A., and Whittington, Dale. "The Economic Efficiency of Water Use in Egyptian Agriculture: Opening Round of a Debate." An unpublished paper read at the 17th International Conference of Agricultural Economists, Banff, Canada, September 3–13, 1979.

Food and Agriculture Organization. *FAO Production Yearbook 1974.* Rome: Food and Agriculture Organization, 1974.

Food and Agriculture Organization. *FAO Production Yearbook 1978.* Rome: Food and Agriculture Organization, 1978.

Food and Agriculture Organization. *Report on the 1960 World Census of Agriculture.* Rome: Food and Agriculture Organization, 1971, pp. 92–97.

Food and Agriculture Organization. *State of Food and Agricultural Production, 1977.* Rome, Food and Agriculture Organization, 1977.

Foster, P. "Land Reform in Algeria." *Spring Review of Land Reform* 8 (1970):1–45.

Fraenkel, Richard M. "Introduction." In *The Role of U.S. Agriculture in Foreign Policy,* edited by Richard M. Fraenkel, Don F. Hadwiger, and William P. Brown, pp. 1–16. New York: Praeger Publishers, 1979.

Fukuyama, Francis. "The Future of the Soviet Role in Afghanistan." Mimeographed. Rand Report no. 1579, September 1980.

George, Susan. *How the Other Half Dies – The Real Reasons for World Hunger.* Montclair, N.J.: Allanheld, Osmun & Co., 1977.

Griffin, Keith. *The Political Economy of Agrarian Change.* Cambridge, Mass.: Harvard University Press, 1974.

Gubser, Peter. *West Bank and Gaza Economic Development: Now and the Future.* Middle East Problem Paper no. 20. Washington, D. C.: Middle East Institute, 1979.

Haider, A. S., and Khan, D. A. "Agricultural Policy Reconsidered." An unpublished paper. U.S. Agency for International Development, Islamabad, Pakistan, March 1976.

Hajda, Joseph, Michie, A. N., and Sloan, Thomas, eds. *Political Aspects of World Food Problems.* Manhattan: Kansas State University, Agricultural Experiment Station, 1978.

Halliday, Fred. *Iran: Dictatorship and Development.* New York: Penguin Books, 1979.

———. "Revolution in Afghanistan." *New Left Review,* no. 112 (November–December 1978), pp. 3–44.

Harik, Iliya. "Mobilization Policy and Political Change in Rural Egypt." In *Rural Policy and Social change in the Middle East,* Edited by Richard Antoun and Iliya Harik, pp. 287–314. Bloomington: Indiana University Press, 1972.

———. *The Political Mobilization of Peasants: A Study of an Egyptian Community.* Bloomington: Indiana University Press, 1974.

Hazelton, Jared E. "Land Reform in Jordan: The East Ghor Canal Project." *Middle Eastern Studies* 15, no. 2 (May 1979):258–269.

Herring, Ronald J. "The Rationality of Tenant Quiescence in Tenure Reform: Production Relations and the Liberal State." An unpublished paper read at the annual meetings of the American Political Science Association, Washington, D.C., September 1, 1979.

Herring, Ronald J., and Chaudhry, M. G. "Land Reforms in Pakistan and Their Economic Implications: A Preliminary Analysis." *Pakistan Development Review Quarterly* 13, no. 3 (Autumn 1974):245–279.

Herring, Ronald J., and Kennedy, Charles R., Jr. "The Political Economy of Farm Mechanization Policy: Tractors in Pakistan." In *Food, Politics, and Agricultural Development: Case Studies in the Public Policy of Rural Modernization*, edited by Raymond F. Hopkins, Donald J. Puchala, and Ross B. Talbot, pp. 193–226. Boulder, Colo.: Westview Press, 1979.

Hirashim, Sigemochi. "Interaction Between Institutions and Technology in Developing Agriculture: A Case Study of the Disparity Problems in Pakistan Agriculture." Ph.D. dissertation, Cornell University, 1974.

Hopkins, Raymond F. "The Politics of Agricultural Modernization." In *Food, Politics, and Agricultural Development: Case Studies in the Public Policy of Rural Modernization*, edited by Raymond F. Hopkins, Donald J. Puchala, and Ross B. Talbot, pp. 1–20. Boulder, Colo.: Westview Press, 1979.

Hopkins, Raymond F., and Puchala, Donald J. "Prospects on the International Relations of Food." *International Organization* 32, no. 3 (Summer 1978): 581–616.

Hooglund, Eric J. "The Khwushnishin Population of Iran." *Iranian Studies* 6, no. 4 (Autumn 1973):229–245.

Huddleston, Barbara, and McLin, Jon, eds. *Political Investments in Food Production*. Bloomington: Indiana University Press, 1979.

Hudson, Michael. *Arab Politics*. New Haven: Yale University Press, 1977.

_____. "The Scars of Occupation." *Journal of Palestine Studies* 9, no. 2 (Winter 1980):32–49.

International Food Policy Research Institute. *Meeting Food Needs in the Developing World: The Location and Magnitude of the Task in the Next Decade*. Report no. 1. Washington, D.C.: International Food Policy Research Institute, February 1976.

International Labour Office. *Yearbook of Labour Statistics, 1971*. Geneva: International Labour Office, 1971.

_____. *Yearbook of Labour Statistics, 1972*. Geneva: International Labour Office, 1972.

_____. *Yearbook of Labour Statistics, 1979*. Geneva: International Labour Office, 1979.

Iowa State University. *Proceedings of the World Food Conference of 1976*. Ames: Iowa State University Press, 1977.

Iran, Embassy Of. *Iran Voice*, September 19, 1979.

Islam, Nasir. *World Food Shortages: Ethics, Politics, and Policies*. Lahore, Pakistan: Progressive Publishers, 1976.

Kaikati, Jack G. "The Economy of Sudan: A Potential Breadbasket of the Arab World?" *International Journal of Middle East Studies* 11 (February 1980):99–123.

Kanovsky, Eliyahu. *The Economy of the Israeli Kibbutz*. Cambridge, Mass.: Harvard University Press, 1966.

Kazami, Fahad, and Abrahamian, Ervand. "The Unrevolutionary Peasants of Modern Iran." *Iranian Studies* 11 (1978):259–304.

Keddie, Nikki R. "Oil Economic Policy and Social Conflict in Iran." *Race and Class* 21, no. 1 (Summer 1979):13–29.

_____. "Stratification, Social Control and Capitalism in Iranian Villages, Before and After Land Reform." In *Rural Politics and Social Change in the Middle East,* edited by Richard Antoun and Iliya Harik, pp. 364–402. Bloomington: Indiana University Press, 1972.

_____. "The Iranian Village Before and After Land Reform." *Journal of Contemporary History* 3 (1968):69–91.

Khouri, Rami G. "Israel's Economics." *Journal of Palestine Studies* 9, no. 2 (Winter 1980):71–78.

Kielstra, Nico. "The Agrarian Revolution and Algerian Socialism." *MERIP Reports* 8, no. 4 (May 1978):5–14.

King, Russell, *Land Reform: A World Survey.* Boulder, Colo.: Westview Press, 1977.

Ladejinsky, Wolf. *Agrarian Reform as Unfinished Business.* Edited by Louis J. Walinsky. New York: Oxford University Press, 1977.

Lambton, A. K. *The Persian Land Reform 1962–66.* Oxford: Clarendon Press, 1969.

LaPorte, Robert, Jr. "The Public Sector and Economic Development in Pakistan." Mimeographed. American Institute of Pakistan Studies, Pakistan Report Series no. 1, May 1980.

Looney, Robert E. *The Economic Development of Iran.* New York: Praeger Publishers, 1973.

Malik, A. "A Quarter Century of Agricultural Development in Pakistan." An unpublished paper read at a meeting of the Western Economic Association, Anaheim, Calif., June 1977.

Marr, Phebe A. "The Political Elite in Iraq." In *Political Elites in the Middle East,* edited by George Lenczowski, pp. 109–149. Washington, D.C.: American Enterprise Institute, 1975.

Mellor, John W. *The Economics of Agricultural Development.* Ithaca, N.Y.: Cornell University Press, 1966.

Merriam, John G. "U.S. Wheat to Egypt: The Use of an Agricultural Commodity as a Foreign Policy Tool." In *The Role of U.S. Agriculture in Foreign Policy,* edited by Richard M. Fraenkel, Don F. Hadwinger, and William P. Browne, pp. 90–106. New York: Praeger Publishers, 1979.

*Middle East Yearbook 1980.* London: IC Magazine Ltd., 1980.

*Middle East Annual Review 1980.* London: World of Information, 1979.

Nelson, Harold D., ed. *Algeria: A Country Study.* Foreign Area Handbook Series. Washington, D.C.: American University. 1979.

_____. *Morocco: A Country Study.* Foreign Area Handbook Series. Washington, D.C.: American University, 1978.

*New York Times* staff. *Give Us This Day: A Report on the World Food Crisis.* New York: Arno Press, 1975.

Nicholson, Norman K. "The Political Economy of Agricultural Research in Developing Countries: The Case for the Farming Systems Approach." An unpublished paper read at a U.S. Department of Agriculture–sponsored conference on Farm Structures and Rural Policy, Iowa State University, Ames, Iowa, October 20–22, 1980.

Nicholson, Norman K., and Esseks, John D. "The Politics of Food Scarcities in Developing Countries." *International Organization* 32, no. 3 (Summer 1978):679–719.

Nicholson, Norman K., and Khan, Dilawar Ali. *Basic Democracies and Rural Development in Pakistan.* Ithaca, N.Y.: Center for International Studies, Cornell University, 1974.

Nyrop, Richard F., ed. *Area Handbook for the Hashemite Kingdom of Jordan.* Foreign Area Handbook Series. Washington, D.C.: American University, 1974.

_____. *Iraq: A Country Study.* Foreign Area Handbook Series. Washington, D.C.: American University, 1979.

_____. *Israel: A Country Study.* Foreign Area Handbook Series. Washington, D.C.: American University, 1979.

_____. *Syria: A Country Study.* Foreign Area Handbook Series. Washington, D.C.: American University, 1979.

Paarlberg, Robert L. "The Failure of Food Power." In *The Role of U.S. Agriculture in Foreign Policy,* edited by Richard M. Fraenkel, Don F. Hadwinger, and William P. Browne, pp. 38–55. New York: Praeger Publishers, 1979.

Paddock, William, and Paddock, Paul. *Time of Famines: America and the World Food Crisis.* Boston: Little, Brown and Company, 1976.

Paige, Jeffery M. *Agrarian Revolution.* New York: Free Press, 1975.

Parvin, Manoucher, and Zamani, Amir N. "Political Economy of Growth and Destruction: A Statistical Interpretation of the Iranian Case." *Iranian Studies* 12 (Winter-Spring 1979):43–78.

Paulson, Barry W., and Wallace, Myles. "Regional Integration in the Middle East: The Evidence for Trade and Capital Flows." *Middle East Journal* 33, no. 4 (Autumn 1979):464–478.

Radwan, Samir. *The Impact of Agrarian Reform on Rural Egypt (1952–75).* World Employment Program Research, ILO WEP 10-6/WP-13. Geneva: International Labour Office, January 1977.

Richards, Alan. "Egypt's Agriculture in Trouble." *MERIP Reports,* no. 84 (January 1980), pp. 3–12.

_____. "The Agricultural Crisis in Egypt." *Journal of Development Studies* 16, no. 3 (April 1980):303–321.

Richards, Helmut. "Land Reform and Agribusiness in Iran." *MERIP Reports,* no. 43 (December 1975), pp. 3–18.

Rothschild, Emma. "Food Politics." *Foreign Affairs* 54, no. 2 (January 1976):285–307.

Schulz, Ann T. "Food in Iran: The Politics of Insufficiency." In *Food, Politics, and Agricultural Development: Case Studies in the Public Policy of Rural Modernization,* edited by Raymond F. Hopkins, Donald J. Puchala, and Ross B. Talbot, pp. 171–191. Boulder Colo.: Westview Press, 1979.

Simmons, John L. "Agricultural Development in Iraq: Planning and Management Failures." *Middle East Journal* 19 (Spring 1965):129–140.

Sinha, Radha. *Food and Poverty.* New York: Holmes & Meier Publishers, 1976.

Sloan, Thomas J. "The Political Role of U.S. Grain Exports in a Hungry World." In

*The Role of U.S. Agriculture in Foreign Policy,* edited by Richard M. Fraenkel, Don F. Hadwinger, and William P. Browne, pp. 19–37. New York: Praeger Publishers, 1979.

Springborg, Robert. "Baathism in Practice: Agriculture, Politics and Political Culture in Syria and Iraq." Paper read at the meetings of the Middle East Studies Association, Washington, D.C., November 1980.

_____. "New Patterns of Agrarian Reform in the Middle East and North Africa." *Middle East Journal* 31, no. 2 (Spring 1977):127–142.

Stevens, Robert D. "Comilla Rural Development Programs to 1971." In *Rural Development in Bangladesh and Pakistan,* edited by Robert D. Stevens, Hamza Alavi, and Peter J. Bertocci, pp. 95–128. Honolulu: University Press of Hawaii, 1976.

Tai, Hung-Chao. *Land Reform and Politics: A Comparative Analysis.* Berkeley: University of California Press, 1974.

Talbot, Ross B., ed. *The World Food Problem and U.S. Food Politics and Policies: 1972–76.* Ames: Iowa State University Press, 1977.

_____. *The World Food Problem and U.S. Food Politics and Policies: 1977.* Ames: Iowa State University Press, 1978.

Taylor, Alan R. "The Euro-Arab Dialogue: Quest for an Interregional Partnership." *Middle East Journal* 32, no. 4 (Autumn 1978):429–441.

Taylor, Charles, and Hudson, Michael. *World Handbook of Political and Social Indicators.* 2nd ed. New Haven: Yale University Press, 1972.

Tendler, Judith. *Inside Foreign Aid.* Baltimore: Johns Hopkins University Press, 1975.

Tuma, Elias H. "Agrarian Reform in Historical Perspective Revisited." *Comparative Studies in Society and History* 21, no. 1 (January 1979):3–29.

_____. "Agrarian Reform and Urbanization in the Middle East." *Middle East Journal* 24, no. 2 (Spring 1970):163–177.

_____. *Twenty-Six Centuries of Agrarian Reform: A Comparative Analysis.* Berkeley: University of California Press, 1965.

United Nations. *Assessment of the World Food Situation: Present and Future.* New York: United Nations, 1974.

U.N. Commission for Western Asia. *Studies on Development Problems in Western Asia.* 1975.

U.S., Agency for International Development. *U.S. Overseas Loans and Grants, 1978.* Washington, D.C., 1978.

_____. "The U.S. Assistance Program for Egyptian Agriculture." A preliminary report prepared by the U.S. Department of Agriculture survey team, February 1978.

_____. "U.S. Economic Assistance to Egypt." A report of a special interagency task force, February 15, 1978.

U.S., Central Intelligence Agency, National Foreign Assessment Center. "Communist Aid to Less Developed Countries of the Free World, 1977." Research paper ER 78-10478U, November 1978.

_____. "Communist Aid Activities in Non-Communist Less Developed Countries, 1978." Research paper ER 79-1012U, September 1979.

_____. "Communist Aid Activities in Non-Communist Less Developed Countries, 1979 and 1954-79." Research paper ER 80-10318U, October 1980.

U.S., Congress, Joint Economic Committee. *Economic Consequences of the Revolution in Iran.* Washington, D.C.: Government Printing Office, 1980.

U.S., Department of Agriculture. *International Food Policy Issues, a Proceeding.* Foreign Agriculture Economic Report No. 143. Washington, D.C.: U.S. Department of Agriculture, January 1978.

U.S., General Accounting Office, *U.S. Assistance to Egypt: Slow Progress After Five Years.* Report to the U.S. Congress. Washington, D.C.: General Accounting Office, March 1981.

Voll, Sarah P. "Egyptian Land Reclamation Since the Revolution." *Middle East Journal* 34, no. 2 (Spring 1980):127–148.

Wallerstein, Mitchell B. *Food for War—Food for Peace.* Cambridge, Mass.: M.I.T. Press, 1980.

Warriner, Doreen. *Land Reform and Development in the Middle East: A Study of Egypt, Syria and Iraq.* 2nd ed. London: Royal Institute of International Affairs, 1962.

Waterbury, John. "Aish: Egypt's Growing Food Crisis," *American Universities Field Staff Reports,* Northeast Africa Series 19, no. 3 December 1974.

_____. "The Balance of People, Land, and Water in Egypt." *American Universities Field Staff Reports,* Northeast Africa Series 19, no. 1, January 1974.

_____. "Egyptian Agriculture Adrift," *American Universities Field Staff Reports,* Africa Series, no. 47, October 1978.

_____. "Land, Man, and Development in Algeria, Part I: Problems of Trained Manpower, Industry and Agriculture," *American Universities Field Staff Reports,* North Africa Series 17, no. 1, March 1973.

_____. "The Opening, Part I: Egypt's Economic New Look," *American Universities Field Staff Reports,* Northeast Africa Series 20, no. 2, June 1975.

_____. "The Sudan, In Quest of a Surplus, Part II: Domestic and Regional Politics," *American Universities Field Staff Reports,* Northeast Africa Series 21, no. 9, August 1976.

_____. "The Sudan, In Quest of a Surplus, Part III: Capital Packages and Regional Prospects," *American Universities Field Staff Reports,* Northeast Africa Series 21, no. 10, August 1976.

Waterbury, John, and El Mallakh, Ragaei. *The Middle East in the Coming Decade.* New York: McGraw-Hill Book Company, 1978.

Weinbaum, M. G. "Agricultural Policy and Development Politics in Iran." *Middle East Journal* 31, no. 4 (Autumn 1977):434–450.

_____. "Dimensions of Elite Change in the Middle East." *Comparative Political Studies* 12, no. 2 (July 1979):123–150.

_____. "The March 1977 Elections in Pakistan: Where Everyone Lost." *Asian Survey* 17 (July 1977):599–618.

Weinbaum, M. G., and Sen, Gautam. "Pakistan Enters the Middle East." *Orbis* 22, no. 3 (Fall 1978):595–612.

Weinbaum, Marvin G. "Agricultural Development and Bureaucratic Politics in Pakistan." *Journal of South Asian and Middle Eastern Studies* 2, no. 2 (Winter 1978):42–62.

_____. "Food and Political Stability in the Middle East." *Studies in Comparative International Development* 15, no. 2 (Summer 1980):1–26.

_____. "Structure and Performance of Mediating Elites." In *Elites in the Middle East,* edited by I. William Zartman, pp. 154–195. New York: Praeger Publishers, 1980.

Weingrod, Alex. *Reluctant Pioneers: Village Development in Israel.* Ithaca, N.Y.: Cornell University Press, 1966.

Weitz, R. *From Peasant to Farmer: A Revolutionary Strategy for Development.* New York: Columbia University Press, 1971.

Wickwar, Hardy W. "Food and Social Development in the Middle East." *Middle East Journal* 19 (Spring 1965):177–193.

Wolf, Eric. *Peasant Wars of the Twentieth Century.* London: Faber, 1971.

Wortman, Sterling, and Cummings, Ralph W., Jr. *To Feed This World.* Baltimore: Johns Hopkins University Press, 1978.

World Bank. *Annual Report 1978.* Washington, D.C.: World Bank, 1978.

_____. *Annual Report 1979.* Washington, D.C.: World Bank, 1979.

_____. *Annual Report 1980.* Washington, D.C.: World Bank, 1980.

_____. *Land Reform.* Washington, D.C., May 1975.

_____. *World Development Report, 1979.* New York: Oxford University Press, 1979.

_____. *World Development Report, 1980.* New York: Oxford University Press, 1980.

# Index